PRAISE FOR TONY
LIFE IS A SERIES OF P

"Whether you are in sales or are the CEO of a billion-dollar corporation, let Tony Jeary be your personal coach."

—MARK VICTOR HANSEN, AUTHOR OF *CHICKEN SOUP FOR THE SOUL*

"Speaking is a skill, which simply means it can be learned, particularly if you have the right teacher. Tony Jeary is the right teacher."

—ZIG ZIGLAR, AUTHOR OF *SEE YOU AT THE TOP*

"This remarkably thorough book extends the art of presentation."

—*PUBLISHERS WEEKLY*

"We discovered Tony Jeary over five years ago and his principles have raised our level of competence and confidence to be more connected to our associates, our members, and our families."

—CELIA SWANSON, EXECUTIVE VICE PRESIDENT, SAM'S CLUB, MEMBERSHIP, MARKETING, AND ADMINISTRATION

"Tony shows us presenting is not about being on stage, it is about communicating our ideas in ways that inspire the enthusiastic support of others in all aspects of our lives. This is an important lesson for any winner."

—DENIS WAITLEY, AUTHOR OF *THE PSYCHOLOGY OF WINNING*

"I have found Tony's insights into inspiring audiences to be both practical and helpful."

—JAMES O'CONNOR, PRESIDENT, FORD DIVISION

"Presentation effectiveness has made a huge impact on both my personal and professional life. Tony Jeary and his practices can help everyone in this often overlooked area of life."

—MIKE REEVES, SENIOR VICE PRESIDENT, NEW YORK LIFE

"A life-changing book for anyone who's ever sweated the small stuff before and during a presentation."

—RICHARD CARLSON, AUTHOR OF DON'T SWEAT THE
SMALL STUFF . . . AND IT'S ALL SMALL STUFF

"It is a pleasure to acknowledge Tony Jeary and his fantastic work as a first-rate business consultant and personal trainer. He is a man with a deep well of skills and a treasure trove of abilities found only in those few who have persevered to achieve great success."

—DR. ROBERT SCHULLER

"Novel, well-written, and heartily recommended."

—LIBRARY JOURNAL

"Almost nothing good in life happens without a presentation of some sort. Helping others understand that is what Tony Jeary is all about."

—SCOTT KLEIN, PRESIDENT, EDS RETAIL

"A great book for all of us who interact with people on a daily basis. Simplify the communication process and enrich your life: read *Life Is a Series of Presentations*."

—ELAINE ST. JAMES, AUTHOR OF SIMPLIFY YOUR LIFE

"Wow! Here is another home run from the master of presentation. Thanks, Tony, for giving me practical ways I can improve my speaking."

—LINDA SWINDLING, JD, CSP, AUTHOR OF GET WHAT YOU
WANT, SET THE STANDARD & MEET THE CHALLENGE

"Any strategy can be dramatically enhanced, and execution intensified, when an organization has clearly articulated and communicated their strategies and tactics throughout all levels of the organization. Tony Jeary's methods are the most critical and final step in assuring maximum success in any organization, be it the largest corporation or even your household. Without utilizing his methodology, even the best strategy will be suboptimized!"

—MIKE GADE, CHIEF MARKETING OFFICER, 7-11

"Realizing that life is a series of presentations is the first step toward personal and professional success. Reading this book is the second. Implementing the powerful suggestions is the third. Tony makes it as easy as 1, 2, 3."

—AL LUCIA, PRESIDENT, ADL ASSOCIATES

"Tony Jeary is a true student of success—and a man who lives out his studies. This work is full of simple ideas that will help you attract success faster."

—JIM ROHN, AUTHOR OF *THE FIVE MAJOR PIECES TO THE LIFE PUZZLE*

"No endorsement can do this tremendous book justice. Please, please read and share it."

—CHARLIE "TREMENDOUS" JONES, AUTHOR OF *LIFE IS TREMENDOUS*

LIFE IS A SERIES

of

PRESENTATIONS

Eight Ways to Inspire, Inform, and
Influence Anyone, Anywhere, Anytime

TONY JEARY

with Kim Dower and J. E. Fishman

A FIRESIDE BOOK
PUBLISHED BY SIMON & SCHUSTER
New York   London   Toronto   Sydney

FIRESIDE
Rockefeller Center
1230 Avenue of the Americas
New York, NY 10020

This Fireside Edition 2005

FIRESIDE and colophon are registered trademarks
of Simon & Schuster, Inc.

For information regarding special discounts for bulk purchases,
please contact Simon & Schuster Special Sales at
1-800-456-6798 or business@simonandschuster.com.

3-D Outline, Mr. Presentation, Mr. Presentation Wizard and Presentation Mastery Profiler
are registered trademarks of Tony Jeary High Performances Resources, LLC.

Designed by Jan Pisciotta

Manufactured in the United States of America

9   10   8

The Library of Congress has cataloged the hardcover edition as follows:
Jeary, Tony.
Life is a series of presentations / Tony Jeary with Kim Dower and J. E. Fishman.
       p.   cm.
Includes bibliographical references and index.
1. Business presentations.   2. Public speaking.   3. Interpersonal communication.
4. Business communication.   5. Success.   I. Dower, Kim.   II. Fishman, Joel E.
III. Title.
HF5718.22.J433   2004
651.7'3—dc22   2003063004
ISBN-13:   978-0-7432-5141-9
ISBN-10:   0-7432-5141-5
ISBN-13:   978-0-7432-6925-4 (Pbk.)
ISBN-10:   0-7432-6925-X (Pbk.)

Acknowledgments

First and foremost, my coauthors and I wish to thank our families for helping us learn how to make the most important presentations of our lives—the ones we make to the people we love.

I would also like to thank the many people who have contributed insights that have influenced my work as a trainer, coach, and author, specifically Brian Tracy, Zig Ziglar, Kyle Wilson, Marc Harty, Robert Rohm, Dick Clipp, Mark Magnacca, Jim Norman, Nonie Jobe, Tawnya Austin, Myra Ketterman, Dave Freeborn, Jeannette Smith, Chris Cole, Bob Gerold, John Davis, and Jim McKenna. Deserving of special mention are my colleagues and partners at Tony Jeary High Performance Resources: Todd McDonald, Al and Michele Lucia, Carson Thompson, and Jeff Presley. Our core thesis, *Presentation Mastery*, co-written by my two partners George Lowe and Greg Kaiser, formed the basis for a good deal of what I have written here on that subject. George in particular has assisted greatly in making sure our ideas were presented consistently and thoroughly. These two, plus Dr. Michael O'Connor, have designed and developed the presentation assessment direction and deserve a big thanks.

A very special thanks also goes to my assistants, Sara Bowling, Bobbie Presley, and Christie George, all of whose dedication to me and enthusiasm for the cause of Presentation Mastery cannot easily be repaid. Thanks also to three of my longtime trusted advisors, my business manager Dan Miller, my business coach Mark Pantak, and my attorney Buz Barlow.

Kim and I owe great thanks to Kim's media training partner, Bill Applebaum. We also owe a debt of gratitude to our agent, Brian DeFiore, for introducing us to Joel E. Fishman, a man with true writing talent, who provided the pieces to the puzzle that we were otherwise missing. All three of us extend our thanks to Brian for his belief in this book. We also want to thank our editor, Caroline Sutton, who initially saw our vision, and to Mark Gompertz, Chris Lloreda, Marcia Burch, and other publishing team members who rallied the troops at Simon & Schuster and who arranged for the presentation of my publishing life, which won over the sales force and put us on the road to success. Finally, Kim and I are grateful to all the clients we've had over the years who have helped us learn how to do our very best coaching. In our cases, life has been a series of presentations shared with a series of wonderful people.

God bless all whom we've listed here, as well as those we may not have mentioned. None of us travels alone. We are all the products of the many wonderful relationships that life has been kind enough to direct our way.

Contents

PART II
HOW IT WORKS: EVERYDAY ESSENTIALS OF SUCCESSFUL INTERACTION

Introduction

Live and Learn . . .
and Share It All

Sometimes, in rare quiet moments, I sit around and wonder about the presentations that have shaped our world: King Solomon delivering his verdict in the most famous custody dispute in human history, Jesus testifying before Pontius Pilate, Henry V urging on his troops at Agincourt, the future Elizabeth I begging Queen Mary to spare her life in the aftermath of a Protestant plot, Thomas Jefferson exhorting his patriotic brethren to fight for their freedom, John F. Kennedy inspiring a generation to reach the moon, and Martin Luther King, Jr., motivating a million people on the Mall in Washington to fulfill his dreams of equality. Often these presentations have pertained to matters of life and death for masses of people. In some cases they have even decided the fate of the presenters themselves.

I sincerely hope you never have to make a presentation with your life hanging in the balance. More likely you think of your presentations as less threatening moments in the work week when you have to get up in front of a group. (If the audience is big enough, you may be so nervous that you want to die, but that's another matter.) Maybe you have to pitch a product to your sales reps or, if you are a rep yourself, to a roomful of customers. Perhaps you're an executive or manager who has to present the company direction to a set of employees or a chief executive who has to make quarterly presentations to her board of directors. If you're reading this you probably have some kind of preconceived notion about what it means to make a presentation. It's a formal occasion in a conference room, lots of chairs, a few sleepy colleagues, or maybe even a sea of faces staring up at you. White boards. Overhead projectors. PowerPoint slides. Coffee and danishes on the side table. A printed agenda. Right?

Well, yes, sort of. Frequently, presentations do contain those things. And, in similar fashion, frequently a movie contains music. But does the absence of music mean that it's not a movie? No, of course not. So the absence of an overhead projector doesn't mean it's not a presentation. Making presentations isn't about the props. It's about the context. I have learned this over the years, and I think most people know it in their hearts, even if they don't spend a lot of time thinking about what exactly constitutes a presentation.

In the most literal sense, I make presentations for a living. I speak before groups of people, sometimes thousands at a time, almost every day. And I get paid to do this, so you might think of me as a professional presenter. But what if I told you that those presentations are only a fraction of the number of presentations I deliver in a day? In fact, when I talk to large groups on my subject of expertise, I often begin by asking the audience how many presentations they make in a twenty-four-hour period. Usually these men and women are from the ranks of management, so their first thought is of the laser pointers and the other toys, of the sales calls and the pitches to colleagues. One or two a day might be their initial answer. But then, with a little prompting, a thought begins to dawn on them. What exactly is a presentation, anyway? Is a presentation defined by the size of the group and the coldness of the room, or is it defined by what you are trying to accomplish at that moment?

As the light of recognition begins to shine in the eyes of my audience, they reevaluate their initial answer. Maybe every time they formally communicate to a superior or customer, that's a presentation—meaning they make presentations dozens of times a day. Maybe every time they need to win a colleague over to their point of view over the phone or by e-mail is a presentation—meaning they make presentations scores of times a day. Maybe every time they attempt to convince anybody, anywhere, of anything—in business, at home, on the phone, in person, one-on-one, or in groups—that's a presentation. In which case, they might actually make *hundreds* of presentations a day!

Your life is full of opportunities. And these opportunities are a reflection of the choices you make daily, weekly, monthly, and yearly. I'd even say your life consists of the choices you make every minute. Do I get up when the alarm clock rings or do I stay in bed late this morning? Do I go for the bacon and eggs or do I eat the bran cereal? Do I kiss my child before I put him on the bus or do I scowl at him because I haven't had my coffee yet? For that matter, do I allow my mood at this very moment to be dictated by the presence or absence of a cup of java?

Your success in life depends upon how you approach the millions of opportunities before you. The person who sleeps late every morning, for example, might be well rested, but she surely isn't going to be the early bird catching the worm. For the purposes of this discussion, though, I'm not concerned with whether sleeping late is a good choice. I'm more interested in one particular type of frequent opportunity: your chance to make an impression upon people who will affect the course of your life. What I spend my time teaching smart people just like you is that they don't even realize the opportunities they miss every day by not stopping to think about their presentation strategy. And this is a significant loss to all aspects of their well-being, from their monetary success to their personal happiness.

Unless you're a hermit living on a mountaintop, your life largely consists of your interactions with the people around you. In the office, unless you're everyone's boss, you can't choose all your colleagues (in fact, it's more likely you haven't chosen any of them). You can't usually pick your superiors. And rarely can you choose your customers. Yet all these people hold tremendous sway over your daily progress through the workday and, as important, the ultimate success of your career. So you might not have chosen to work with them, but—consciously or not—you would like to have a degree of power over how much you can sway them.

In our personal lives, we often have more influence over those people with whom we surround ourselves, but even then we cannot assume complete control of their moods or thoughts. If a person in the family unit does not wish to cooperate in the family's daily activities, that's going to affect all their happiness. If the members of a family cannot convince one another to behave in compatible ways, then they're all going to be miserable.

Think about some of the opportunities you have every day to win people over to the thoughts and actions that will help you improve your own life. Your son doesn't want to put his clothes on for school, and if he persists much longer you'll be late for work. You've got too much to accomplish at the office, so you desperately need to convince your boss to allow you to hire an assistant. At lunchtime you want to talk a clerk into letting you return a brand-new VCR to the store, even though you lost the receipt. On the way, you're pulled over by a police officer for failing to make a full stop before turning right on red, and you'd really like to be sent on your way without a ticket.

Imagine how much your time on earth would improve if you could prevail at most of these crucial moments. Not a single one of them may change the entire course of your life, but winning that other person over to your point of view with regularity almost certainly will help take you where you want to go. *The way in which we present our thoughts and ideas to people—from our colleagues at work to our spouse and even the person waiting on us at the grocery store—could have a profound effect on the shape of our own lives.* So one sure way to accomplish the things we want to accomplish is to improve our success rate in these kinds of circumstances. If we can do that, then we can advance the quality of our existence. Because, as I like to say, *life is a series of presentations. Mastery of the art of making presentations takes us closer to the outcomes we desire.* It also provides a powerful confidence boost that will guarantee you more success in all aspects of your life.

Never thought of it that way? Take heart. It's not your fault!

Contact with Impact

Whenever I have the opportunity, I ask educators in the Dallas area, where I live, what kind of instruction they offer their students in the art of presenting. I've asked this of university professors, and I've asked it of high school principals. As parents, we all want our children to have confidence in their abilities and possess high self-esteem, so I asked the head of my two girls' elementary school this question as well. The best answer he could think of was speech class, which is for children with pronunciation issues!

Of course a kid with a speech impediment should get special attention, but what about helping the rest of us be all that we can be? The fact is that our formal education systems usually lack any instruction in the more practical skills of life. But I'm not talking about reinstituting defunct home economics classes. Rather, I am confronted every single day with intelligent, well-educated, and often exceptional people—my clients or people who work for them—who have never been offered one iota of information about what should be the fourth pillar after reading, writing, and arithmetic. I call it *presentation skills,* but we might as easily call it *people skills.* As my friend and colleague Jim Rohn—a motivational speaker, author, and business philosopher—has said: "It's not the matter you cover so much as it is the manner in which you cover it."

In the course of my life, I've had the privilege of getting to know many interesting folks, not a few of them people of great accomplishment. I've met and trained famous entrepreneurs and politicians and the executives, presidents, and CEOs of Fortune 500 companies. Some of these people had enough God-given talent to sell sand to a desert nomad. Most of them—however they came to it—had the ability to connect well with the people around them and frequently to win colleagues and customers over to their point of view. But the interesting thing is that these men and women weren't necessarily all that much better at this than their closest rivals. In most cases, in fact, they were just marginally better than their colleagues at some of the skills that define great communicators. Did that small difference really matter? You bet it did.

In this book you'll learn about what my organization calls the Presentation Impact Curve, which suggests that incremental improvements in presentation skills will pay disproportionate dividends with regard to your influence upon others. By being just a little bit better than their peers, the successful individuals I know achieved enormous results. And if I had to write a profile of each of those people who were successful, I could probably explain to you exactly how their presentations differ from those made by millions of equally smart and well-intentioned workers who never could seem to achieve their own highest ambitions.

In corporate America, awareness of the value of presentation skills to business success is just breaking the surface. In the not-too-distant past, most of my clients were the top executives at major companies—people who often had to speak to large groups of employees and shareholders, or those who often found themselves in front of the media. Or they were teams of sales professionals trying to get an edge with their customers.

Today, by contrast, my clients increasingly appreciate the importance of presentation skills at *every* level of their organization. Wal-Mart, for example, has 98,000 managers apart from the top executives in the home office. If those managers can't motivate or communicate well to their teams, the efficiency and responsiveness of the entire organization—1.4 million employees—suffers.

As more and more top executives come to recognize the crucial role of efficient personal communication throughout their companies, I believe they will begin to institutionalize the ongoing learning and refinement of the important skills we'll talk about in this book. The greatest manager of his generation, Jack Welch of General Electric, used to say he considered himself a teacher—a job that is largely about presentation, when you consider it. In similar fashion, Steve Jobs of Apple computers and Bill Gates of Microsoft may be old rivals, but they have many traits in common. Both men, I believe, are at the leading edge of a movement toward increasing involvement by chief executives in the presentation skills that they hope will permeate their corporations. Jobs and Gates have changed their official titles in the past couple of years. If they keep to the paths they've chosen, I believe they may soon come to refer to themselves as the chief presentation officer (CPO) of their respective companies. *Acknowledgment of the importance of the CPO role may represent the next phase of the so-called Learning Organization.*

But no individuals should wait for their bosses, seeking a corporate edge, to give them an advantage in their own day-to-day lives. The historical references that I opened with are just a few among thousands of stories I might find where great presentation skills have already made the difference between success and also-ran status. Where did Elizabeth I and Henry V and JFK and Martin Luther King, Jr., acquire their presentation abilities? Some of the greatest leaders in history certainly may have possessed extraordinary talents, but I strongly believe that *delivering good presentations requires more skill than talent.* What makes me so sure? I now earn my living making presentations, yet I was once just about the worst presenter you could ever want to hear!

Bounce When You Hit Bottom

If you have attended one of my seminars for corporate executives, you might find my background a little surprising. The people I've helped often have advanced degrees and work at the top echelons of American business. They've attended the best colleges and training courses and benefited from the advice of the greatest consultants in the world, and now they run things at such companies as Ford, Wal-Mart, and New York Life. As for me, I've read and studied thousands of works. The foundations of my program rest firmly on a core of book knowledge, as well as life experience. My story, I think, is relevant to the enterprise at hand.

About forty years ago, I was born into a middle-class family in Oklahoma City. We lived in a nondescript house not unlike millions of modest houses you find in the hardworking neighborhoods of any American town. My father's father was a small-time entrepreneur with his own candy route. My mother's father, Cliff Smalley, started his own car detailing business in 1943 (a bad hand kept him out of World War II), and my father later went to work for him. Including my younger brother, Randy, we were a happy family. I went to public school until the fifth grade, then to nondenominational Christian schools, then to a Catholic high school. I learned to make God the priority in my life, and that is still true today.

But what distinguished me, I guess, was having two grandparents and parents who lived by their entrepreneurial instincts. All I knew my whole life was to be an entrepreneur, to serve people, and, ultimately, to be blessed to earn a whole lot of money. My family never quite achieved the last part. But the family business, the Auto Beauty Shop, did perform well enough to keep us all very well fed. Dealers would send us cars to be spotlessly cleaned, and my father, my grandfather, and even my grandmother would work right alongside a group of hardworking men and women six days a week, doing the same car-cleaning chores as their employees without regard to economic status or race, at a time when people had strong feelings about both.

After watching this activity while growing up, all I ever wanted to do was work. I started mowing yards when I was ten or twelve, and pretty soon I was holding down three jobs. At one job, I was making $20 per hour when kids my age were normally making $2 doing other things. I worked for Target stores, assembling bicycles at night for $5 per bike.

They'd lock me in the store a couple of nights a week and I'd just crank those things out, putting together four bikes an hour and sleeping little. I also worked as a photographer for an insurance company, taking pictures of houses to document them for coverage. And, of course, I helped out at the Auto Beauty Shop. Somehow I made it to school regularly, but my main focus was raking in the bucks—and finding ways to spend them. By the time I was sixteen I owned a '66 Mustang, a '48 Chevy pickup, and a '77 Monte Carlo.

In 1979, before I even graduated from high school, my grandfather agreed to sell me the 49% of his business that he had not already sold to my father. I had my grub stake, and I was going to work like a dog to make it pay off. I woke up before dawn every morning to go pick up the expensive cars from the dealers. Before sunup, I would be driving brand-new Ferraris down deserted streets, minimizing the chance of any mishaps. Then I would work alongside my employees, just as my father and grandparents had, and I'd return the cars the next morning.

I got to know the dealers really well, and one day the manager of the Cadillac dealership, a fellow named Keith Wadley, called me aside. "Son, you're working too hard with your hands," he told me. "You're too smart for that. You need to be using your mind, not your hands."

That simple observation hit me like a strike of lightning from heaven. My dad had been a server. All his life, he had served people with his hands. I was going to do it differently. I would serve people with my mind. So I worked just as hard as ever cleaning cars and managing the Auto Beauty Shop, but I soon began making time for investing in and building businesses, too. In all honesty, I was manic about it. Within three years I owned a residential leasing company, a building company, a grocery store, two lakes for potential development, an office building, and small parts of two banks. At the peak of my fortune in the mid-1980s I had two homes, a chauffeur, six cars, and many of the other possessions of a wealthy man. But in 1986, oil suddenly dropped from $40 to $10 per barrel and Congress changed the laws of depreciation to make real estate speculation far less attractive. My highly leveraged empire collapsed like a cornstalk after a hard frost.

Within a year I was destitute. I had gone from having several million dollars to a negative $500,000 net worth in a matter of months. The foreclosures and lawsuits were coming so fast and furious that I had to marry my wife with a sort of reverse prenuptial agreement—one that would protect her against my creditors. At the worst point I lay in bed for three days, contemplating suicide. Those days were so painful that I never revisit the details, even now. I didn't know what to do, but I had to move on. My wife, Tammy, and I packed up our one remaining car and headed for Dallas to try and start a new life. I thought about taking a spin past the now-shuttered Auto Beauty Shop, but the idea was too discouraging. I just hit the gas pedal and resolved not to look back.

Pretty soon I had scraped up a few bucks to start another business. I was mowing lawns for the first time as an adult, working alongside a small crew that I had assembled. But this time they weren't lawns in my own modest childhood neighborhood—they were the lawns of rich people. I figured that maybe I could meet someone in these upscale areas who might help me find a new opportunity and again steer my business life in the direction of success. Day after day I went home to the bathroom of our tiny apartment and washed the grime off my calloused hands with the words of Keith Wadley echoing through my head: "You need to be using your mind, not your hands."

But how? I had so few dollars left to employ—all I had were those two hands and what I retained between my ears. I thought there must be a way to leverage what I knew, both my good and my bad experiences. While I worked I wondered how many of the people in all those great houses had made it big by doing the same. And whenever I saw a client, I'd tell him or her the story of how a multimillionaire from Oklahoma City came to be mowing lawns in the suburbs of Dallas.

Then, one day, sure enough, I went to pick up the monthly check at a client's house. I had become casually friendly with this fellow over the months, and I had told him my story, as I had done to a hundred others. This time, he invited me in for a cup of coffee, we chatted for a few minutes, and he gave me a tip that would change my life. He said that—never mind my spectacular flameout—my experience at having achieved quick success could make me a hot commodity on the rapidly growing seminar circuit. He invited me to attend a seminar on computers with him, which shortly led to an introduction to the event's promoter.

I had a lot of respect for the seminar world. I had rounded out my hard-knocks education with dozens of visits to seminars, the best of which I found far more efficient communicators of information than an ordinary classroom education. After hearing my story, the promoter, whose name was Gary Cochran, told me I had far more life-experience than most of the seminar speakers he had represented. He agreed to give me a shot, and before I knew it he had scheduled me in dozens of cities.

Now, you have to know a little bit about the seminar business to appreciate the impending disaster. In those days, no one paid admission for seminars. Everyone involved made their living off the sales of books and other paraphernalia in the back of the room. Gary would spend thousands of dollars getting people to attend. It was the speaker's job to inspire them to buy stuff. If the audience didn't visit the table at the back of the room, then nobody involved in producing the seminar would eat.

I wish I remembered my first presentation like it was yesterday. But the reality is that I've blocked most of it out—it has receded into the fog of humiliation. I'm not even sure of the exact topic: something along the lines of how to achieve one's financial goals. What I do recall is how confident I felt before the event. Unlike so much of the seminar talent in those days, I knew I was the real thing—or had been. I wouldn't be speaking theoretically about how to grow wealthy; I had done it on a grander scale than many people ever dared dream of. (Even the bad luck that followed would have lessons people could take away.) I had invested dozens of hours in slick overhead transparencies that would drive home the points of my presentation. I had bought a brand-new suit and tie on my wife's credit card. My shoes were polished and I was ready to rock and roll.

The promoter had efficiently booked me into a dozen cities, and the first gig was an appearance in the ballroom of some mid-level hotel in downtown Seattle. I strutted into the cavernous room with my notes and slides tucked under my arm in a manila folder. Looking up for the first time, I suddenly discovered that Gary had done his job too well. There must have been close to a thousand people in the room. To me, it felt like a million. I haltingly introduced myself and, throwing the first slide up, began to speak. I had spent ten years building an empire, only to go broke, I explained in all sincerity. Now, as I urged them to do, I had decided not to build a business but to build *myself*. This was not hocus-pocus, I thought. I could really bring value to the people in this audience. But if so, why were they tittering in the background? I looked out at them in desperation. To my nerve-blinded eyes they were a monolith, an expanse of incommunicative faces. Somehow, as I droned on, I began to discern that a few hands had gone up, as if trying to throw me a lifeline. They didn't wish to be called upon, though; they were pointing at the screen behind me. I had placed my transparency on the projector upside down!

I'd like to say that that was the low point of my new career as a presenter, but such a statement wouldn't even come close to being accurate. In fact, that moment wasn't even the low point of that day! I continued to fumble along, adrift at the head of the room, completely detached from my audience and, through my awkwardness and ineptitude, putting the lie to my very real life-experiences and the lessons they ought to have taught. But what else could I do? I was passively carried along by the inertia of the moment, which had taken me away from any tangible connection to my audience or the material I was presenting. People weren't just laughing at my slides anymore; they were doing something much worse. They were laughing at *me*—and they were beginning to walk out of the ballroom.

That two-hour train wreck of a seminar was the first of many presentations I made that year that ended in utter failure and humiliation. I don't think I sold a single book or tape in Seattle. And if Gary earned back his expenses on me that first year it had to be a miracle. But, though I was humbled, I also remained determined. I wasn't going to mow lawns for the rest of my life and I had to find a way to pay for that new suit! I trudged through forty cities that year, and after each appearance Gary and I went back to the hotel room to do the postmortem. I also began studying everything I could get my hands on that might improve my presentation skills. I read hundreds of books about public speaking and related topics, watched scores of videos, and attended dozens of seminars to observe and quantify how the masters made excellent presentations. And eventually I began to improve. Then I built upon that improvement. Today, with all due modesty, I am one of the most accomplished presentation coaches in the country. But that result didn't drop from outer space. It came from study and plain old hard work.

The Foundations of Great Presentations

There will always be a little bit of art behind regular presentation success, and we can't control the amount of talent God gives us. But I firmly believe that being a successful presenter involves more craft than talent. In my studies I have identified skills and techniques that run like indelible themes through the lives of successful presenters. No one comes into the world with skills and techniques. They have to be taught and they can usually be learned by anyone with the will to learn them.

I know that it's true, because I learned them myself. In addition, my coauthor Kim Dower (Kim-from-L.A.), who makes her living as a media coach, has taught similar skills to hundreds of high achievers. Her clients are often experts in their field, but they need help in front of a camera or an audience. Often after only a few days or even hours, they leave her office with their pitches much more polished than when they entered it.

Kim and I met at the American Bookseller's Convention in Los Angeles a few years ago. Her company was conducting a raffle that offered a free coaching session, and she ended up pulling my card out of the fish bowl. As we got to talking, we realized that we shared many views on the value of presentations, especially an understanding that **Presentation Mastery** is perhaps the least commonly known factor in people's professional and personal success.

One day, Kim and I were talking about all the ways presentation excellence can improve a person's day-to-day life and the fact that all people are continually presenting to one another throughout the day. We compared stories that we've heard from our individual clients about how the techniques that we teach them for specific presentations have also helped them in their personal lives. We were amazed to find that, although Kim and I work with very different types of clients, the overwhelming similarity is that everything they learn from us rolls over into other aspects of their lives and makes them feel more confident in everything they do. Then Kim looked at me and said, "The truth is, Tony, *life* is a series of presentations." When she said that I knew I had to solicit her help in writing my first big book. And we soon set out down that long and arduous road.

After a while, Joel E. Fishman was introduced to us by our agent. Joel is not only a writer and former editor, he is also a retail business owner.

He found our proposed title, *Life Is a Series of Presentations*, to be one of the most intuitive ideas he'd heard in a long career in the book business.

So our writing team consists of a lifelong entrepreneur and presentation expert, a media trainer, and a business owner and writer. Collectively we have a great deal of life-experience and the expert knowledge needed to help you benefit most from this book. Each in our own way, we all live by the author Harvey McKay's brilliantly simple advice: "Do what you love, love what you do, and deliver more than you promise."

You don't have to read a thousand books or watch nearly as many videos to learn to be a great presenter. I have read them all and I have studied the techniques that universally distinguish good presenters from bad. I have been honing the presenter's craft for more than fifteen years—not only my own approach to presenting, but the skills of many thousands of others whom I've trained and coached. These people knew that having sharper presentation skills would enhance their credibility and respect, which would get more audience buy-in for the points they needed to get across. Few of these people intended to earn a living by making presentations per se. All who applied my practices, however, have improved their outcomes, learning to be more comfortable, confident, and effective when the occasion arises to make a presentation. And, as I mentioned earlier, these opportunities arise many times each and every day.

Throughout this book, I use the word "audience" a great deal. You may be in the habit of thinking of an audience as a large group of people attending a formal presentation or performance. In common usage, you would be right, but one of our main points is to help you understand that when anyone tries to inspire, inform, or influence anyone else, that's a presentation. This means that an audience may be as small as one person. So when I use the word **audience** throughout this book, it may refer to a group of any size or it may refer to a single individual.

I strongly believe that anyone who seeks success in life's endeavors—at work or in other contexts—will benefit tremendously from the Eight Essential Practices of Successful Presenters that you'll find here. If you end up agreeing, I urge you to pass this book along to your friends, so they can benefit too. And if you work for or own any kind of collaborative enterprise—large or small—I encourage you to expose your associates to this book, as well. I know it will make your company function better, because I have seen this with my own eyes in countless situations. It's not overstating the case to assert that *Presentation Mastery is the single biggest key to professional success and personal power,* and this is true no matter your background or education level.

Life Is a Series of Presentations is the culmination of the past decade and a half of my work studying and helping others put into practice the techniques for making great presentations. With the help of my co-authors, I will teach you that, while the differences between a good and bad presentation may seem intangible, many differences can in fact be quantified. For example, all people—whether presenting to a conference or to their spouse—must approach their task in a state of preparedness, must make others want to listen to them, and must then be responsive to their audience. These goals sound so simple. Why don't more folks achieve them? Well, it turns out that most people don't know the Eight Essential Practices of Successful Presenters that you'll learn in the second half of the book. To understand why these practices will be effective, however, you need to appreciate the three core concepts that I'll introduce in the first section: the psychology of persuasion and influence; the principles of Neurolinguistic Programming, which enables people to practice what is called Sensory Acuity; and the organizational foundation that helps you define what I call your Presentation Universe. While some of this terminology may sound complicated, these theories can be summarized relatively simply:

- **Psychology of Persuasion and Influence:** You will have greater influence over people if you understand the prejudices that are hard-wired into all human beings. Once you do, you can easily establish yourself as an authority in their minds, which means you will begin with their full attention.

- **Neurolinguistic Programming and Sensory Acuity:** The vast majority of us have five senses, but we need to learn to use them consciously so as to "read" our audience and make adjustments on the fly. It's all about gaining *attention for retention.* That is, they won't recall what we said if we can't get them to stay focused throughout the presentation.

- **The Presentation Universe:** I have learned over the years that most people give amazingly little attention to the role presentations play in their daily lives. Once they begin to think about it, however, they come to appreciate how many opportunities they're missing. By defining all the presentation opportunities in your world—your Presentation Universe—you begin to set a strategy for how you will conquer the challenges ahead. Then you will have a basis with which to evaluate the way you approach each of your presentations. Before you go into a meeting or discussion—at work or in more casual settings—do you ever ask yourself exactly why you are saying what you are about to say? No? Don't feel bad; remarkably few people do. But if you don't know exactly what the purpose of your message is, then how can you expect your audience to pick up that message fully and clearly? We function in a three-dimensional world, yet most presenters pursue their task in a manner that burdens them with tunnel vision. In order to take our presentation skills to the next level, we need to learn to think of our presentation as a multidimensional exercise. That's why I created a trademarked 3-D Outline, which you will learn about in Chapter 6. In more than ten years of training hundreds of thousands of people, the 3-D Outline has received more positive response in evaluations than any other single concept that I regularly discuss. Understanding and employing this process alone will improve any presenter's success rate exponentially. Combined with the personal perspective of a defined Presentation Universe, it gives unique insights into how to achieve your presentation goals.

Despite the value of the above theories, you need not fully grasp them in order to build your presentation skills. Each of the Eight Essentials in the second part of the book contains practical instruction on how to polish one's craft, regardless of whether the theories are of interest to you intellectually. And you can begin employing these steps in any order you choose. Taken together, however, *the Eight Essential Practices of Successful Presenters will dramatically improve your ability to effectively communicate your ideas to individuals or to groups of any size in both your business and personal lives.*

I have taught these practices to professionals and homemakers, to older folks and kids. My daughters have used them and have had a happier time selling their fund-raising candy than any other children I know. My minister has been using them while he builds the fastest growing congregation in the Dallas metroplex. And, of course, I use them every day, not just when I conduct seminars or training sessions, but when I need to upgrade a hotel room or get a good seat at a restaurant.

To one degree or another, in fact, I have tested the Eight Essentials you'll soon learn about before literally tens of thousands of people. I use them in my own presentations to such an extent that they have all become second nature. Of course, I have also taught them to chief executive officers, salesmen, and mid-level executives. My niece even used some of them to get elected student council president! I know they work.

Maybe the lives of these people don't depend on presentation skills. But their livelihoods and personal happiness very well may. And yours, too. Because, as I hope you've begun to appreciate, life really is a series of presentations. *The better your presentations are, the better your life will be.*

✓
Very Important Points

- Your success in life depends upon how you approach the millions of opportunities before you.

- Unless you're a hermit living on a mountaintop, your life largely consists of your interactions with the people around you.

- The way in which we present our thoughts and ideas to people—from our colleagues at work to our spouse and even the person waiting on us at the grocery store—could have a profound effect on the shape of our own lives.

- Life is a series of presentations.

- Mastery of the art of making presentations takes us closer to the outcomes we desire.

- Acknowledgment of the importance of the Chief Presentation Officer (CPO) role may represent the next phase of the so-called Learning Organization.

- Delivering good presentations requires more skill than talent.

- Presentation Mastery is the single biggest key to professional success and personal power.

- The Eight Essential Practices of Successful Presenters will dramatically improve your ability to effectively communicate your ideas to individuals or to groups of any size in both your business and personal lives.

- The better your presentations are, the better your life will be.

PART I

WHY IT WORKS

Understanding Before Action

CHAPTER 1

What Bill Clinton Has That Gary Condit Doesn't

The Difference between a Good Presenter and a Poor One

Take two Democrats of the same generation with similar political views and similar character issues. One becomes the first man in his party to win reelection in fifty years—despite a sex scandal that later leads to his impeachment trial. The other, after two terms in Congress, can't get elected dogcatcher. Whatever you think of the politics of Bill Clinton and Gary Condit, most people would agree that both behaved inappropriately during crucial moments in their professional lives. Yet Clinton, despite years of jokes and innuendo, managed to walk the fine line between political success and historical infamy (at least while he was in office). By contrast, in the course of one short year, Condit transformed himself before the entire world from a respected congressman to a walking synonym for "unredeemable cad." As is the case for us all, their presentations made a big difference.

Earlier, Clinton's defeat of President George H. W. Bush may have been mostly about "the economy, stupid," but it also seemed obvious to me at the time that Bush did not present himself or his ideas in a completely effective manner. Remember the "town hall" debate of that campaign? Clinton was completely engaged with his audience, hanging on every word, while Bush kept checking his watch—as if he had an appointment that was more important than getting reelected president. Here's a hint that you don't need to read a whole book to learn: If you blatantly peek at your watch during your own presentation, you may have instantly jeopardized any rapport you already established with your audience. History shows that Clinton "won" that debate—and that single sub-par performance on Bush's part might well have sealed his own one-term fate.

Clinton might have been more of a natural with people, but you can't tell me that a man who was as capable as Bush was in other respects had to look at his watch or do the many other things he did to alienate his audience. Despite Bush's excellent qualifications for reelection, if you review that tape you'll see a man who often speaks *at* his audience, not *to* them; who looks uncomfortable in their presence; who rarely involves his audience by redirecting attention to them and taking it off himself; who is not "up" for the moment; and who makes very few adjustments to his approach in order to retain his audience's focus. Somebody failed to sharpen this candidate's presentation skills.

As president, Ronald Reagan became known as the "Great Communicator." He earned this reputation by being the first president in modern times to stay relentlessly "on message" whenever he spoke, in public or in private. You may or may not have agreed with his political views (or, for that matter, with those of Clinton or Bush), but unlike our experience with most other politicians, we always knew where Reagan stood.

Bill Clinton was something different altogether. To the great frustration of his opponents, Clinton proved to be an excellent presenter, even if at times he quite intentionally was not very communicative. How can that be? Because communication and presentation may frequently overlap, but they are not necessarily the same thing. For the purpose of my work and this book, I define **presentation** as *the act of working to change the content of another person's mind at a particular time and place*. Note that I said "to change the content of another person's mind," not "to change another person's mind." The latter has the connotation of getting a person or persons to alter their opinion. But a presentation might do the opposite. It might *reinforce* someone's opinion. Or it might have nothing to do with your audience's beliefs and simply impart information. Or it might spur your audience to take action. In any case, *if successfully executed, presentations fulfill desired outcomes in the presenter's audience—by enhancing a skill, changing or reinforcing an attitude, or imparting information*.

The upshot of all this is that, on some level, any time we have contact with another individual—on the phone, in person, via e-mail or voice mail, etc.—we are making a presentation, whether we like it or not. And Bill Clinton, for all his flaws, liked the presentation process and so became very good at it. George H. W. Bush, for all his strengths, clearly didn't enjoy making presentations. And here's the most important point to keep in mind: because Bush managed for so many years to succeed in life *without* achieving Presentation Mastery, he never felt compelled to build those skills. So when the necessity arose for him to step it up a notch, he had neither the time nor the inclination to do so. And the result for him was a less than satisfactory conclusion to his long political career.

Most of us are more like George H. W. Bush than we are like Bill Clinton. We were probably not born with natural charisma or the gift of gab. The very ubiquity of our presentation opportunities often makes us unaware that they exist as opportunities at all. They're just a part of our day that we don't think about, like walking or talking. Our walking has always gotten us to where we want to go, so why bother to work on improving it? We have areas of mastery in our lives—perhaps the kinds of things we've learned in graduate school or in business training—but when it comes to interpersonal skills we just presume that mere competence is enough. In a very real sense, then, the great opportunities we have to improve our lives through Presentation Mastery continually pass us by.

A lot of the people I know who are Master Presenters have achieved that status either by chance or because at some point they were forced to do so. In many cases they were corporate executives who learned—before it was too late—that their lack of presentation skills was holding them back. So they went for training or coaching. In some instances, as with many of my coauthor Kim's clients, they were requested to refine their presentation skills by a superior or a business partner who needed them to meet an important challenge. But the best story of this kind that I ever heard is about a man who *had* to learn how to present, literally in order to survive. His name is Bill Porter.

Presentation Is an Art

On a recent plane trip I sat next to a man who happened to be a professional chef. When we exchanged pleasantries and he learned how I make my living, he became excited to remark that a big part of what he does also involves presentation. From the compilation of colors and shapes on a diner's plate to the dress of the staff to the lighting and decoration, he noted, the quality of any restaurant patron's experience depends greatly on how well the chef has mastered the art of presentation. My plane companion had become so conversant in the art of restaurant presentation that he told me he could predict half of an unknown restaurant's menu simply by looking at the presentation of their parking lot and front entrance.

Art requires both skill and creativity. For the chef, creativity without skill might result in something beautiful to look at but not very appealing to eat. Skill without creativity could result in a well-executed dish that didn't make for a very interesting dining experience. But when he was able to elevate his vocation to an art, it meant that the chef's skill *and* creativity had joined forces. Beautiful things resulted.

Like the chef, a man named Bill Porter came to understand early on that *the presentations in his life would require equal parts inspiration, skill, and hard work*. And—guess what?—beautiful things resulted.

When he was still an infant in the early 1930s, Bill Porter was diagnosed with cerebral palsy. Though he later proved to be a man of normal intelligence, the doctor predicted that he would be mentally retarded and urged Bill's mother to have him institutionalized. In a pattern that would be repeated over many decades by Bill's parents and then by Bill himself, they ignored the doctor's advice and refused to accept defeat.

As related in the book *Ten Things I Learned from Bill Porter* (written by his longtime friend and employee, Shelly Brady), Porter would go on to graduate from the Grout School for Handicapped Children in Portland, Oregon. More important, he then graduated from the mainstream Lincoln High School, an extremely unusual accomplishment for a physically challenged person of that era. But none of that could change the fact that Porter struggled with a very real and visible disability. At a particularly poignant stage in his life, Porter began looking for a career with the help of a counselor. This effort resulted in little more than a series of humiliations. A job as a pharmacy store clerk lasted less than a day because Porter's trembling hands would not allow him to stock the shelves neatly. A job as a Goodwill Industries cashier lasted three days because Porter's palsied fingers kept hitting the wrong keys. His physical limitations also brought a job at the Salvation Army docks to a prompt end. And his slurred speech soon lost him his job answering phones at the Veterans Rehabilitation Center. After five months of this kind of thing the counselor told Porter that the state considered him unemployable. He suggested that Porter stay home and collect disability payments.

Another person in Porter's position may have taken this advice to heart, but Porter knew deep down inside that he could be a productive member of society—even if he couldn't tie his own shoes without difficulty or button his own shirt cuffs. A few years before, Porter had had some success as a door-to-door salesman for United Cerebral Palsy. He quit that job when he realized he couldn't make a living at it, though. The products were too limited and Porter got the impression that repeat customers were buying as much out of charity as for any other reason. He then tried to freelance for a while, purchasing gift items from a catalog and reselling them door-to-door for a marked-up price. In order to do that, Porter realized he had to create a unique presentation that would compensate for his communication disability. So he meticulously built his own catalog by cutting and pasting, then typing descriptions himself. As Shelly Brady notes: "He wanted to make sure that if verbal communication broke down between himself and his clients due to his speech impediment, the illustrated catalog would do the explaining for him." In other words, Porter—like any good presenter—had *put a great deal of stock in preparation*. Although that preparation paid off in a degree of success, Porter had begun looking for steadier work with a big employer when he met the string of failures mentioned above. When he realized that his physical limitations were too much to overcome in the field of manual labor, he again set his sights on becoming a salesman.

Having exhausted his patience with state counselors, Porter began combing the want ads himself. Naturally, this met with more rejection. Most times he didn't even get past the initial phone call. Then, one day, Porter landed an interview with a company called Watkins Products. "I know I can do this job," Porter confidently told the interviewer. "I've been successfully selling for the past ten years. It's in my blood. My father is a successful salesman. It almost doesn't matter what product I sell, customers enjoy buying from me."

I've never met Bill Porter. I can only imagine how difficult it was for him to deliver this speech at the end of a year of rejection and frustration and while trying to do the things that a non-handicapped person might take for granted: sitting still and upright, allowing his muscles to relax, and forming the words with his lips and tongue. All of these things require incredible amounts of effort for a person with cerebral palsy. Yet in this short speech Porter employed several techniques that are the hallmark of the Master Presenter, which we'll explore in later chapters. He put himself in a positive psychological state by opening with a statement that projected self-confidence: "I know I can do this job." Then he lent authority to that assertion by offering bona fides that the interviewer had to respect: "I've been successfully selling for the past ten years. It's in my blood. My father is a successful salesman." Finally, he used a technique called **Future Pacing,** essentially leading his audience to a picture of the outcome Porter intended to generate: "It almost doesn't matter what product I sell, customers enjoy buying from me."

Don't forget, we're talking about an event that happened in 1961, decades before disability laws, when tolerance for people who were "different" ebbed very low. Porter got his break, but prejudice being what it is, the sales manager assigned Porter to the worst, most hopeless territory in Portland, where people lived in dire poverty and the houses were falling down. And the poor man was working on commission! But more important to Bill Porter, he had himself a job. He packed his briefcase full of color brochures, hit the street at 9 A.M., and hasn't looked back since. Porter didn't sell a single item his first day on the job. But he took time to learn all he could about the Watkins product line and understood human nature enough to use Watkins's money-back guarantee as a major selling point. Eventually, he went on to become one of the top salesmen in the history of Watkins Products, and their top salesman ever in the Northwest. None of his colleagues, so far as I know, had to struggle with Porter's physical challenges. On the other hand, I'll bet that none of them made presentations as masterfully, either.

A Master Presenter

Bill Porter was an only child. When it became clear that, in the natural order of things, his father and mother would predecease him— and that he was not capable of performing work that required manual dexterity—he realized that becoming a Master Presenter was the only chance he had to live a dignified and independent life. What makes me so sure that Porter is a Master Presenter? I'll answer with another question. Tell me, what choice did a man in his position have? Bill Porter never went to college, so he couldn't become a professional. He might, I suppose, have become an office clerk of some kind. But having chosen to be a salesman, how could he possibly succeed if he allowed his presentation ability to cruise along at an average level? People with disabilities usually have to compensate somehow. Like the blind person who listens more attentively, Porter compensated for his weaknesses by building other strengths.

Amazingly, in order to succeed Bill Porter had to overcome one of the most powerful principles that help people connect with one another. As you'll learn in the next chapter, people overwhelmingly like folks who are like themselves and tend to distrust those who are different. Porter—who walks hunched over, has limited use of his hands, and slurs his words—was like very few people upon whose doors he knocked. To achieve success as a commissioned door-to-door salesman in this position required both monumental effort and complete mastery of presentation techniques.

This assertion is confirmed by some of the other elements of Porter's story. I believe it was the business consultant Tom Peters who once said of customer service, "You can pretend to care, but you can't pretend to be there." Shelly Brady tells the story of sitting outside in the sun with Porter at a resort in Palm Springs. They had just given a motivational talk and Brady was feeling relaxed when Porter began fretting about the customer messages that would be piling up on his answering machine. Brady tried to reassure him that his customers, who "are loyal to you," would await his return. "Exactly," Porter said. "Loyal to *me*, not an answering machine." Porter knows that making presentations is the heart of his business, and presentations by definition require some kind of one-to-one contact. (As we'll see later in the book, this is even true when you're presenting to a whole roomful of individuals.)

Another thing Porter knows is that *appearances are a major factor behind one's success in life.* He pays careful attention to grooming habits and the way he dresses. Since he can't easily perform some of these important tasks, he has gone out of his way to befriend the employees of a nearby hotel, who help him polish up by tying his shoes for him and buttoning his cuffs. Interestingly, Brady observes that the hotel's manager and lobby staff "had a good rapport with Bill, too. They all felt they were essentially in the same line of work—pleasing their customers. Bill came to know them all personally; he learned about their birthdays, college applications, marriages, and children." As Dale Carnegie said, "You can make more friends in two months by becoming interested in other people than you can in two years by trying to get other people interested in you." In the course of his work, Brady reports, Porter has committed to memory the habits and personal preferences of more than 500 customers.

A further point of significance is that Porter never uses his master presentation skills as a means of manipulation. He never misleads his customers about his products and he even fastidiously corrects accounting errors down to the penny. Though it is clear that some of his customers have purchased from him more out of respect than necessity, he is never anything other than 100 percent honest and genuine. Is he persistent? You bet. And he understands that *people have different preferred ways of communicating and being communicated to.* As Brady writes, "I learned from Bill Porter that when someone says 'no' they are simply asking you to modify your proposal or change your delivery." Porter has always understood this principle and been willing to adjust his presentation, and he always approaches his audience with positive energy. Brady notes that she heard from some customers who told her that they "had placed orders with Bill on the spur of the moment because they liked his enthusiasm and upbeat attitude, but they later realized that they didn't need them. They just didn't know how to say 'no' to Bill."

In the afterword to *Ten Things I Learned from Bill Porter,* the Master Presenter himself modestly offers this presentation advice:

Think about each person you meet each day of your life and what effect you might have upon them, for good or ill. It isn't always the big decisions that make a difference in our lives; more often it's the little ones. The extra smile or wave; calling a friend who is ill; going out of your way to help someone whether they ask or not. Each of you has the same opportunity to inspire others as I do, simply by living your life as best you can. People tell me that I have touched thousands of lives, but what I think is that hundreds and thousands of people have helped me. Thank you, each of you, and every time you ask yourself if you can make a difference, remember this answer: You bet you can.

Since Porter's story aired on ABC's *20/20* on Christmas Eve 1995 and was later dramatized in an HBO movie starring William H. Macy, there is no doubt that his perseverance and positive thinking have had an impact on many people. It's important that we all appreciate, however, that Porter's success as an independent individual who overcame hardship relies on more than his persistence and positive attitude. It also depends greatly on the skills he learned and honed. Among these was his ability to become a Master Presenter. As one of his many fans wrote: "I once read that the quality of one's life is not measured by the things one acquires, but by the lives one touches." To touch lives in this sense means not simply to bump into people, but to get through to them.

Remember this: *Every time you touch a life you are making a presentation.* Read on and become prepared. Don't get caught looking at your watch!

Your Life Is a Series of Presentations

You know all those twelve-step programs that will cure you of your substance abuse or emotional addictions? First, they always tell you, you have to recognize that you have a problem. This book isn't like that. For one thing, there are only eight steps, and the eight steps aren't actually steps at all, which means you don't need to work through all of them to begin improving, and you don't have to do them in order, either. But most important to understand is that the first step is not to acknowledge that you have a problem, because you *don't* have a problem—you have an *opportunity.* So . . .

First admit that you have an opportunity.

We, the authors of this book, are equal opportunity explorers. The opportunity we've discovered comes along at least once a day. More frequently, it arises a hundred times a day, even if you're not a door-to-door salesman like Bill Porter. It wears many hats and uses many guises. It drops into your home and visits where you work, where you shop, and where you play. Like any true opportunity, this one is only of value if you seize it. It is the opportunity to make an impression on someone—and to do so in a way that might just slightly improve your life, as well. And if you seize every opportunity, it can improve your life much more than slightly. It can improve it exponentially.

Imagine yourself as a typical American woman of normal intelligence and average appearance. You went to college and used to punch the clock in an office, but now you're working part-time in order to spend more quality hours with your one and a half children. Yes, No. 2 is due in four months! Since your husband is a freelancer, you took a job for twenty hours a week as a barista at Starbucks. Even though you're overqualified, you need the health insurance, and how many part-time jobs does anyone know of with these kinds of perks? . . . pardon the pun. Besides, you love the coffee and it's the one stimulant you're allowed a little of in your present condition.

The alarm clock rings at 4:30 A.M. Ugh! You've got the opening shift. Your husband, Hal, gives you the hairy eyeball. You can scowl back, but where would that get you? Your first presentation is a smile, a warm hand on Hal's shoulder, and a silently mouthed, "I'm sorry." Hal went to bed at midnight, so it's a near miracle that your initial presentation of the morning elicits a smile in return. On such exchanges are great marriages built.

After slathering toothpaste on your brush, you lift your eyes to the mirror and see a groggy-eyed, puffy-faced woman with a head that has witnessed a sustained visit from the Hair Fairy. You could allow this to depress you, but you're four months from giving birth and you know nature will have her way with your body no matter what you think. You decide to laugh it off by brushing your teeth in a silly way, as you did when you were a kid. You know this act will literally change your physiology, which will impact your mood in a positive way. You make yourself laugh as you watch this crazy, wild-haired woman mugging for the mirror, and just like that your second presentation of the day ends in a great success. Two for two and it's not even sunrise!

After showering you choose black slacks and a tan turtleneck that you know will suggest competence and professionalism when half-covered by the green apron of the barista. You shout a good-bye to your husband, who is now in the shower. Just as you grab your bag to go, however, the phone rings. It's your sister in New York, the one who is in the throes of a divorce. As usual, she is ranting about the latest stunt her soon-to-be ex has pulled. You glance at your watch—it's okay to look at your watch when it's impossible for your audience to see you doing so. You don't have time for this, but you love your sister and feel her pain. Fortunately, you know your audience. In a sense, you have been preparing for this presentation all your life (in fact, you've been *making* this presentation all your life). You let your sister know that you really, really, really, really, really care, but you have to go or you'll lose your job and Hal will be delivering your baby instead of the doctor—and no one even wants to try to picture that one. The first part sounds completely sincere, because it is. The second part makes your sister snicker, and the conversation ends with her just a little happier on the other end of the line. Mission accomplished.

When you turn to head for the garage, however, you are brought up short by a little person at the kitchen door. Your five-year-old son, Zach, heard the phone ring and is now up an hour early, rubbing his eyes and looking a tad forlorn. He starts to whine and cry, begging Mommy not to leave, and your options are these . . . You could start to cry, too, allowing his sadness to rule your mood. You could just turn and walk out the door, knowing his father will look after him. You could yell. You could even give him a spanking. None of these would be an effective presentation— not if your goal is to get to work on time and leave behind a happy child. So you kneel down on the floor and take his little hands in yours, as you've done very many times before for comfort, a memory you hope to evoke in him now. You look into his eyes, which are already beginning to brighten. "You know, Zach, that Mommy sometimes has to go to work early," you say. "That's what I do so we can pay for all the fun times we have together, like going to the mall this afternoon and riding on the merry-go-round." "The merry-go-round? This afternoon? Yeah!" Despite the words, he's still pouting a little, but you can tell he'll soon be over it. Having carried your son to a better future with this presentation, you go forth to conquer your world.

In reality, you're a little nervous this morning, because you plan to ask the manager for a promotion from barista to assistant manager. You feel that you've performed well for the company over the past year, and while your background and experience probably would qualify you to manage a store yourself, you want to keep it part-time and you don't want to move to another location. In short, you're not a threat to this manager, only an asset. But she can be a little gruff and you really want this next big presentation to go well, because you could use the raise. You envision where this presentation will take place. Having a firm picture of it in your mind will remove some uncertainty and increase your confidence. Rather than do it in the confines of the manager's cramped office, you plan to try to sit down by the fireplace with a latte. The manager, you know, will have a mocha grande created by your own hand; she loves the way you make the mochas. Then you'll spring a little surprise on her, after which you'll ask for the promotion.

But first things first. You stride confidently into the store as you always do, greeting your colleagues by name—the easiest two-second presentation ever invented, since people love to hear their own names. Then you're on to the dramatic presentation that is the barista's role: the *clip, twist, hiss, pour.* You look every customer in the eye and smile. *Clip, twist, hiss, pour.* You comment on the weather or compliment them on their tie or hat when you can. *Clip, twist, hiss, pour.* When you know a customer's name, you use it. When you are in command of other facts about them, you hold a brief conversation about *their* interests. *Clip, twist, hiss, pour.* There's a reason the manager gets more compliments about you than about any other employee, even more than for some baristas who have worked here for years. You know that life is a series of presentations, and you are up for the challenge.

When the morning rush ends and the store quiets down you clean your station and then spend a few minutes handing out coupons for an upcoming special offer. Before you know it, your shift is over. The manager is leaning against the counter, looking a little burnt out. You offer to fire up that mocha for her just as the table by the fireplace springs free. *Clip, twist, hiss, pour.* Already the manager, watching over your shoulder and taking in the aroma, has begun to relax. You maneuver over to the table in a way that positions her back near the warmth of the fireplace, just as you had planned. You give her the surprise: a paperback novel you bought that you know she'll love. It is received well—perhaps the best eight bucks you've spent in a long while. As she rests one hand on the book and sips, you make your pitch for the promotion. She takes it pretty well, but wonders what's going to happen when you have the baby. Well, you explain, that's exactly *why* you want the promotion. Not only do you deserve it, but it will enable you to pay for the additional child care. The manager seems to like what she hears and says she'll think about it. That's fine. You knew this presentation would be an ongoing process.

You stop at the cleaners on the way home and ask to speak with the owner, who is a nice but unambitious man. You have a problem in the form of an upcoming wedding. You had two formal maternity gowns, but this man's business ruined one. You need to make sure that the one you're bringing in now can not only be ready for the party but treated with extra TLC. You don't want to have to buy any more maternity clothes, if you can help it. Rather than berate the owner for the ruined gown, you focus on the present, telling him that he's often done terrific work, that you really need his help, and that you're counting on him. Though you do mention the ruined dress in your presentation, you don't dwell on it. You're here to inspire, not to criticize. The owner picks up the cues. He is apologetic and promises to do right by you this time.

At home you sink into a comfortable desk chair and pop off four or five e-mails to friends and former business associates. You're just touching base, for the most part, but you're careful to make sure that you strike the appropriate tone with each recipient, because you realize that e-mails, too, are a form of presentation. Then you get to thinking about your sister. You'd like to make sure your mother isn't being too hard on her during the divorce. You'd rather not call just now, but an e-mail to your mother won't cut it either. So you decide to write a letter by hand, your mother being an old-fashioned lady.

A look at the clock and you see that it's time to go out and meet Zach's bus. It soon pulls up and the door swings open, followed by Zach bounding down the steps. In a brief conversation you thank the bus driver in advance for dropping Zach off at his friend's house tomorrow. You remember that the driver loves dogs and owns a boxer, so you ask after it and relate his answer to your own dog. Then a warm wave goodbye, and he's off again.

At the mall, you are waiting in line with Zach at the merry-go-round when you both spot his soccer coach. You've been preparing for this impromptu opportunity for a while, because Zach believes he isn't getting enough playing time and Hal, who can be a little hot-headed, just can't bring himself to raise the issue with the coach in a calm way. You start by mentioning that you've attended every game this season, establishing some authority, but quickly follow that with the observation that the coach has a difficult job and seems to be doing well with the kids. Then you tell him how much Zach loves soccer and, lowering your voice, note that he's been working really hard at it and hopes you'll soon give him a little more time on the field. The coach manages to take all this without seeming to receive it as criticism. As he departs, you're hopeful that your point got across to him.

Back home, Zach is off watching post-dinner TV when you decide to broach a sensitive subject with Hal. You've been thinking for a long time that the three of you should go on a short vacation before the baby comes. But you know this means having to plan last minute, which always makes Hal a little nervous. Rather than bring it up as an abstraction, you did the research and got the brochure on a great resort in Mexico that's having an early spring special. While Hal lingers over his favorite dessert—Mississippi mud pie—you slide the brochure across the table. When his eyebrows lift, you remind him how tough the first six months will be with a new baby and recall the romantic time you both had in that part of the world before Zach was born. You paint a word picture of the two of you spread out on the sand while Zach spends time in the excellent day camp the resort is said to have. "How much?" Hal wonders, and you have the answer on the tip of your tongue. It's cheap and you've already saved for it. The man is sold—just pick a date. He finishes his mud pie with a big grin on his face.

Now the homeowner's association beckons. There's an issue of allowed paint colors, about which the association has historically been very strict. You'd like to add one itsy bitsy color to the palette, just for a little variety. Prior to the association meeting, you took the liberty of mailing a paint chip to each of the board members and some other opinion leaders, along with a stunning picture of a house in Colonial Williamsburg painted in that exact color. It's conservative and classy. After the mailing, you polled a few members of your audience by phone to see how they would react to the suggestion, so you've got a pretty good handle on the potential responses your proposal might receive in the actual meeting. Finally, you invited along the board chairman from a pricier neighborhood association down the road to report on the experience they had when they took up a similar proposal. By the time you're actually asked to speak, it's almost as if this presentation makes itself. The new color choice passes with a vote of acclamation.

At home at last for good, you snuggle on the couch with Hal, who put Zach to sleep before you returned. Darn it! You missed an opportunity to read a story to the boy. Hal tells you that he did and Zach went to bed imagining he was a pilot, soaring over the clouds. Hal, you figure, must have made a pretty good presentation himself. . . .

How many presentations did you spot in this fictional woman's day? I counted—well, a lot! Now take a look at your average day at work, at home, or around the neighborhood. Look for three types of presentations, the three I's.

The first type of presentation aims to **Influence** or persuade, bringing an audience around to one's point of view. George W. Bush's 2002 speech before the United Nations about Iraq falls into this category. So does convincing your family to wake up early on Saturday morning and go on a hike or getting your spouse to agree that it's time for new furniture. Our barista had several opportunities to persuade people during her day, asking for a promotion and trying to convince her husband to take a vacation, to name just two.

The second type of presentation is intended to **Inspire.** Many of Martin Luther King's speeches come easily to mind when we recall inspirational presentations. In your own life, you might think of what you would say in a eulogy at the funeral of a good friend. But I also think of the efforts of Bernie Marcus, cofounder of The Home Depot. His presentations were so inspirational that they often moved employees to tears. Now, getting people to cry for freedom is a great accomplishment—but making them cry over hardware? That's got to bring presentation skills to a whole different order of magnitude!

But sometimes inspiration can be less grand. One might say that our barista had the opportunity to inspire her cleaner to get her dress done right this time. Rather than yelling, she took a more positive tack. Making people feel good about themselves is almost always a better motivator than fear.

The third type of presentation seeks to **Inform.** If that sounds dry, it can be. But consider the difference between your best college classes and your worst. The lecturer who presents well can get you to retain far more than the professor who drones on interminably.

Of course, many presentations combine two or all of these elements. When the barista presented to her homeowner's association, for instance, she wanted to change the minds of the board in order to allow another paint color. In order to do so, however, she employed techniques that both informed (by introducing a neighboring board member who could report on his experience) and inspired (by showing them the picture of Colonial Williamsburg).

Some opportunities to present are scheduled or planned, such as the barista's approaches to her husband about the vacation and to her boss about the promotion. In many cases, however, our presentations are *impromptu*. Depending upon what you do for a living and your hobbies, you can go weeks without having to make a planned presentation, but impromptu presentations arise on a daily basis, forcing us to think on our feet. Such was the case with the barista's presentation to the soccer coach.

Paradoxically, *the key to a successful impromptu presentation is to be prepared long before the occasion arises*. First, of course, we must recognize the kinds of presentation opportunities that will come up throughout our day. Then, we must build an arsenal upon which we can draw on the spur of the moment. Sometimes people almost subconsciously rehearse stressful scenarios, planning what they might say. Have you ever talked yourself out of a parking ticket? If so, there's a good chance that you had rehearsed this scenario to yourself many times before facing the actual situation. So your impromptu presentation had a degree of planning behind it.

Now that you've had time to count, how many presentations do you suppose you make in a day? Ten? Twenty? A hundred? And how many are you truly prepared for, viewing them not just as chores or meaningless moments but as opportunities to advance your life's agenda? All the above types of presentations, taken collectively, create the basis by which people form impressions of us. And impressions do matter! At the heart of this book lies the premise that *we have more control over the impressions people form of us than we often realize*. Too often we go through life like the blindfolded child swinging at a piñata.* Just because we make contact and some candy falls out now and then doesn't mean we're really giving it our best whack. So let's resolve to take the blindfolds off, to make what we sometimes succeed at unconsciously into a conscious act.

The next two chapters reveal some of the hidden elements of presentations and how we influence people. Once we've brought these principles to light, we will be in a better position to create practices that will help us become successful presenters every day of our lives.

---

*Go to http://www.tonyjeary.com/mistakes for a list of the most common presentation mistakes.

✓
Very Important Points

- A presentation is the act of working to change the content of another person's mind at a particular time and place.

- If successfully executed, presentations fulfill desired out- comes in the presenter's audience—by enhancing a skill, changing or reinforcing an attitude, or imparting information.

- Good presentations require equal parts inspiration, skill, and hard work.

- Put a great deal of stock in preparation.

- Appearances are a major factor behind one's success in life.

- People have different preferred ways of communicating and being communicated to.

- Every time you touch a life you are making a presentation.

- The key to a successful impromptu presentation is to be pre- pared long before the occasion arises.

- We have more control over the impressions people form of us than we often realize.

CHAPTER 2

Listen Up!

*What the Psychology of Compliance Says
about How We Persuade People*

One Saturday morning not long ago, I went into my garage to fetch a tool around 8 A.M. and was startled to find a sparrow fluttering desperately against the panes of a closed window. The poor little guy must have snuck into the garage late the preceding afternoon and become trapped. Now my presence had him severely agitated, and he was trying with every fiber of his feathered being to escape. Somehow, despite all evidence that the window was closed, he kept pounding against it, pausing only when overcome by a moment of exhaustion, then resuming his exercise in futility with a wet fluttering sound that sent a chill down my spine.

Every time I moved, it launched him into a new spasm of panic. His instincts clearly told him to fly to the light. That might work in a forest when a hawk is swooping down toward you, but it was of little use in the environment of a modern garage.

I soon opened the garage door to let him out, but that bird was so focused on the light on the other side of the window that he didn't even notice; he still kept pounding and pounding at the immovable panes. Finally, I walked over to the window with my arms flailing. At that point, I guess he perceived that he had to relocate. He launched himself abruptly into flight and—finally seeing the big space of the now open garage door—made for clear sky. Phew . . . I felt almost as relieved as he did!

Before I read an outstanding book by Dr. Robert B. Cialdini, I might have dismissed the sparrow's behavior as, well, the result of having a bird brain. But since studying his insightful book, *Influence: The Psychology of Persuasion*, I have come to realize that the sparrow's preprogrammed actions have their parallels in all animal behavior—including the human animal. Dr. Cialdini's explanation of our susceptibility to different means of persuasion has been a huge influence on my own work. I have studied and recommended his book continually over the years and have lectured on it in the context of building presentation skills. Once, his wife even popped up in the back of the room at a seminar I was conducting in Toronto for Meeting Professionals International. She professed amazement at how thoroughly I had absorbed her husband's work and thanked me. But the real gratitude is mine, because the ideas that Dr. Cialdini has identified lie at the core of our understanding of what makes many good presentations succeed.

According to Dr. Cialdini, the brains of all animals are hardwired with what he calls *fixed-action patterns,* so that certain stimuli almost always elicit a particular response. I honestly don't know a whole heck of a lot about sparrows, but it seems pretty clear that a sparrow's first instinct when it sees a large mammal moving in its direction is to get out of Dodge. In its mind, light equals open space, so in an enclosed garage it flies toward the window. And this reaction is so deeply embedded in its genes that it continues to seek the light even in the face of evidence that that is *not* the way toward freedom.

As humans, we may know enough not to batter ourselves repeatedly against a closed window, but we in turn can be slaves to our own "trigger" mechanisms. Whether we like it or not, *our receptivity to messages often depends upon certain core biases that are embedded in the human psyche.* These biases produce what Dr. Cialdini calls **automatic compliance.** In other words, when another person hits one of our triggers, we're most likely to respond in a certain preprogrammed way without really thinking.

One example cited by Dr. Cialdini as automatic compliance involved the work of a researcher at Harvard named Robin Langer. Ms. Langer, a social psychologist, set up a simple experiment where she asked people waiting in line at a library copy machine whether she could cut ahead of them. First she merely said, "Excuse me, I have five pages. May I use the Xerox machine?" When she put it this way, 60 percent of people allowed her to cut in front of them. Then she tried, "Excuse me, I have five pages. May I use the Xerox machine, because I'm in a rush?" This elicited the consent of 94 percent of the people asked, a 50 percent improvement. The jump in compliance may have been easily predicted by psychologists, who know from numerous studies that people on average are much more cooperative when given a reason for the request. But the surprising part of Ms. Langer's study came when she made her request a third way, by saying: "Excuse me, I have five pages. May I use the Xerox machine because I have to make some copies?" This request did not provide a reason why, but it still received a compliance rate of 93 percent! The conclusion psychologists draw is that the word "because"—in and of itself—is a trigger for nearly automatic compliance, even without the explanation that usually follows use of this word. It's as if the reasoning part of the mind shuts down when it hears the word "because," and therefore does not significantly pay attention to the explanation that follows.

Intrigued by observations like this, Dr. Cialdini set out to study what he calls Weapons of Influence. He spent three years working in various jobs among people whose livelihoods depend upon influencing others, and he observed the tools they employed to win compliance from their customers. After more careful study, he then concluded that *most successful techniques for influencing people fall into one of six categories:*

- *Reciprocation*
- *Commitment and Consistency*
- *Social Proof*
- *Liking*
- *Authority*
- *Scarcity*

"Each of these categories is governed by a fundamental psychological principle that directs human behavior and, in so doing, gives the tactics their power," he summarizes. In other words, the techniques he studied succeed because they exploit essential qualities that have been ingrained in all humans. Before you conclude that you are above these influences, you may want to consider that a recent study found that the human and mouse genomes contain counterparts on 99 percent of their chromosomes. If, like the rest of us, you're 99 percent mouse, then you are that much more like other humans and most certainly just as susceptible as the next guy to Dr. Cialdini's influencers.

More than fifty years ago, in *How to Win Friends and Influence People*, Dale Carnegie anticipated these studies by writing: "When dealing with people, let us remember we are not dealing with creatures of logic. We are dealing with creatures of emotion, creatures bristling with prejudices and motivated by pride and vanity." Later researchers turned this observation into a science.

Since the order of Dr. Cialdini's categories doesn't matter, I've created a mnemonic device to help me remember them: **CLASS R:** Commitment and Consistency, Liking, Authority, Social Proof, Scarcity, and Reciprocation. While you don't have to memorize these influencers to become a good presenter, successful presenters inevitably draw upon every one of them every day. To have at least a passing understanding of them is to begin to comprehend what people are hearing when you talk.

Commitment and Consistency

Famously, the author Tom Wolfe always wears a white three-piece suit out in public. Somewhat less famously, I always wear black. While I've never heard Wolfe expound on exactly why he chose the white suit, I am well acquainted with my own motivation. Some years ago, I was so busy with work and family that I found it hard to pack my clothing in a leisurely fashion for the dozens of business trips I took every quarter. Consequently, I often would find myself on the road with mismatched clothes and have to waste time shopping last-minute in unfamiliar cities just to fill out my wardrobe. So one day I decided that I would only wear black to business meetings. It may seem odd to you, but if you looked in my closet today you'd find substantial rows of black shirts, black slacks, and black shoes. Open the correct drawer and you'll find a pile of black socks. There are, of course, subtle differences among these garments in terms of fit, weight, fabric, and style, and I do pause like anyone else when choosing what to wear. But my decision-making process takes seconds, not minutes, and when I open my bag in some far-off hotel, there's no anxiety. I know everything has to match.

When it comes to choosing our dress, of course, Wolfe and I each made conscious Commitments, and we have stuck with them. But the real reason I raise this story is to illustrate why Consistency (and, to some extent, each of the other influencers) is hardwired into our brains.

Imagine if you had to think fresh every day about every action you take in the morning. Should I reach for the alarm clock with my left hand or my right? Which leg should I swing off the bed first? Would it be better to shower before shaving or vice versa? Should I start brushing my teeth on the top left or the bottom left or the top right or—you get the idea. If we had to consider these decisions anew every day, we'd probably never make it past the breakfast table. There might be a thousand little things we do in our daily lives that we can do differently—maybe even perform in a way that would be slightly better or more sensible. But we decided to do them in a certain manner long ago, and we've stuck with that way, for the most part, through thick and thin. Why? Because we couldn't function productively if we had to go around reinventing the wheel every minute. While this was undoubtedly true thousands of years ago when we were fleeing predators and scavenging for nuts, it is probably even more crucial in the fast pace of our over-stimulated modern lives. Just as I made a conscious decision that always wearing black would increase the efficiency of my business travel, we have made these thousands of unconscious decisions in order to increase the efficiency of our daily lives. So it's a good thing that we have evolved to quite practically exploit the advantages that Consistency brings, but like so many other parts of the human genome, this one comes with consequences.

One consequence is that *we love and respect Consistency in ourselves and others—and we loathe inconsistency.* As a practical matter, this has two major implications for how we may or may not allow ourselves to be influenced. First, it means that we are usually reluctant to change our ways of doing things, even in the face of quite logical arguments to the contrary. Second, however, it means that once we do take even a tentative step toward a Commitment to change, our instinct toward Consistency will push us deeper and deeper into that decision.

A fellow I know owns a retail store that, like most every store, accepts credit cards. For various reasons, he was displeased with the company that provided him with the credit card processing. Their customer service was terrible and he knew that he could find a better rate if he just went and looked for one. In short, he had no reason at all to use this particular credit card company—except that he had always used them in the past. So he allowed the situation to drag on for years. Consistency.

One day, however, a representative of the credit card company was particularly unhelpful with regard to a certain issue my friend was trying to resolve. And that very day a salesman from a competing company happened to walk through his door. My friend is a pretty good businessman, so he wasn't going to sign up with a strange company right away—he was going to analyze the numbers first, carefully comparing the complex schedules of competing fees that these two companies presented. But it turns out that comparing the fees of credit card companies, at least for a small businessman, is such a confusing process that it's like trying to compare apples and oranges. He had no idea at the end of it which company would be charging him less.

That simple fact might lead us to the easy conclusion that my friend would stay with the original company for Consistency's sake. But instead he decided to switch. What happened? I'll let him tell it:

"Well, I had told this fella from the new company that I was dissatisfied with my current situation. And I really went on about how bad that company was to work with. Once I'd told him that, it was like getting a load off my chest. Even though I had sworn I would only move if the numbers proved the case, in my heart I was already tipped over the edge. I suppose the mere act of comparing the two companies, not the analysis itself, drove me to the decision to switch."

Imagine that! Merely having articulated to himself a desire to change had pushed my friend toward a change, even though that step was not the easiest from a business perspective. Now he would have to go through all new paperwork with the new company, get new credit card machines set up in his store, train his people to use them, etc.—all much more difficult than the effort he had expended up to that point. Yet once he had his toe in the water, the rest of him rapidly followed. Commitment. Among salesmen, the approach that exploits this tendency has long been known as the "foot in the door" technique. Good salesmen know that getting you to make even a small purchase will tickle your sense of Commitment and make you much more likely to do business with them again, next time perhaps on a much larger scale.

My friend with the retail store hit upon a further point that Dr. Cialdini emphasizes as an enormous influence on our sense of Commitment. Once we articulate to another person that we intend to change, and especially if we commit our intentions to paper, our sense of Commitment grows much more powerful. As Dr. Cialdini puts it in his book, "Whenever one takes a stand that is visible to others, there arises a drive to maintain that stand in order to *look* like a consistent person." Because it is considered a poor reflection on us to be perceived as inconsistent people, we usually "try to avoid the look of inconsistency," he continues. "For appearances' sake, then, the more public a stand, the more reluctant we will be to change it."

This may be why it is increasingly common for students to be asked to sign contracts with regard to abstaining from certain behaviors. It used to be that many after-school programs asked the parent to commit to controlling inappropriate behaviors. Today, many schools ask the kids to sign their own contracts. As my coauthor Kim points out, her son, Max, has been asked to sign several contracts requiring him to follow certain rules in his middle school—with regard to the library, sports teams, and the like. Because Max is a minor, he cannot be legally bound by these contracts, yet the school asks for his signature anyway. And experience has shown that Max and his fellow students do take these commitments more seriously once they have been requested to write them down.

When I was discussing the point about public Commitment with my coauthors, one of them thought of a friend who had struggled with an alcohol problem. This person, let's call her Virginia, had suffered silently for a decade. As with so many alcoholics, the situation got worse and worse by the year, until her husband had to confront her about driving drunk to pick up their child from day care. He convinced her to go to a rehabilitation center, where she dried out for a week without anyone else's knowledge. Pretty soon Virginia was back home, and nobody—not her friends or siblings or parents—was any the wiser. But it didn't take long for her to fall back into the same old habits. One drink would lead to another, as it often does for substance abusers, and her husband watched in frustration as his wife began hiding bottles of vodka all over the house, continuing to drink frequently and denying she had a problem.

When this crisis hit its breaking point, Virginia's husband finally called a close friend of his wife and asked her to help him intervene. They confronted Virginia and convinced her, after many emotional days of argument, to seek treatment again. This time, however, there was something different—she had verbally committed to her friend that she would never drink again. Also, as part of the Alcoholics Anonymous program, she went many steps further. She acknowledged not only to strangers but to most of her closest friends that she had a problem that she was seeking to beat. She even wrote letters to her siblings, who lived in different states, reiterating her Commitment to stay dry. And this time the results turned out quite differently. Today, four years later, Virginia is still on the wagon. This is so, I think, largely because she made a public Commitment the second time around, and that triggered something in her brain that was much more forceful than simply having made a promise to herself.

Liking

Recently when I went to pick up my daughter at Tae Kwon Do class, another parent, Jim, came up to me and began to make conversation. Pretty soon he revealed the main reason for his approach: He was looking for a new church to attend and thought I might have some ideas. Reflexively, I began to sing the praises of Cross Timbers Community Church, the house of worship my family attends near our residence in Flower Mound, Texas. I noted how dynamic and interesting I thought the pastor, Toby Slough, was and related proudly that the congregation had just put the finishing touches on a beautiful new addition. I mentioned that my daughters enjoyed the instruction and that we found our fellow parishioners to be very warm and friendly.

Jim smiled with appreciation, but choosing a church is among the most personal things we do. Something in Jim's eyes betrayed a sense of doubt. "The thing is," he said, "my parents were Catholic."

"No kidding? I went to Catholic school," I quickly replied.

"But I go to a Methodist church now."

"I was raised a Methodist," I said truthfully.

Warming to the conversation now, Jim allowed that he had tried one of the big churches in town called Fellowship. I responded that my wife and I had attended that church five or six times, that we enjoyed the services there, and that we had chosen our current church because it had many similarities to Fellowship, but with a smaller congregation.

Finally, now completely comfortable, Jim decided to give our church a try.

Why was I not surprised? Though our conversation began with Jim's approach to me, I realized quite quickly that he had put me in the position of making a presentation to him in favor of our church. And though it may seem to the reader that Jim and I coincidentally had a lot in common that would lead to a smooth conclusion, remember that our conversation might easily have unfolded in a hundred different ways that would not have revealed the similarities in our backgrounds. Imagine if when Jim had said he now goes to a Methodist church, for example, I had simply thought to myself that I currently go to a Baptist church, which might not be relevant to this conversation. I might easily have followed that train of thought instead—and Jim would never know that he had Methodism in common with me. When I make one-on-one presentations, these kinds of commonalities come out more frequently precisely because I am on the lookout for them and I am quick to reinforce them. In this way, I drive rapport, because I know that people are more open to hearing from those they perceive to be similar to them.

"Few people," writes Dr. Cialdini, "would be surprised to learn that, as a rule, we most prefer to say yes to the requests of someone we know and like. What might be startling to note, however, is that this simple rule is used in hundreds of ways by total strangers to get us to comply with *their* requests."

"Liking," as he sees it, has a number of elements. First, we all have a tendency to like people who are physically attractive. It's not fair, but in study after study researchers have concluded that most people instinctively assume that physically attractive people have other positive personal traits, even when there is no evidence to support this assumption. Psychologists call this the *halo effect*.

Second, we tend to like people who like us, especially if they openly indicate so. As Dr. Cialdini argues, "We are phenomenal suckers for flattery. Although there are limits to our gullibility—especially when we can be sure that the flatterer is trying to manipulate us—we tend, as a rule, to believe praise and to like those who provide it, oftentimes when it is clearly false."

The nineteenth-century pragmatist philosopher William James once said: "The deepest principle in human nature is the craving to be appreciated." This phenomenon has been so well understood for so long as an opportunity to influence others that Dale Carnegie even addressed it in 1936. After quoting James, he went on to tell the story of Charles Schwab, whom Andrew Carnegie chose to be the first president of U.S. Steel in 1921. "There is nothing else that so kills the ambitions of a person as criticism from superiors," he quotes Schwab as saying. "I never criticize anyone. I believe in giving a person incentive to work. So I am anxious to praise but loath to find fault. If I like anything, *I am hearty in approbation and lavish in my praise.*"

Golly, everyone's mother or grandmother has always known that "if you have nothing nice to say about someone . . . don't say anything at all." Right?

Third, we respond best to people whom we perceive to be similar to us, especially if we believe we are engaged in a cooperative effort with them or people like them. With all due respect to Groucho Marx's assertion that he would never belong to a club that would have him as a member, most people join clubs that are populated with those we assume are like us. And it doesn't have to be a club, per se, of course. We make friends more easily with folks who share our values; as kids, we hang out in the cafeteria with others who belong to our "crowd"; we go to restaurants and vacation spots populated with people who dress similarly to us; we even tend to choose careers based upon the types of people we will be surrounded by most of the time.

Fourth, the inclination toward Liking is so second-nature to us that we make a semiconscious effort to associate ourselves with those whom we believe will reflect well upon us. As Dr. Cialdini observes, "We purposefully manipulate the visibility of our connections with winners and losers in order to make ourselves look good to anyone who could view these connections." And the corollary, of course, is that, "There is a natural human tendency to dislike a person who brings us unpleasant information, even when that person did not cause the bad news. The simple association with it is enough to stimulate our dislike."

Those who sell for a living, of course, nailed down the power of Liking ages ago. Anheuser-Busch puts stunning women in beer commercials, the ladies working the cosmetics counter at Saks Fifth Avenue tell us how beautiful we look, salesmen often dress like their customers, and sneaker companies spend millions to make us believe we're just like professional athletes. *When it comes to influence, there's nothing like the Liking principle.*

Authority

One of the most popular films of 2002 was Steven Spielberg's *Catch Me If You Can*, based on the raucous real-life story of Frank Abagnale, Jr. (The book of his story was also a best-seller that year and back in 1980.) Abagnale was a con man in the late 1960s who managed to pass himself off, in turn, as a Pan Am airline pilot, a hospital physician, and an attorney. Amazingly, he accomplished this feat not only with no prior knowledge of any of those professions, but as a teenage runaway. And though he did get caught eventually, he was never fingered as an impostor by any of his "colleagues." Rather, the act of floating millions of dollars in fraudulent checks created a paper trail that ultimately led to his arrest.

Abagnale knew instinctively what experimental psychologists have studied formally: To quote Dr. Cialdini, *"There resides a deep-seated sense of duty to authority within us all."* Our inherent respect for Authority is, like our sense of Consistency, a shortcut through life that allows us to function more efficiently. Without a fairly universal deference to our "superiors" and other experts, it would be impossible to construct a functioning society. "A multilayered and widely accepted system of authority confers an immense advantage upon a society," writes Dr. Cialdini. ". . . The other alternative, anarchy, is a state that is hardly known for its beneficial effects on cultural groups and one that the social philosopher Thomas Hobbes assures us would render life 'solitary, poor, nasty, brutish, and short.' Consequently, we are trained from birth that obedience to proper authority is right and disobedience is wrong."

Shrewd operators can turn the Authority principle into a Weapon of Influence. And that's exactly what Frank Abagnale, Jr., did. Whether by design or by sheer luck, Abagnale found a way to brilliantly exploit the three main elements of Authority: titles, clothes, and trappings. To begin with, he had the gall to impersonate professionals whose stature in society commanded immediate respect. Then he created an image for himself that was consistent with society's expectations in regard to dress, whether with the uniform of a pilot or the "uniform"—a conservatively expensive suit—of the attorney. He soon found that by his clothing alone he could command a degree of deference that ordinary people could not ever achieve. Then, for the coup de grace, he created the trappings of whatever office he was pretending to: as an airline pilot he carried credentials and ID badges, to play the role of a doctor or lawyer he created fake diplomas, etc. All of this gave him an air of Authority that was nearly impenetrable. Even his father-in-law to be, an attorney himself, never fully suspected the truth.

All of this went to prove Dr. Cialdini's assertion that "we are often as vulnerable to the *symbols* of authority as to the *substance.*" This had to be true for people to accept Frank Abagnale, Jr., because there was no real substance behind his impersonations at all.

Marketers the world over appreciate and regularly exploit our susceptibility to Authority. They pay professional ballplayers millions of dollars to promote their sports drinks and they bury real doctors in free samples. Remember the commercials that claimed Tylenol was the No. 1 brand used by hospitals? A pure Authority play all the way. But in the world of presentations, there is a less cynical way to use the Authority principle to win your point.

While I was in the process of writing this book, my grandmother died of old age. This sad but not unexpected event led to what I suppose is the usual series of painful but necessary steps to settle her estate. Among other things, I found myself helping my mom to facilitate the sale of some shares of stock that my grandmother had owned in a closely held corporation. Unlike shares of, say, DuPont, in which there is a fluid market, stock owned in a closely held company can be difficult to dispose of. So all kinds of rules and regulations have grown up around this issue—technical stuff that is irrelevant to this discussion. But the bottom line is that my mother had to sell my grandmother's stock, and I had to convince the corporation's general counsel to allow me to do the transaction in a certain fashion—in a manner, in fact, that would have tax benefits both for her estate and for the company itself. In more than one phone conversation with the company's attorney I explained what I wanted to do, but I sensed that he was dragging his feet, probably because he had never executed a deal quite like this one and was beset by uncertainty.

I was mulling over this dilemma when it occurred to me that the attorney might be far more receptive to the proposition if I could introduce a voice of Authority. So I contacted my accountant and asked him to get on a three-way call with me and the attorney. I introduced them over the phone, reminded both of the reason for our call, and turned the accountant loose. I can't say that he said anything to the attorney in that conference call that I hadn't already said many times myself. But within fifteen minutes we had our deal. Such is the power of a voice of Authority.

Social Proof

There is a famous tale—almost certainly untrue, but still instructive—about the Great Crash of 1929. Supposedly, some months before that tragic October, the financier Bernard Baruch went down to the sidewalk in front of his office to have his shoes shined. Like many men of his stature, Mr. Baruch undoubtedly enjoyed this frequent ritual, which helps a well-dressed gentleman maintain an appearance of control over his own person. In the big city, this routine event can also afford a moment of peace in an otherwise busy day, a moment when you have to sit still and might take the opportunity to reflect on the big picture, to sneak a peek at the sports pages, or to have a chat with the person of more humble status who is engaged in the somewhat dirty job of rubbing down your wing tips.

On this occasion, as the story goes, Mr. Baruch offhandedly inquired after the shoe-shine man's state of mind. The shoe-shine man said he was feeling very well indeed, as his stock portfolio was growing rapidly, and he even offered Mr. Baruch some suggestions on a hot stock.

Without another word, Mr. Baruch finished having his shoes shined, calmly returned to his office, and instructed his colleagues to liquidate all his stock market positions. Asked why he was taking such a dramatic and unprecedented step, he declared that when a shoe-shine man on the street starts giving stock tips it's time for the wise investor to get out of the market. And, of course, he was right. A short time later the market came crashing down to earth and only the shrewdest of Wall Street were spared.

As we know from past market bubbles and from the more recent one, most of us are less like Bernard Baruch and more like the shoe-shine man.

That is to say, to quote Dr. Cialdini, "We view a behavior as more correct in a given situation to the degree that we see others performing it."

About ten years ago I recall reading in *The Wall Street Journal* about an analysis by a psychologist who studies market behavior. For one study, he focused on investors in the famed Fidelity Magellan fund, which during a certain ten-year period was the best performing mutual fund on the planet. You would expect investors in Magellan to have done very well indeed during the period studied, but in fact the average investor in the fund during that time *lost money!* The explanation is simple. While the fund was most successful over a ten-year span, like any other financial instrument its shares fluctuated. Most Magellan investors were not in the fund for the entire ten years. Some were invested there for just a few years; others went in and out several times in that period. What did the average investor do? Apparently, he watched the fund appreciate and felt left out. So then he bought in high. But when the shares dropped he panicked and sold—most likely just before the fund was set for another round of appreciation.

The problem with the average investor, of course, is that he or she is not a stock market professional with all the time in the world to study a given investment. So—whether consciously or not—he turns to another one of those shortcut mechanisms we've been talking about, in this case the principle of Social Proof. As Dr. Cialdini explains, "In general, *when we are unsure of ourselves, when the situation is unclear or ambiguous, when uncertainty reigns, we are most likely to look to and accept the actions of others as correct.*"

The late 1990s were a time of great optimism but also a time of unsettling change, when many businesspeople feared for their own existence while others claimed to be reinventing the very business cycle itself. Everything seemed to be up for grabs. There was talk in the business magazines that people would no longer have one career, working for one or two companies in a lifetime. Rather, we were told by the experts, they might have to reinvent themselves every decade. Meanwhile, everywhere we went people were talking about the stock market, even quitting their jobs to become day traders or to found Internet companies based upon a far-out idea and some seed money. My coauthor Joel founded one such company. When the money ran out and he had to close it down, one consultant told him that his very *failure* would be an asset if he became a consultant, because failure was more instructive than success. In other words, the world had turned topsy-turvy. All of it was very unsettling—uncertainty reigned.

Meanwhile, anyone sitting the market out was watching in amazement as the subject of every cocktail party became the transformation of business and the rise of the stock market. Few people felt qualified to try to out-guess these market conditions on their own. What did they do, then? As we now know, they blindly relied upon Social Proof: Everyone was investing in high tech so it must be the right thing to do. "As slaughterhouse operators have long known," writes Dr. Cialdini, "the mentality of a herd makes it easy to manage. Simply get some members moving in the desired direction and the others—responding not so much to the lead animal as to those immediately surrounding them—will peacefully and mechanically go along." We weren't so much emulating Amazon.com founder Jeff Bezos as we were our friends and neighbors.

Of course, the principle of Social Proof does not just apply to stock market bubbles. It is a tool that smart businesspeople and presenters employ to their advantage on a regular basis. For example, I used to do a lot of work for Chrysler, which caused me to visit their dealerships all over the world. Many of these dealers—from Europe to Japan to America to Korea—would take pictures of their customers getting into their new cars and then post those photos all over the walls of the dealership. This technique engaged the mechanism of Social Proof in existing and new customers. When you see your friends and neighbors buying a car from that dealership, it adds credibility and confidence to your own purchase.

Scarcity

The other day I got a call from a woman—we'll call her Beth—who recognized the use of a Scarcity technique in a pitch she had just received from a salesman. Beth, who owns a small business, had attended a seminar of mine in Chicago just a few weeks before and had begun to put the things she had learned into practice in order to increase her rapport with her own customers. Now, however, she had witnessed a brilliant presentation from a fellow who was trying to sell some software to her. She was so excited that she had to tell me about it.

The salesman began his pitch to Beth by reminding her that her friend had suggested that this software might be a good fit for Beth's company, thus invoking the Liking principle. Then he mentioned that he had examined some of the other aspects of her business and observed that she did everything first-class. Therefore, she would want the best computer system to support that effort (Consistency). What made him so sure his system was the best? He cited quotes from computer magazines (Authority) and ticked off a dozen companies in Beth's field that were using aspects of the system (Social Proof). But—and here the salesman paused for effect—the enterprise software business is a complicated one. He had instructions from his sales manager not to sell their software to just any business. He had to make sure that she was *qualified* to carry it.

Naturally, Beth felt herself at a certain advantage for being able to recognize the Weapons of Influence this salesman was employing. Yet, even with that knowledge, she almost couldn't control herself. She wanted to jump out of her chair and begin to make an argument for why her company was worthy of receiving his product. Wait a minute! Then she recognized his reluctance for what it was: use of the Scarcity principle. By leading Beth to believe that the software had a sort of limited availability, the salesman hit one of those triggers that would make her desire the product more.

As Dr. Cialdini writes, "The idea of potential loss plays a large role in human decision making. In fact, *people seem to be more motivated by the thought of losing something than by the thought of gaining something of equal value.*"

This particular response is so classic that instances of its exploitation abound. We are surrounded by advertising messages that promise certain deals "For a Limited Time Only" or "While Supplies Last" or "Offer Expires Next Week." Car salesmen never seem to have more than one car on the lot with just the options you want. Realtors always have a competitive bid on the verge of coming in. TV pitchmen promise a special promotional price to only the first fifty callers.

Ironically, one of the main reasons we respond viscerally to these come-ons is that we cherish our freedom to choose. According to a field of study called *reactance theory*, writes Dr. Cialdini, "Whenever free choice is limited or threatened, the need to retain our freedoms makes us desire them (as well as the goods and services associated with them) significantly more than previously. So when increasing scarcity—or anything else—interferes with our prior access to some item, we will *react against* the interference by wanting and trying to possess the item more than before."

This might at least partly explain a collector's lust for a rare coin or painting, as well as the perennial runs on the hot toy of the year. It seems that every holiday season some toy manufacturer underestimates demand for its product and ends up being caught with too little supply. Then the Scarcity principle creates enough surplus demand to carry sales well into subsequent incarnations of that item, turning it into an even bigger hit. What luck! But often, as legendary baseball executive Branch Rickey said, "Luck is the residue of design." One of the most brilliant exploiters of the Scarcity principle in our time was Ty Warner, the creator of Beanie Babies. Toy crazes come and toy crazes go, but none seems to have lasted as long as the near tulip mania that surrounded the little stuffed animals produced by Ty, Inc. While Beanie Babies may have been intelligently priced for their audience and cleverly positioned both in their engineered cuteness and the personal stories that accompany each figure, the real shrewdness behind their marketing was the simple decision to "retire" each Beanie Baby at particular intervals. Thus the resulting Scarcity stoked demand to a frenzy that carried these small plush creatures from toys to collectibles and beyond. Some people even began to think of them as investments—hey, they weren't making any more of this model, right? But the only one who truly got rich from this wholly manufactured craze was master marketer Ty Warner himself.

More interesting and relevant to our purpose than the way the Scarcity principle operates on demand for goods is the way it can affect our perception of information. Studies have shown, according to Dr. Cialdini, that "we will find a piece of information more persuasive if we think we can't get it elsewhere." Thus, for example, we might be more inclined to act on information to which we believe ourselves to be exclusively privy—a "hot" tip from our stockbroker, say—and less likely to act based upon that same information coming from a more universal source, like the evening news.

Reciprocation

In the mid- to late 1980s, before Rudolph Giuliani became mayor of New York, there was a period of time in that city when panhandling took on a whole new angle. All over town, people found themselves the recipients of unwanted—or at least unrequested—services. If you emerged from Penn Station or Grand Central Terminal carrying a piece of luggage, seemingly kind men would offer to hail you a taxi and even help you load your luggage into the trunk. Similar people held doors open as you entered an office building or bank. When a traffic light turned red, the now-famous "squeegee men" would jump out in front of your car and begin to clean your windshield. Sometimes they even used aerosol cans of cleansing foam. Somewhere along the line, all these individuals had discovered the benefits of the Reciprocation principle.

Like the principle of Authority, Reciprocation is probably as much trained into us as it is hardwired, but the results are the same: When wielded correctly, this weapon creates an often irresistible force on our decision-making process.

In similar fashion to the Consistency principle, *we are trained from birth that when someone does us a favor, we have an obligation to repay.* This behavior lies at the root of a civilized society and is the engine of human progress. Without it, we would never be able to trust one another, and without trust there is no cooperation. Without cooperation it becomes every man for himself. That undoubtedly explains why the Reciprocation rule manifests itself in every civilization on earth. As Dr. Cialdini puts it, "Each of us has been taught to live up to the rule, and each of us knows about the social sanctions and derision applied to anyone who violates it."

Consequently, we find it very difficult to allow the stranger to put our luggage in the taxi trunk or to clean our windshield without invoking a sense of obligation on our part to reciprocate the favor. Of course, the squeegee man does not desire to have you clean his windshield in return—he doesn't even have a car. We all know what the squeegee man wants: money. And often enough in the 1980s in New York, that's exactly what he got.

So why do we allow the squeegee man to wash our windshield or another stranger to hold the door for us with his hand out in the first place? Because, as Dr. Cialdini writes, "Although the obligation to repay constitutes the essence of the reciprocity rule, it is the obligation to receive that makes the rule so easy to exploit. The obligation to receive reduces our ability to choose whom we wish to be indebted to and puts that power in the hands of others." Thus, before we were trained to avoid them completely, we often allowed airport Hare Krishnas to force flowers on us and then felt compelled to "donate" a dollar. And, similarly, studies have shown that the plying upon us of free food samples by marketers makes us more likely to buy their product—*even if we don't really like the taste of it!*

Some time ago, I found a clever and fun way to invoke this technique in presentation situations. I go to the bank, acquire crisp new dollar bills, take them to a printer, and have them glued at one edge into a pad. When I'm presenting to a group, I good-humoredly "reward" people for making valuable contributions to the discussion by peeling off these dollar bills and handing them over. And while this always gets a laugh and seems all in good fun, one of my intentions is quite serious. Even though they frequently presume, at first, that the dollars are fake, these audience members become indebted to me in some small way. They know that my presence before them is a request for their engagement and cooperation, which they find is an easy thing to give me in return for the dollar I've just given them. As a result of having invoked the Reciprocation principle, I have obtained something that is infinitely more valuable to me than the few dollars it cost, something that allows my speaking sessions to move into more entertaining learning experiences.

An interesting corollary to the Reciprocation rule is that we often are willing to pay people back even for intangibles. Writes Dr. Cialdini: "We have already seen that one consequence of the rule is an obligation to repay favors we have received. Another consequence of the rule, however, is an obligation to make a concession to someone who has made a concession to us."

Psychologists, marketers, and shrewd negotiators speak of the "rejection-then-retreat" technique. Quite simply this involves asking for more than you want in order to settle to the point where you planned to be all along. So, for example, an agent might request $100,000 for his client when he knows he's willing to settle for $75,000. Or a salesman may introduce you to the most expensive car on the lot, knowing it would make you more likely to choose a vehicle in the middle of the line rather than the cheapest one. The reason this technique works is that we view the concession (the agent's willingness to adjust his requested number downward in response to rejection) as a favor that requires a reciprocal concession.

The Influencer's Edge

When we understand what makes people receptive to influence, we are in a position to be a motivating force in their lives—even if it's only for a moment. Presenters who grasp these fundamental concepts of human behavior have an enormous advantage over those who are ignorant of them. If you don't think knowledge of these techniques can have a major impact on people's lives, consider the story that my coauthor Joel recently related.

A few years ago, Joel received a series of urgent phone messages from a good friend of his, Dr. Jeffrey Oppenheim, who is a neurosurgeon. Dr. Oppenheim was desperate to get in touch with Joel and requested an immediate callback. Naturally, Joel hurried to comply, and when he reached his friend in his office Dr. Oppenheim related a tragic story. Apparently, he had been the neurosurgeon on call one night about a week before when his beeper sounded and another physician asked him to speed to the emergency room of a local hospital. A young man in his twenties had been involved in a car accident and had sustained severe damage to his spinal cord. Dr. Oppenheim evaluated the patient and rushed him in for a delicate operation to stabilize his spine, but the spinal cord had been severed very high up. Once the young man had recovered from the surgery, Dr. Oppenheim had to inform him that he would be paralyzed from the neck down. It was almost a certainty that he would never walk again, and also quite likely that he would not have the use of his arms. Needless to say, this news left the young man severely traumatized emotionally, and by the time Dr. Oppenheim called Joel the patient had been refusing food for several days.

While Dr. Oppenheim empathized with the patient's severe depression—and even, to some extent, with his wish to die—he also knew that many quadriplegics go on to lead productive lives. He didn't want this young man to make a decision to die while in a state of understandable agitation. Furthermore, he knew that if the young man would have any

chance to maximize his recovery, he had to be transferred to a rehabilitation hospital immediately. He pleaded with the young man, and when
that didn't work he had the patient's other doctors, nurses, parents, and
relatives beg him not to refuse further treatment. All of this, however, fell
on deaf ears.

As he was groping for a solution it suddenly occurred to Dr. Oppenheim that his friend Joel lived near the actor Christopher Reeve. Dr.
Oppenheim didn't know explicitly about the Weapons of Influence, but
he figured that a person who had lived through a similar trauma might
have more standing than anyone else in the eyes of his patient.

Joel didn't know Mr. Reeve personally, but he reached out to some of
his contacts in the neighborhood and within an hour managed to obtain
the phone number of the actor's home office. Figuring it was a long shot,
but a shot worth taking, Dr. Oppenheim immediately called the number,
spoke to Mr. Reeve's secretary, then his nurse, and by that evening Mr.
Reeve himself was on the phone to Dr. Oppenheim's patient. I can only
imagine how gut-wrenching that conversation must have been for both
parties. When it was done, the young man agreed to begin taking food immediately and to be transferred to the rehabilitation hospital the next day.

Having read this chapter, you now ought to appreciate that Dr.
Oppenheim employed several of the principles we outlined above. As
had been well documented in the press by the time of this story, since the
occurrence of his tragic accident Mr. Reeve had become something of an
authority on injuries of the spinal cord, testifying before Congress and
speaking out often on the issue. So Dr. Oppenheim was invoking the
Authority principle by getting him involved. Also, as a fellow sufferer Mr.
Reeve had set an example of how a spinal cord injury may disable the
body but need not cripple the soul. By the rewarding life he led—and by
reminding the young man of what he could continue to accomplish with
his own life—Mr. Reeve called upon the principle of Social Proof to
guide the young man away from fatalism and toward recovery.

Lastly, I would suspect that Mr. Reeve's phone call (and, by the way, a
subsequent personal visit that I'm told he made) inadvertently invoked
the Reciprocation principle. A reasonable person would presume that a
man like Christopher Reeve has many demands on his time. Furthermore, we all know that famous people often become standoffish just out
of the need to survive emotionally. So—though I'm sure he didn't look at

it this way—by reaching out Mr. Reeve was doing a "favor" for the young man. All he asked in return was for the young man to take a little food. And once that food had been received, of course, it would be that much more difficult not to take some more—because of the final principle involved in this story, the principle of Consistency and Commitment.

Dr. Oppenheim and Mr. Reeve might not have known about the Weapons of Influence, but they had to understand that they were confronted by a life-and-death presentation. Fortunately for the young man, they seemed to know in their hearts how to approach the situation and win the day. I continue to study and share Dr. Cialdini's book because I believe *the success of our presentations should not be a random event, but the result of conscious actions.*

✓
Very Important Points

- Our receptivity to messages often depends upon certain core biases that are embedded in the human psyche.

- Most successful techniques for influencing people fall into one of six categories: Commitment and Consistency, Liking, Authority, Social Proof, Scarcity and Reciprocation (CLASS R).

- We love and respect Consistency in ourselves and others—and we loathe inconsistency.

- When it comes to influence, there's nothing like the Liking principle.

- "There resides a deep-seated sense of duty to authority within us all."

- "When we are unsure of ourselves, when the situation is unclear or ambiguous, when uncertainty reigns, we are most likely to look to and accept the actions of others as correct."

- "People seem to be more motivated by the thought of losing something than by the thought of gaining something of equal value."

- We are trained from birth that when someone does us a favor, we have an obligation to repay.

- When we understand what makes people receptive to influence, we are in a position to be a motivating force in their lives.

- The success of our presentations should not be a random event, but the result of conscious actions.

CHAPTER 3

Did You Say Something?

The Importance of Sensory Acuity

The newly hired executive vice president of a Fortune 500 company once asked me to help her improve her presentation skills. Specifically, she was about to make her first speech to a large group of employees, and while she had delivered hundreds of presentations to small groups over the years, she had only presented a handful of times before entire auditoriums. As it happened, she had already written this speech, so a few colleagues and I suggested that she stand on the mock stage at the front of my studio and give it a whirl.

From the moment I first met this woman, call her Jane, I could see why she had excelled in her company. She was smart and personable, well dressed, and obviously focused. When we made small talk, she was relaxed and confident. And her speech was intelligently written—all of which made it more amazing that she had managed to bore us all to the verge of tears in about ten minutes.

Wait a minute! What went wrong?

Jane knew enough to understand that burying her face in the paper before her and reading in a monotone would make her look like an amateur. She clearly had thought about putting different emphasis on certain words and lifting her eyes to the room now and then. But every time she looked up, she wasn't meeting the eyes of her audience—she was looking *past* us. We might have put wax vampire teeth in our mouths and I doubt she would have noticed until the speech ended.

It unsettles people when we don't meet them in the eye, but that wasn't the real problem with Jane's presentation. More important, she hoped her audience would respond to her speech, but because she was not really connected with the audience herself, she was not in a position to respond to *us*. The result was a complete lack of rapport.

When you have a conversation with somebody, you subconsciously read cues from them—and you tailor your level of receptivity accordingly. Say you're home alone and a stranger knocks on the door. If that person is a trembling, disheveled mess with a hole in his coat and dirty untied sneakers, your goal even before he opens his mouth is to end the conversation as quickly as possible. But if he's well dressed and well spoken, you will relax your mind just a bit further. And that person, before saying a thing, is already a step closer to getting what he wants.

We call the full employment of one's senses **Sensory Acuity.** The thing Jane needed to understand is that she was not engaged in a one-sided event. In fact, although she as the presenter may have been doing all the talking, she was still having a "conversation" with the audience. But if she wasn't listening to them, why should they bother listening to her? And if they weren't listening to her, it follows that they were not in a position to retain much of what she said. Or, worse, she may inadvertently have been sending the opposite message of what she truly hoped to communicate.

The good presenter needs to bring all her senses to the task at hand—and to do so consciously. For example, one of the little things I do to make small groups more comfortable is to use writing markers that have pleasant scents. Last time you wrote on a white board, did you notice the noxious odor? People don't like the smell of chemicals; it puts them on edge. And meetings become more productive when attendees are focused on the subject of the meeting, not wondering whether the marker is killing their brain cells.

We don't stop to think about it all the time, but the fact is that *our entire perception of the world is a reflection of what we absorb (or have absorbed in the past) through our five senses.* Even our emotional experiences and memories are, in a way, bits of data stored in our brains. As the psychologist Mihaly Csikszentmihalyi writes in his landmark book, *Flow*, "Everything we experience—joy or pain, interest or boredom—is represented in the mind as information." Furthermore, "If we are able to control this information, we can decide what our lives will be like."

Csikszentmihalyi's book is about understanding and harnessing the psychological elements that create optimal experiences. He uses the word "flow" to describe these states, but most of us are more familiar with the terminology used by athletes, who speak of being in "the zone." If you're lucky enough to have experienced what it's like to be in the zone, you know it as a feeling that you never forget. Basketball players, for example, describe this feeling as being one with the rim, believing for that moment that nothing else in the world matters and you know every shot will go in even before you release it. On the golf course in this state you are oblivious to distractions—those inside your own head as well as those in range of your peripheral vision—so that every swing is perfect and the balls you hit seem to have eyes of their own, focused on the hole. Such feelings are most common in sports, but they can occur whenever you accomplish any challenging thing in a way that is so focused and pure that your entire being becomes bent to that single purpose: playing a difficult violin passage especially well, for example; painting a picture in complete harmony with your creative side; losing yourself in the construction of a model; or even standing at the stove and juggling pots as you cook a perfectly timed meal. When we're in flow, doing these things may constitute the happiest moments of our lives. As Csikszentmihalyi writes, ". . . in the long run optimal experiences add up to a sense of mastery—or perhaps better, a sense of *participation* in determining the content of life—that comes as close to what is usually meant by happiness as anything else we can conceivably imagine."

What interests me most as a presenter is not so much our sense of mastery of any particular skill; rather it is the flow we may feel when we're communicating well with another person. In the course of an especially intense conversation—perhaps a brainstorming session with a business partner or while making life plans with a spouse—have you ever gotten to the point where you found yourself completely on the other person's wavelength? In a case like that you almost feel as if you know what the other person is going to say before he says it. You might find yourselves finishing each other's sentences or speaking in a kind of short-hand that someone outside the conversation would never be able to follow. At such moments, it may almost feel as if you're talking to yourself or that you're inside each other's heads.

Stop and think about that. How can you know what someone is about to say before their lips begin moving? Have you become a mind reader? No, but you have engaged in a period of Sensory Acuity—a time when your perceptiveness of the other person's verbal and physical cues is so acute that you are influencing that person (and in turn being influenced by him or her) in an intensely heightened way. For the most part, the elements of that kind of communication fall under the category of a practice called Neurolinguistic Programming.

Neurolinguistic Programming

"Neuro" refers to the study of the brain and nervous system; "linguistic" refers to language and its characteristics; "programming" is the development and implementation of a strategy or plan. So **Neurolinguistic Programming** (NLP) is a long-winded way of describing *the study and use of language as it impacts the brain and, therefore, our behavior.*

I came across Neurolinguistic Programming when Tony Robbins facilitated its popularity with his book *Unlimited Power* in the mid-1980s, and I quickly became fascinated with it. While this discipline interested me in its own right, I really got into it when I began to realize the implications NLP had for presentation effectiveness. But I approached this aspect with great caution, because I strongly believe effective presentations must come from the heart, must be genuine, and must not be manipulative of the audience. More so than some other presentation tools, NLP has the potential to undermine one's genuineness. In any case, where it descends into manipulation, I would find the outcome to have come about immorally and would urge you to stay away from it. Even when judged solely from the perspective of effectiveness, manipulation may succeed in the short-term, but will often undermine long-term relationships. Nevertheless, like any tool, in my opinion NLP can be a force for good as well as bad. If used with a light touch, it can truly magnify the impact of our presentations without crossing the line into manipulation. Keep in mind, as you read on, that that is our sole intention.

Like many intellectual disciplines, NLP can get very technical, and many aspects might not apply to what we endeavor to do here. The remainder of this chapter will lay the groundwork for your understanding only of those aspects of NLP that I feel are appropriate for achieving Presentation Mastery. If you want more, there are many books you can read that are totally dedicated to NLP. Those books tend to be more exclusively devoted to *communication*, where our purpose ultimately is excellence in *presentation*.

Later in *Life Is a Series of Presentations*, we will get into the utility of the ideas in this chapter and this section. While I will mention some more prescriptive aspects of NLP by way of example, keep in mind that we will be much more rigorous in Part II about applying these concepts. By the end of this chapter, you should have an appreciation for the following broad principles of NLP:

1. *We must respect different perspectives.* People view the world differently, depending upon their life experiences: what they've read, seen, and felt; their religious experiences; their formal education; what their parents have taught them; where they've lived and continue to live; and what kind of people and environment they've been exposed to. As a result of these varied experiences, different people use different—and sometimes conflicting—frames of reference to analyze and respond to what's going on in the world. So, while we may not agree with the way some other people see the world, we must respect their views as having been legitimately arrived at based upon what they know and don't know of life. If we are to communicate effectively, we must do justice to these differences, because such an understanding makes us more flexible and, therefore, more effective.

2. *Our communication goes beyond the words we choose.* The way we say things and the way we receive information are as important as the actual words we use. While we should never lose sight of *why* we are communicating with our audience and *what* we are communicating, we also must always be conscious of *how* we are communicating. Our verbal vocabulary is just one piece of this puzzle.

3. *When we become like our audience, our message is better received.* As we learned in Chapter 2, people are much more receptive to messages from those whom they consider to be like themselves. As a consequence, the presenter who appears to be similar to his audience has a much greater opportunity to achieve rapport. So we should strive to create sameness with our audience.

4. *People receive information differently.* While most people appear to have all their senses, it turns out that individuals have different preferences for receiving information. If you were bilingual and went to a foreign land where you knew the language, you would likely communicate better in the native tongue than by persisting in English. So it is with the ways people receive information. Once we discover their preference, we must endeavor to adjust the "language" of our presentation for optimal understanding.

5. *We also reject information based upon subconscious personal preferences.* Just as people have preferences for the way they wish to receive information, they have inclinations about what information they would prefer not to receive at all—or will only agree to receive in an altered way. By understanding the way our audience filters information we have another means to adjust our approach for better rapport.

6. Finally, *generalizations and other loaded phrases can work against our message.* We must choose our words with precision and understand which words and phrases hamper or defeat our ability to communicate effectively. Clarity of language can be as important as clarity of purpose.

Originally a model for psychiatric therapy, NLP was first articulated by a language expert and a computer programmer at the University of California at Santa Cruz. These two men, Richard Bandler and John Grinder, developed their model by closely observing the incredibly successful work of contemporary therapists such as Virginia Satir and Milton Erickson. Bandler and Grinder found that these therapists paid close attention to their patients' means of communication, including both the words they used and the way they used them. By closely observing the way patients communicated, Satir and Erickson were able to better understand what was going on inside their patients' minds—their thoughts and mental images. They called these *internal representations.*

Bandler and Grinder agreed that the way patients communicated revealed their internal representations. Then they took this idea a step further. They reasoned that if a skilled communicator could learn through observation the specific ways an individual forms internal images and thoughts, he could use that information to have a more direct effect on how that individual receives his message.

Of course, this only works to the extent that the communicator is willing to adjust to his audience. As such, it is imperative that we accept the following proposition: *The person with the most flexibility has the best chance of achieving the outcome he or she desires.* Many years ago I attended a seminar called The ACT Training that was devoted to certain technical aspects of NLP. One of their handouts put this concept of flexibility very well, explaining in part: "In cybernetics there is a law called the **Law of Requisite Variety.** In simple terms, the law states that ' . . . in any system of machines (or human beings) the element (or person) with the widest range of variability will be the controlling factor in that system.' The widest range of flexibility is going to allow you to elicit the OUTCOMES you want and, thus, control any situation in which you find yourself. Therefore, as long as you maintain flexibility in your behavior, you will always be the controlling element in your environment (or in your communication)."

We must accept the assumption that at any given moment everyone is doing the best he or she can. Think about it. Do you ever say to yourself, "I plan to react poorly to this next turn of events"? Of course not. You might realize you have done so upon reflection, days after the event, but by then you are a different person. You've had more experience. Your best is now a little better. And so it is for us all. We do everyone an injustice if we assume otherwise. As Dale Carnegie wrote: "You deserve very little credit for being what you are—and remember, the people who come to you irritated, bigoted, unreasoning, deserve very little discredit for being what they are. . . . Pity them. Sympathize with them. Say to yourself: 'There, but for the grace of God, go I.' Three-fourths of the people you will ever meet are hungering and thirsting for sympathy. Give it to them, and they will love you."

A number of assumptions underlie the effective use of NLP:

- *You should respect the way the other person views the world.* Does this sound a great deal like a point I already made twice above? Well, it bears repeating because we so rarely accept this simple proposition. People come from a wide variety of experiences, locations, and backgrounds. All these factors, in various permutations, combine in each person to form a unique internal idea of what they believe the world is really like. We all see the world through different eyes.

- *The substance of your communication is the response it generates.* In other words, it doesn't really matter what you meant to communicate. All that matters is the response of the other person to what he or she understood you to mean.

- *The words we use to describe things have different meanings to different people.* You must keep in mind that the words we use conjure unique internal images of what they describe. The word "boat" might raise images of a dinghy in one person's mind and an ocean liner in another's. If you want to be a master communicator, you must be sure that the other person's internal image is as close to yours as possible.

- *The mind and the body influence each other.* What you are thinking at a given moment affects your posture, breathing, skin tone, and even your overall feelings of ease or anxiety. In her book *How to Talk to Practically Anybody About Practically Anything* Barbara Walters writes, "When people recall a time when they were happier and more articulate, they become happier and more articulate." Taking the people across from her to that place on a consistent basis has helped Ms. Walters' subjects open up in front of the camera and made her arguably the best interviewer of celebrities on television.

In many ways, NLP is nothing more than a formalized approach to empathizing with the person to whom you are trying to communicate, and then leveraging that connection in order to get your point across. Remember again that one of the most powerful forces that act upon our receptivity to a message is the Liking principle. We like and trust people who are like us. NLP exploits this principle in certain ways that we'll discuss in just a few pages. For now, let's keep in mind that we will largely succeed in our presentations to the degree that we can successfully be like our audience.

Having learned the above assumptions, we are ready to begin understanding some more specific elements of NLP.

It's How You Tell It

We receive communication through one or more of our five senses, the most important of these being our visual (sight), auditory (hearing), and kinesthetic (touch or feeling) senses. While, of course, most of us have all of our senses, it is also true that most people tend to have a bias in the direction of one of the senses or another. Once we uncover this bias in our audience, we can begin to tailor our presentation strategy to have the greatest possible impact.

There used to be an American Express commercial featuring the comedian Jerry Seinfeld on a trip to London. He gets up on stage in front of a British audience, and his act is so laden with American colloquialisms that he can't get a laugh. He's dying up there, so he runs from the theater and jumps into a taxi. Seinfeld then uses his charge card to feverishly travel the city and familiarize himself with the natives. When he returns to the stage, his stand-up routine—now full of Britishisms—results in triumphant laughter. Every comedian knows that *what* you say is only half the battle. As the expression goes, it's not the joke itself that knocks 'em dead. It's how you tell it.

In fact, research indicates that, on average, about 38 percent of what you communicate to others has to do with the way you say something rather than the words you choose. As it turns out, usually only about 7 percent of what you communicate is comprised of the word selection itself. Seven percent! (The remaining 55 percent of the message comes from your body language.) Does this mean you should throw away the speech? No. But you must always be aware that *how* you say something is potentially five times more powerful than what you say.

There are four core elements of *How* to keep in mind. First is the Tone of your voice. Tonality has an enormous impact on the degree to which others like to hear you speak, and listeners tend to assign certain tonality to specific cultural groups. So it makes sense that people who speak with matching tonalities are more greatly inclined to find rapport with one another.

A second factor is the Rhythm with which you speak. Many people do not take the time to really examine why they form a particular impression about another person, good or bad. They form their impressions unconsciously. So it's up to you to be sure to match their tempo if you want to be in rapport with them.

Third comes Volume, or how loudly you speak. Matching vocal volume helps you establish rapport on two levels. On the surface, you sound like the other person, which as I've mentioned is very powerful. And on a deeper level, by modulating the volume of your voice you become able to match the other person's mood. As William James observed a century ago (and clinical psychologists have confirmed): "Action seems to follow feeling, but really action and feeling go together; and by regulating the action, which is under the more direct control of the will, we can indirectly regulate the feeling, which is not."

The last vocal element involves the words and phrases you use—not so much the content of your message, but the Way you say it. Achieving the greatest rapport with your audience will depend upon your finding out how they prefer to receive information—through the visual, auditory, or kinesthetic mechanism. A person who prefers to see things will use phrases such as "I see" or "that is clear to me." People who prefer to hear messages will say things like "I hear you" or "that sounds wonderful." And people who prefer to use feelings to understand messages may say things like "this doesn't feel right" or "how touching." Once you know how a person prefers to receive messages, you can tailor your conversation for maximum rapport by making use of words and phrases that are congruent with his or her personal view of the world.

Be Like Mike

One of the most famous scenes ever to air on the *I Love Lucy* TV show began when Lucy, dressed as Harpo Marx, walked by a doorway in her hotel room only to see as her "reflection" the real Harpo Marx. Each character then proceeded to test the "mirror" they were staring into by executing a perfectly timed sequence of identical gestures while facing each other. While this scene is still hilarious, practitioners of NLP would not consider it to be **mirroring,** but mimicry. And mimicry in real life is far from funny—it's usually insulting, which is no way to communicate. The kind of mirroring we're talking about is always respectful of the audience and never mocking. In fact, like the finding of flow it is frequently done inadvertently.

A friend of mine named Mike Perkins is a master at mirroring his audience. At least partly as a result of this skill, he has succeeded quite significantly in the financial services business, where he works for a large corporation. Mike has the greatest instant rapport I've ever seen. Over the years, I've watched in awe as he climbed to the top tier of his company based largely upon his instinctive ability to mirror whomever he's talking to. Was that the only factor in his success? Of course not. Mike is a highly competent and together fellow in many respects. Yet he quickly jumped to the top of his firm while others of similar talent advanced more slowly. And I am convinced that much of his success derives from his ability to present himself very well—something he does by effortlessly achieving sameness with associates and superiors alike. As a result of this skill, Mike has acquired a real following.

I once witnessed Mike's presentation style in front of a large group at a company sales conference in Dallas. At most companies, there exists a natural tension between the home office and the field reps. Typically, people in the field harbor a degree of resentment for natural reasons: The home office is a bureaucracy making decisions that directly affect the reps, who feel that they're slugging away in the trenches while having to follow orders from people who are less in touch with the customers. Field reps at large firms often exist almost in a different universe from their office-bound peers. Their days are structured differently, they have a language all their own, and they often even dress differently from the company's office workers. At Mike's firm, it was no different. Yet Mike, a straightlaced home-office worker who was at ease in the halls of power, never had any trouble connecting with his people in the field. When he was talking to the suits, he was like the suits. But when he was talking to the reps one-on-one, he could backslap with the best of them. And when he stood up in front of a large audience filled with people from "out there," I saw all signs of difference evaporate. Mike used the words they used, talked about his visits out in the field, easily illustrated how what he did in his office linked to their world, and got his audience involved. In short, Mike became like his audience, and his audience loved him for it. At the end of Mike's presentation he received resounding applause.

All good presenters must endeavor to be like Mike, in spirit and in practice. Without even realizing it, Mike has built his career upon one of the foundation stones of NLP.

Whenever you have a high degree of rapport with another person, you will almost always find that you are sitting or standing alike and that you are each mirroring the other's facial expressions and gestures in a completely natural fashion. One of the easiest ways to mirror another's body language is to mirror his or her stance or sitting position. Matching the other person's leg and lower body positions is a simple way to increase rapport.

As for the upper body, people generally position their shoulders in a way that allows them either to face you directly or to face you at an angle. If you are consciously looking for this type of positioning, you'll find that it is very easy to recognize and mirror. Simply pay attention to the position of their shoulders and the gestures they make with their arms and hands.

It is also relatively easy to mirror the tilt of another person's head. The facial expressions can be a little more challenging. It helps to recognize that there are two distinct areas of the face: the region including the eyes and everything above them, and the region below the eyes, including the nose, mouth, and chin. In the upper portion, look for wrinkling and other muscle movement. It's fairly common for people to wrinkle their fore-heads or squint their eyes in response to certain messages. They might also open their eyes more widely than normal. You can mirror these changes easily. In the region below the eyes, pay close attention to the other person's mouth. Of course, the simplest gesture of all is the smile. One of Dale Carnegie's most basic rules for making friends and influencing people was to smile. He quoted University of Michigan psychology professor James V. McConnell as observing that, "People who smile tend to manage, teach and sell more effectively, and to raise happier children. There's far more information in a smile than in a frown. That's why encouragement is a much more effective teaching device than punishment." A spiritual principle comes to mind, found in Proverbs 17:22: "A cheerful heart is good medicine, but a crushed spirit dries up the bones." If your audience is smiling, you'd best be smiling back.

Remember Jane, with whom we began this chapter? Her audience— my colleagues and I—sat down with open ears and hearts and with smiles on our faces. But Jane never smiled back. By getting lost in the paper on the stage, rather than reaching for rapport with her audience, she failed to jibe with the psychological state that we had brought to the room. This shortcoming led to alienation from her audience.

State is *the sum of all the thoughts, feelings, and experiences a person has at any one instant.* Since time began man has attempted to alter his state by various methods, from the use of music to the ingestion of food or drugs. Any of those things might work, but as William James suggested and science has subsequently proved, we don't need outside influences or foreign objects to change our mental state. We can do so merely by changing our physiology—our posture, breathing, and biochemistry. For example, simply sitting up straight in your chair and putting a big, goofy smile on your face can actually lift your spirits.

One of the most effective ways to increase rapport is by matching another person's breathing pattern. You don't literally have to breathe in and out with the other person. Look at breathing as just a rhythmic body function that everyone does constantly. With that in mind, you can easily see that tapping a pencil or moving your foot in the same rhythm as the other person's breathing will work as well as actually breathing in and out when he or she does.

If you stop to think about it, then, mirroring another person's state is relatively straightforward. Observe that person's posture, facial expressions, and vocal quality. Then subtly match these things as closely as you can. But be careful. Matching a person who is in a state of limited power or enthusiasm is not conducive to helping that person do great things. So match his or her state to gain rapport, but once you've gained that rapport be prepared to lead him to another, more powerful, state.

How? When we have a conversation with someone, our inner thought processes are constantly seeking common ground with that individual. This tendency—like our receptivity toward Social Proof—derives from our deep desire for understanding and belonging. Practitioners of NLP refer to *the entire process of matching behaviors* as **Pacing.** While we all may pace other people in order to increase our mutual comfort levels during a conversation, the accomplished presenter employs this method with a purpose in mind. Once she's established that rapport, she then uses it to lead her audience where she wants them to go.

Leading is about *exhibiting behavior that differs from the other person's as a way of generating some new response on his or her part.* In effect, Pacing is reactive while Leading is proactive—rather than imitating, you take the lead in generating a different behavior. Consider the following rather amusing old story about a slightly nutty Englishman named Lord Berners.

About seventy years ago, the famous Australian ballet dancer Robert Helpmann had been invited to take tea at the home of Lord Berners, a composer whom a biographer recently labeled "the last eccentric." Ushered into the drawing room of the peer's mansion near Oxford, Helpmann found Lord Berners with an elegant silver tea service resting on a table next to a live horse. He greeted Helpmann, asked whether he took cream and sugar, and all the while fed buttered scones to the horse. Offering no explanation, he finally told the horse that it had had enough, and a servant led the animal out through the large French window. Much later, apparently, Helpmann screwed up the courage to inquire about the horse's presence.

"I'm very nervous," Lord Berners explained. "When people see the horse, they become as nervous as I am, so that after a while I get over it. Then we can have a normal conversation."

So Berners had essentially forced his guest to pace him and then led him where he wanted him to go emotionally! Fortunately, you don't usually need to bring a horse into your living room in order to lead your audience. Once you have paced a person for a few minutes, test the level of rapport you have by attempting to lead him. Rather than following his gestures, try initiating some new gestures. Then watch closely to see if he is following your lead. If so, he is now unconsciously being paced by you.

The key to Pacing and Leading is conscious control over your behavior, moods, and beliefs, coupled with sufficient flexibility to change them in order to match or mirror the other person. By pacing, you establish an atmosphere of acceptance and understanding. It's almost impossible to match and mirror another person without acquiring some degree of empathy for him. So the whole process of Pacing and Leading has another positive effect: It takes the attention off of you and puts it where it belongs if you want to maximize communication—on the other person. How important is that? As Henry Ford said, "If there is one secret of success, it lies in the ability to get the other person's point of view and see things from that person's angle as well as your own."

Receiving is Believing

The fifth habit in Stephen R. Covey's great book *The 7 Habits of Highly Effective People* is "Seek First to Understand, Then to Be Understood." Noting that "this principle is the key to communication . . . the most important skill in life," he goes on to observe that when another person is speaking, we exercise one of five levels of listening: *ignoring, pretending, selective listening, attentive listening,* and *empathetic listening.* I hope you understand by now that empathetic listening is the most important and useful of these five.

One of the ways we achieve empathetic listening in our audience is by tapping into the power of NLP to directly access that person's preferred way of receiving information. As we noted above, each of us has a favorite—but usually subconscious—**sensory modality.**

Suppose I put the following otherwise identical packages on a desk in front of you: a FedEx, an Airborne Express, a UPS, an apparent form letter, and a hand-addressed package. Which would you open first? The Federal Express package, maybe? Or the hand-addressed one? Most people would have a preference that would probably give you a small insight into their personality. A rudimentary analysis might infer, for instance, that the person who opens the FedEx package first is more inclined to be a Type A personality while the person who opens the hand-addressed one might be more inclined to value human contact. In similar fashion, whether we do so consciously or not, we all allow various preferences to rule our lives. As presenters, it helps to understand a very particular aspect of this behavior: the way we prefer to receive information.

The easiest way to spot which mode a person prefers is by listening to the words and phrases he or she uses. The action words, or predicates, that a person employs to describe the world are like a window opening directly into what he or she is thinking. Paying attention to which mode people prefer is a lot like recognizing that some people prefer the phone while others would rather receive letters. When you send your message (i.e., make your presentation) using the right medium, communication and rapport are bound to be improved.

Recall the three main modalities: **visual** (seeing), **auditory** (hearing), and **kinesthetic** (feeling). The person who prefers visual images is the most common type of communicator in our society. Visual people are much more mobile than auditory or kinesthetic people. They are in constant motion, as is their thinking process. That's because images are much easier for the brain to process than sounds or feelings. "Visuals" are the fast, impatient people of the world.

Ross Perot is probably a visual. His presidential campaign was replete with charts and graphs. And though that gave the comedians some fodder, it also helped propel Perot to one of the best showings of any third-party candidate in U.S. history. Perhaps that's because more people, like Perot, prefer to receive their information visually than in any other way.

The breathing of visual people tends to be shallow and from the chest. They also frequently stop breathing for a moment while accessing internal images. It's like a power drain when the movie projector comes on. Visuals are actually seeing themselves in the pictures playing across their minds. Where a person's eyes move also tells you a lot about what type of thought process he or she is currently using (this is called eye accessing).* Visual people will most often look up, either to the left or right, when asked a question that requires some thought. Most right-handed auditory people, by contrast, will direct their eyes to the right if trying to remember a familiar sound or to the left if asked to construct a sound that is unfamiliar.

Do you ever think that people sometimes don't hear what you mean? Do you prefer to talk on the telephone rather than read letters? Do you become especially irritated by noise or sounds that others seem able to ignore? If so, you may be an auditory communicator. You probably enjoy

---

*Go to http://www.tonyjeary.com/eyeaccess for a free copy of the eye-accessing chart.

dialogue and discussion, either with others or with yourself. In fact, some auditory people become so engrossed in inner dialogue that they appear to be unfriendly or even withdrawn. Sometimes an auditory communicator will stop mid-sentence when talking because he has to listen to some internal sound or dialogue. This interrupts what he's saying. On the other hand, most auditory communicators love to listen to other people's ideas and stories.

The breathing rate of auditory people tends to be deeper and more from the diaphragm than that of visuals. It also has a more rhythmic pace. Auditory people tend to slouch their shoulders somewhat, and they often turn their heads to one side in order to facilitate hearing. Especially important is to recognize who among your friends and coworkers is most disturbed by harsh sounds or most enjoys melodious sounds or good music.

Finally, there are people for whom feelings and sensitivity are everything. These feeling-based, or kinesthetic, people translate visual and auditory input into feelings in order to process that information. People who prefer to interpret the world this way are usually not as quick to make decisions or reply to pointed questions as are visual people. Sometimes they seem maddeningly slow to decide things, especially to visuals who are able to evaluate criteria literally at the speed of light. But this doesn't mean kinesthetic people are any less intelligent than the rest of us; they simply value depth more than speed.

When people wait for feelings and intuition to become fully apparent, they usually look down and to the right. At that point they often show other clues, such as small smiles, tightening around the eyes, or even scowling (if the feeling is an unpleasant one). It's not uncommon for kinesthetics to ask the same question, worded differently, at several points in a short period of time. They listen in a very intense way, and their breathing comes from low in the chest or stomach and is very measured. They look keenly into your eyes, seeming to soak up everything being said. Internally, they are working hard to generate feelings to go with what you are telling them. This takes concentration and intensity.

Kinesthetics make up the smallest portion of our population. They are the people who seem to be most interested in how others feel about things—and in how they themselves feel. Often they enjoy human contact more than the rest of us. Huggers might be kinesthetic people.

Keep in mind that it is not important to become an expert at reading people's every sensory cue—or even at other aspects of NLP—in order to become a great presenter. I think of NLP as a language that most people don't happen to know and often aren't even aware is being spoken. Imagine being dropped among one of those African tribes where the people communicate partly by clicking their tongues. If you'd never heard of this, you might not even realize at first that they were talking with one another. But once you learned a few words of their language, even if you never became fluent or nailed the grammar down completely, you would begin, at times, to have a sense of what was being communicated. Now another visitor drops out of the sky. Wouldn't you have an advantage over that person when it came time to influence your newfound friends? A passing knowledge of NLP gives you a similar advantage.

The Mind Is Truly Like a Sieve

When you reflect on the elements of what you consider a good job, house, or relationship, what are some of your criteria? If you begin the list of your answers with what you *do* want, chances are good that you're the type of person who moves toward pleasure. On the other hand, if you start your list with the things you *don't* want, chances are that you prefer to move away from pain rather than toward pleasure.

Most people prefer one kind of response or the other, and this preference results from deep subconscious filters called **metaprograms**—*mental patterns that we use to form internal images and ideas when we are confronted with a choice that must be made.* Like the mental shortcuts that Dr. Cialdini talks about, these metaprograms enable the brain to efficiently sort the data brought to us by our senses. The mind, in other words, is like a sieve that tries only to let the important stuff through. So next time someone says glumly that they have a mind like a sieve, tell them they're right!

In order to most effectively communicate with another person, it helps to understand their metaprograms and how to present to them in a way that will make it through their filters. It's common that people who move toward pleasure are annoyed by those who present ideas to them as a way to move away from pain. They often see this approach as pessimistic or negative. On the flip side, people who prefer to move away from pain see ideas presented as avenues to fun and pleasure as overly optimistic, unrealistic, or frivolous. For these people you must phrase your message as an opportunity to move away from pain.

People filter information differently. There are many different kinds of filters, and it's not that important to have a comprehensive understanding of each one. What's more relevant to us as presenters is to have an awareness that these filters are one way that people process information. Consider, for example, the relative amount of input different people need from others—whether they use an external or an internal frame of reference. Some people "just know" when they have done something well, for example. Others require a good deal of affirmation and congratulations. The simplest way to determine whether a person has an external or internal frame of reference is to ask, "How do you know when you've done well? Can you just tell, or do you wait for others to tell you?"

If you were making a sales presentation, the key phrase for a customer who has an internal frame of reference would be, "You be the judge." This person already feels that he or she is the only important judge anyway, so acknowledging this builds rapport. Conversely, for a customer with an external frame of reference, the most effective approach would be to talk about others who have used your product or agreed with your idea. Even better is to patch one of these people into a three-way call, which lends a voice of Authority or Social Proof, depending upon who you have selected as the third party.

Another filter pits necessity versus possibility. The people who are motivated by necessity tend to look at choices as limited. In fact, they often don't even see some options that might be available. They interact with others on the basis that "this is the way it is." Alternatively, people motivated by the possibilities and options that life offers are ever in search of another way, another idea, or another situation. They are not motivated by what they *have* to do as much as by what they *could* do. They are very interested in things that are not yet known.

While many of us may intuitively think that the person who prefers options and possibilities would be more interesting, it's important to keep in mind that the people who are motivated by necessity have more depth of knowledge than those who are motivated by opportunity. That's because, taken to extremes, the opportunity-motivated person spends a great deal of time sorting through all the possibilities available. The trick in identifying a person's necessity versus possibility filter is to listen to *why* he or she chose to do something. Then phrase your message accordingly.

Yet another filter determines whether a person is a serial or parallel thinker. Some people—those with a parallel thinking style—prefer to understand the big picture before they embark on a project. Others (serial thinkers) need to know how the details will be handled. The best way to uncover whether a person prefers details or the big picture is simply to ask them at an appropriate time. This is not a filter that is well hidden from its owner; people know immediately what they prefer. And once you as the presenter know, you can respond accordingly. Giving details first to a person who prefers to understand the big picture is worse than useless. On the other hand, people who prefer details first will not be convinced that you have "thought the project through" unless you can first explain the details.

Similar to the detail-oriented people, some folks can only be convinced something will work when they see it in operation—they are "show me" people. Some "show me" people will automatically accept a thing they see functioning once or twice. But others will be convinced only by consistency. Still other people are willing to assume something will work unless it is demonstrated to them that it doesn't. All of these types of people, given a little thought, can tell you their preferences.

Finally and importantly, some people seek out similarities while others seek differences. The former we call **Matchers** and the latter **Mismatchers**. Matchers are always on the lookout for sameness. They say things like, "It boils down to this." In other words, there is a pattern here that ties this vast array of differences together. Matchers are bound and determined to find that pattern. They will tend to ignore information that supports the theory that there are many significant differences among things. The only information they pay attention to is that which supports the theory that "all this stuff is somehow related." Matchers also love regularity and routine. Moving them out of a routine is painful and causes them to be disconcerted until they are able to find that ever-present pattern and hook back into it. President George W. Bush is most certainly a Matcher, as evidenced by his faith in daily routine and his approach to Iraqi evasions on disarmament.

Mismatchers are not terribly common, but it is helpful to know when you are dealing with one. These are the people who notice those things that are not in place, no matter how small. They often seek to make changes to things just for the sake of the change itself. They locate differences for the sake of differences.

Matchers are motivated to find things that are alike. So give them options that fit the patterns they have established. Point out how your idea is just like their current set of ideas and beliefs. Mismatchers, on the other hand, are looking for differences, so point out how your idea differs from any other. Paying close attention to whether a person matches or mismatches is very useful in understanding why they see things certain ways.

Mean What You Say

Yogi Berra, as famed for his malapropisms as for anything he did on the baseball field, once remarked, "I really didn't say everything I said!" Sadly, neither have most of us.

If the discipline of Neurolinguistic Programming teaches us anything it is the importance of precision in our communications. Study after study has shown that *the more precise a person is in communication, the more successful he or she becomes*. The best managers and leaders in the world are those who are able to clearly convey their abstract visions and ideas to almost anyone.

Many of us speak in generalizations. But phrases such as "too many," "too much," and "too expensive," for example, have no meaning unless they are further defined. Consequently, it's very important that you work to establish what benchmark is being used for comparison.

Let's say you and a friend were discussing cars in 1989, the year that Toyota introduced its Lexus. The Lexus line eventually went on to take market share away from European luxury car makers because, while it was expensive in relation to other Toyotas, it was comparable in quality and quite reasonably priced next to certain Mercedes and BMW models.

"That car is too expensive," says your friend.

"Compared to what?" you reply.

"Well, compared to the car I currently drive."

"What kind of car is that?" you ask.

"A 1988 Oldsmobile."

"In what ways is your Olds like that Lexus?"

"In some ways, I suppose. They both have a V-8 engine and four doors," says your friend. "But in other ways it's apples and oranges."

"Do you think that Lexus is too expensive in general? Or are there maybe instances when it might be a bargain?"

"Actually," your friend comments, "I've heard that the Lexus is as good as but cheaper than similar cars from Mercedes-Benz and BMW."

By encouraging your friend to turn away from generalizations and toward specifics, you've just come a whole lot closer to selling him on the idea that the Lexus might be a good value. So when you hear comparison words used—or feel inclined to use them yourself—remember to ask, "Compared to what?"

Another good question to ask is, "Who or what or how, specifically?" Unspecified nouns are usually the result of lumping all parts of some larger system or process together. The problem arises when we make a judgment about the whole based on our assessment of one of the parts. For instance, a teacher might sigh, "They are driving me crazy today!" A concerned principal might then ask, "Who are *they?*" The teacher could respond, "Those kids in my third period class." That's certainly more useful information than simply "they."

In this example, the principal might wish to seek more clarification: "Which kids specifically are causing the trouble?" The teacher replies, "Those two new kids. They are very undisciplined."

By asking the question two times, the principal has narrowed the focus down from every kid in the school to the two new kids in a certain class. That's a huge difference.

Unspecified nouns can include obvious ones like "them," "those people," or "that group." They can also be words that describe an entire process, such as "your idea" or "those rules." For example, suppose a person tells you, "Your idea is not going to work." You could reply, "Sure it will. Just look at how well it's put together." But in this instance you are being combative, and as Dale Carnegie wisely observed, arguing is among the least effective means of communication. "Nine times out of ten," he wrote, "an argument ends with each of the contestants more firmly convinced than ever that he is absolutely right."

So let's have another go at it by asking, "What specifically about my idea won't work?" The other person will most likely respond something like, "Well, that part about public speaking. I don't speak publicly, so your idea makes no sense to me."

Aha! This person's objection is really about just one small part of your idea. Now you are in a position to ask, "What if you didn't use it for public speaking. Could it work for you in other areas?" Chances are that it could, and you've resolved the conflict much more elegantly, without being argumentative.

One of the most common ways people allow themselves to lapse into generalizations is through use of words like *all, always, never, everybody,* and *nobody.* If you have kids, as I do, then you experience this kind of usage practically on a daily basis. My two daughters are always coming in and saying—wait a minute! Always? No, not always, just when they really want something.

The key to helping the other person—or yourself—break down the generalization is to repeat the generalized word as a question, as I did above. If you want to persuade another person (or yourself) to take a new course of action, generalizations can become a barrier to clear reasoning, since they usually have the effect of closing off alternative courses of action. Repeating the generalization as a question forces the speaker to examine it more closely, which is the first step toward breaking it down.

Similar to our habit of often speaking in generalities is people's tendency to create rules of conduct or communication for ourselves or others. Over time, we all subconsciously build up rules and regulations that are designed to help us avoid experiences that we expect will cause us pain. But this kind of filter in your audience can be like a blunt instrument mindlessly batting away the influence you are trying to exert.

When we use words such as "wouldn't" and "must" we are revealing our inner rules and regulations. Similar words are *ought, can* or *can't, should* or *shouldn't, necessary, appropriate,* and *have to.* We use these words when speaking to others (or to ourselves) as a way to close off consideration. They're shortcuts that have often worked for us in the past, but that does not mean they will lead us (or our audience) to the correct decision in the present. So we need to short-circuit this trigger by asking a question like, "What would happen if you didn't?" In most cases, the only major upheaval that would occur would be a change in one's beliefs. And that is exactly what this question is meant to accomplish! But if more tact is required—as it often is when challenging another person's beliefs—soften the question with an opening phrase such as, "I'm wondering . . . ," "I'm curious . . . ," or "Would you be willing to consider . . ."

An understanding of NLP concepts and practices will allow any person to communicate better in life. The techniques we reviewed above can help good presenters get their point across with clarity and overcome the knee-jerk defenses of their audience. Though we often do these things *subconsciously*, it is essential that we have come to understand the basics of this process, because its *intentional* use undergirds many of the practices we will learn in later chapters. In the second half of the book, we will examine some easy ways to employ our knowledge of NLP.

Even if we do not remember or have the opportunity to use all the aspects and techniques discussed above, we must take away a more important lesson from our understanding of NLP. *Any time we are making a presentation—whether it's to an audience of hundreds or to a single individual—we are engaged in a two-way conversation.* As is the case in any conversation, we should expect not only to talk, but to listen and respond. We need always to carry with us an awareness that even when our audience is not speaking, they are communicating. We need to approach all our presentations with Sensory Acuity—that is to say, with our own senses in a heightened state of awareness. If we do that, we will better understand the unspoken conversation as well as the spoken. This will make it more likely for us to achieve rapport and communicate with clarity and effectiveness.

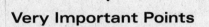

Very Important Points

- We call the full employment of one's senses Sensory Acuity.

- Our entire perception of the world is a reflection of what we absorb (or have absorbed in the past) through our five senses.

- Our communication goes beyond the words we choose.

- When we become like our audience, our message is better received.

- People receive information differently.

- We also reject information based upon subconscious personal preferences.

- Generalizations and other loaded phrases can work against our message.

- The person with the most flexibility has the best chance of achieving the outcome he or she desires.

- You should respect the way the other person views the world.

- The substance of your communication is the response it generates.

- The words we use to describe things have different meanings to different people.

- The mind and the body influence each other.

- The more precise a person is in communication, the more successful he or she becomes.

- Any time we are making a presentation—whether it's to an audience of hundreds or to a single individual—we are engaged in a two-way communication.

CHAPTER 4

A Miss Is as Good as a Mile

*The Impact of Mastery and
How to Define Your Presentation Universe*

We have seen that the typical person's life is a series of presentations and that, on occasion, these presentations might even pertain to matters of life and death. So you know by now that presentations are important to people's lives and to their success, no matter how they define success. Decades ago Dale Carnegie observed that "even in such technical lines as engineering, 15 percent of one's financial success is due to one's technical knowledge and about 85 percent is due to skill in human engineering—to personality and the ability to lead people."

In the past two chapters we have also learned that effective presentations do not have to be random events. Our receptivity to influence is grounded in the biology and psychology of the human mind, even to the point where on occasion we generate unconscious automatic responses to certain verbal and visual stimuli. And, as we have seen, it follows that the most potent presentation practices are those that we employ with a sincere appreciation of the strengths, vulnerabilities, and inclinations of the human mind—both our own and the ones that reside in our audiences.

Now the time has come to relate these observations to the particulars of your situation. The first thing to appreciate is the frequent power of small differences. Scott Klein, for example, has understood for many years that being at least slightly better at presenting than his peers would yield big payoffs professionally. When we spoke about this he was forty-five and already president of the $1-billion Consumer Industries, Retail and Energy division of the giant corporation EDS.

I asked Klein when he first realized how important good presentations are to success and happiness. "Since I was about five years old," he answered without hesitation. "When I was really very young I got involved with both magic and music, which gave me the opportunity to get up and perform in front of groups of people on a fairly regular basis. So I got the chance early on to hone my presentation skills, and it made a big difference in everything I did. For example, my parents were involved in fund-raising activities, and they'd send me around to sell candy bars for charity. By the age of six or seven I was outselling all the other kids by a mile because I was always very comfortable making those presentations. Those skills, which were learned at a very young age, really helped me thrive not just as a kid growing up but straight through college and on to every aspect of my adult life."

Klein's first full-time job was as an entry-level brand-management trainee with Procter & Gamble. His first day on the job he got into a conversation with two other newly hired trainees as they waited in the personnel department for processing. One mentioned that he was fresh out of Harvard Business School, and the other said he had just received his MBA from Wharton. "Where'd you graduate from?" they asked Klein. When he told them he was an accounting major with an undergraduate degree from Syracuse, they laughed at him, but Klein suspected that he had some skills that they don't teach at Harvard or Wharton business schools.

As an entry-level brand-management person working on the Dash detergent account, Klein says he was called upon to do "a tremendous amount of writing, but there were only two times a year that you actually had an opportunity to present in person to senior management. Most of my peers lived in fear of those two presentations. Me? I eagerly counted down the days to when they would take place, because I knew they were opportunities to shine. When I did the first presentation the general manager of the division was so blown away by what he saw from a relatively young guy that he took a tremendous interest in my career, and when I made my second presentation a few months later, management was so impressed that they quickly promoted me."

The next stop in the Procter & Gamble program was to go out on the road for sales training. As a result of his strong presentation skills, Klein became the first in his "class" of about ninety trainees to advance. He moved on to that step after only nine months with the company, easily beating the promotion record of fifteen months set by a previous entry-level employee. And when Klein returned from the field after his three-month stint, his friends from Harvard and Wharton were still in their original positions.

Klein went on to help make Tide detergent the company's first billion-dollar brand, then moved to the sales and marketing side of Pepsi, which he calls "a total presentation environment." Needless to say, he was promoted very rapidly there, and by the time he was twenty-six Klein had become the director of marketing for the eastern region. He later became COO of PrimeSource Building Products and president of PC Mall, before joining EDS and making the most important presentation of his life. That came when he sat down with Jeff Heller, then–vice chairman of EDS, in an effort to convince him that the company needed to increase its emphasis on consumer packaged goods companies and retailers by treating that market as a separate business segment within the company. His presentation proved so convincing that EDS not only decided to segregate that business into a separate division as Klein recommended—they gave him the job of leading the organization.

Presentation competence, by Klein's definition, "is the ability to be in front of an audience, whether of one or one thousand, and make points in a convincing manner. Mastery is when you can do those same things in such a way that your audience is energized and can't wait to get out of their seats and do something exciting about what you've just said."

He laments the fact that most in-person business presentations lack that extra oomph. "I've been a big believer my entire life that if you want to just provide information you can write it up in a memo and hand it out. What makes an on-site presentation special is that it's going to change the way a company is doing something or the way people in the audience are conducting themselves. Too many times with presentations a bunch of information is conveyed and people sit in the audience and listen and kind of nod their heads, but an hour later the audience has forgotten 80 percent of what they heard. Any time I'm in front of a group one of my key objectives is to make sure that as I'm talking, people are physically or mentally making an action plan—that people are chomping at the bit to follow through on what I have to say."

Klein likens the difference between presentation competence and Presentation Mastery to the distinction between management and leadership, a subject he speaks publicly about a great deal. *"Leadership,"* he observes, *"is the ability to teach people and organizations to surpass themselves.* It's about maximizing human potential and about the ability to see what others don't see. Leading is the ability to find where people or an organization should be going, while managing is handling a collection of tasks. Leading is what's possible, while managing is what's necessary."

The main factor that enables Klein to "teach people and organizations to surpass themselves" is his mastery of the presenter's art. That element has led both to his own success and that of every company he has had the opportunity to lead.

What's the lesson for our presentation strategy from Scott Klein's story? That *most of the time, stuff doesn't just happen to us—we make it happen by what we do and by the way we are.* And here's the real nub of it: The result of our action (or inaction) can be disproportionate to the action itself, depending partly upon luck and partly upon how crucial the circumstances are to our goals in life.

If we want to maximize our new effort to make masterful presentations, we must do two things. First we must understand how much Presentation Mastery can specifically advance our own agenda for success and contentment. Then we must identify our own opportunities for improving our skills and outcomes.

Impact!

On rare occasion, national or world events leave such an impression on us that they sear themselves into our memory in a unique way. If you're old enough, you probably recall exactly where you were or what you were doing when John F. Kennedy was shot, when Neil Armstrong first walked on the moon, and, more recently, when terrorists attacked the World Trade Center and the Pentagon. I remember exactly what I was doing when I found out that the space shuttle *Challenger* had exploded over Cape Canaveral. I was delivering a newly detailed Ferrari back to the dealer when the deejay announced it on the radio. My coauthor Kim tells me she was pitching an author over the phone to a producer in San Francisco when the news came over the wire. Joel was working at a trade magazine company, and he remembers all the employees piling into the conference room to watch the replay on the television set there.

Naturally, the space shuttle is a very complex piece of equipment. Its design has resulted from the work of literally thousands of scientists and engineers, and every flight involves not only a team of astronauts but many people on the ground. It contains hundreds of thousands of parts, almost every one carefully engineered to a particular purpose. Hundreds of sensors monitor its every operation, and redundant systems back up crucial functions. So at first no one could believe that a single, relatively inexpensive part could have led to such complete catastrophe. But as the scientist Richard P. Feynman notoriously demonstrated in a presentation before Congressional investigators, the decision to launch on a cold morning caused the booster rocket O rings to become brittle and to leak rocket fuel after takeoff. The failure of this single part among many thousands led to a rapid cascade of events that cost the lives of the crew and traumatized a nation.

Our physiology and the systems that make up our world are more complicated than the space shuttle or anything man has ever designed. Yet in our lives, too, the success or failure of a relatively small part can have grave consequences for our ability to achieve the outcomes that we seek. Until you began to read this book you might not have realized the importance of everyday presentations to your happiness and success. After all, unless you're solely in the business of doing presentations— and most of us are not—then how often will anyone compliment or criticize you on your presentation style? Rarely. As a result, you are walking around oblivious to the importance of that O ring in your life—the part you never pause to think about, but the importance of which contains the ability to decide between success and failure. Before you began reading this book, my friend, you may have walked through life as an unconscious incompetent.

Whoa! What did I just call you? Incompetent?

Don't be insulted. You didn't know!

In the training world from which I hail, we talk about there being **four stages of learning:** unconscious incompetence, conscious incompetence, conscious competence, and unconscious competence. We might summarize these stages as follows, taking as an example the process of tying one's shoes:

Unconscious Incompetence. The one-year-old child is an unconscious incompetent on the subject of shoe tying. While he may have observed laces attached to shoes, he could look at them as strings to be played with but remains blissfully unaware of their relationship to keeping shoes on one's feet. Or perhaps he hasn't even noticed the laces on shoes at all. In any case, he doesn't think of shoe tying as something he wants to do because he simply has no concept of what shoe tying is. Similarly, you may not even have thought of the important role presentations play in both your personal and professional lives until you picked up this book.

Conscious Incompetence. The three year old knows a lot more about shoes. He knows that most shoes need to be fastened on and that he can do the Velcro ones himself. Still, he can't tie his own shoes. Mommy or Daddy has to do it for him. So the three year old understands that shoes with laces require tying, knows that others have the ability to tie shoes, and is conscious of his own inability to do this. He is a conscious incompetent. And, having read about a third of this book, you've achieved the same status with regard to presentations. Your awareness has been heightened, but you haven't yet become conversant with all the practices that will make you a Presentation Master.

Conscious Competence. The five-year-old child, if she is like my daughters when they were younger, practically considers herself an expert on her own shoes. She knows the difference between the party shoes and the everyday shoes. She has her favorite shoes and her least favorite, her comfortable shoes and the shoes she wears to impress. She even thinks she can well match her shoes to her outfit, and sometimes she's right. Most important, however, she has learned to tie her own shoes. She is very proud of this at times, but she also understands that she is not as competent at the shoe tying thing as her mommy is. The five year old, as we know, still labors over her shoe tying. She can do it all right, but she must always work at it and often think about it. Moreover, if she tries to do it without thinking about it, she is likely to mess it up and have to do it again more deliberately. She is competent, but that competence comes at the price of her having to pay some attention to the task. In similar fashion, as you begin to put into practice what you learn from this book, you will at first be self-conscious and may choose to apply these lessons selectively and with great planning.

Unconscious Competence. I am pleased to inform you that, when it comes to shoe tying, long ago I achieved more than competence. When I need to tie my shoes, my fingers coordinate themselves like lightning and before I even know it my laces are perfectly tied. Once I decide to tie my shoes, I never even think about which way to put the loop or how to make the knot. It just happens—without any conscious effort on my part. When I'm tying my shoes, I can devote 100 percent of my conscious brain to other things. My fingers might have to do some work, but as far as my brain is concerned shoe tying for me has become completely effortless. When it comes to shoe tying, I am unconsciously competent. And after you have studied the Essentials of the Master Presenter and made them into habits, your presentations will no longer be labored. Like your shoe tying, they will have become automatic.

As you can see from these examples, despite the loaded associations we have when anyone refers to our "competence," this terminology does not imply value judgments. There are so many things to know in the world that in many instances we may not even have a sense of what we don't know, and there's nothing wrong with that.

Our goal as presenters ought to be unconscious competence—or to be operating in automatic mode. Why? First of all, in the long run it will be easier. If every time we make a presentation we are like the five year old tying her shoes, then to a degree we will always sweat our way through it, which will make us less sure of ourselves and leave us fewer mental resources to concentrate on our message. Second, we live in an interrupt-driven world, where presentations often arise unexpectedly and we must meet challenges on the fly. The unconscious competent is more prepared to meet this challenge than anyone else. But, when it comes to presenta-

tion skills, it turns out that there are more people with conscious competency than we might care to admit. They are, in a sense, our competition.
So in order to excel at winning the support of others, we must exceed
them. As Tom Peters noted, referring to the world of business, the success
of excellent companies depends upon ordinary people achieving extraordinary things. Being good just ain't good enough.

Today my colleagues and I call this phenomenon and its application to
our work the Presentation Impact Curve.* As George Lowe, Greg Kaiser,
and I describe in a shared thesis for our clients called *Presentation Mastery*, the Impact Curve might look like this:

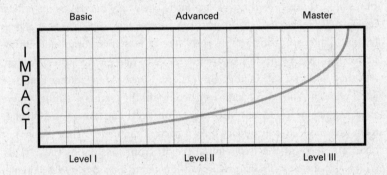

What this simple model describes is that early on in our skill development, small advances produce proportionately small improvements.
But once we've mastered the basic and intermediate components of a
skill set (Levels I and II), incremental improvements begin to yield
exponential results (Level III). This might best be exemplified by the
careers of Hollywood movie stars or television personalities. Tom
Hanks commands something like $20 million per picture and has won
several Academy Awards. Other actors who are almost as talented and
have also won Oscars often earn a fraction of what Hanks makes. Is
Tom Hanks a better actor than these people? That's a subjective question, of course, but judging by his popularity and Oscars, the answer
might be yes. Is he twenty or thirty times better? The dollar figure
would suggest so, but a more probable explanation for the discrepancy

---

*Go to http://www.tonyjeary.com/impactcurve for a free electronic copy of this model.

is that Tom Hanks is incrementally better than many other potential leading men, but there's very little room at the top, so to speak, so Tom Hanks (like only a handful of peers) gets compensated disproportionately for that incremental difference.

My colleagues and I have studied the feedback we get from corporations that are facing the most competitive environment in history. The senior management of these companies consistently tells us that, when all other things are equal, Level III competency in presentation skills will give them results that run off the chart.

In the corporate presentation world, most people and businesses generally focus on becoming "good enough" or having "adequate" presentation skills. *At this primary level, presenters don't fully appreciate the critical impact that presentation effectiveness can have on their success or that of their business.* They are "comfortable with"—or, at least, not completely intimidated by—getting up in front of an audience and giving a presentation, and they find that satisfactory. But other businesses realize that that isn't good enough. They send their key people on for further training, where they acquire more advanced presentation skills and a measure of platform presence. That secondary level is better than the first, but it does not take into account the exponential payoff from *mastery* of these skills, which produces *a disciplined user of advanced processes and techniques that are effective virtually 100 percent of the time.*

Mastery, you may now realize, is synonymous with unconscious competence. Like the unconsciously competent shoe tier, the Master Presenter accomplishes her task with fluidity and seamless confidence virtually every single time. While the presentation might feel effortless, however, a great deal of effort has gone into the achievement. This feeling is analogous, I think, to what those who train athletes call **muscle memory.** Coaches will tell you, exaggerating the point just a little, that no one ever got better by playing—you get better by practicing. Practice allows us to focus on one element of our skill set—something we cannot do well in the midst of a competitive situation, where all elements must be brought to bear. But practice has a much higher purpose. It teaches us what it *feels* like to make a winning move—hit a passing shot in tennis, say, or put a golf pitch close to the hole. The more times we perform this maneuver in practice, the more deeply ingrained it becomes in our muscle memory. So when the moment comes to use it in a match, we don't have to think about it. Like shoe tying for adults, all the hard work lies behind us and the immediate execution becomes effortless.

Why is it important to achieve this feeling of effortlessness and mastery in our presentations? Because, like the Hollywood food chain, as we succeed in life there are fewer and fewer slots to fill and proportionately more equally matched candidates to fill them. The difference between the guy who gets chosen to be CEO and the one who never makes it past executive vice president is often infinitesimal. Some of that difference might well be intangible, but let's remember that business ultimately is about people, and I can almost guarantee you that the person with better people skills—with better presentation skills—always has an edge in an otherwise even matchup.

Where do *you* need that edge? With your bosses and colleagues? With your customers or subordinates? Perhaps in your personal life as much as at the office? In social situations or around town conducting chores? Maybe with your family? Before we go further you must honestly evaluate your situational goals with regard to the presentation opportunities in your life. Look at the simple chart below:

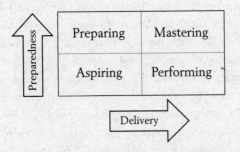

**"Mastering" requires both preparedness
and delivery effectiveness.**

Now that you realize your life is a series of presentations you may have begun to hope for greater impact during the opportunities that arise in the course of the day. But if all it took to succeed was aspiring then you wouldn't need the rest of this book. It's easy to aspire; you can sit in a comfortable chair at home, pop open a bottle of wine, and just picture yourself knocking down that difficult presentation. While it certainly won't hurt you to do this—and it *is* a necessary first step—if what you're aspiring to is mastery then you still have a considerable way to go. As the chart shows, Presentation Mastery requires BOTH the utmost preparedness and the utmost delivery effectiveness.

Now let's evaluate whether we demonstrate mastery during all our presentation opportunities. Though I have spent a good deal of my adult life quantifying and analyzing the role presentations play in our lives, I have to admit that my colleagues and I have had trouble coming up with a definitive way to categorize all the presentation opportunities the average person faces in a week or a year. Presentation opportunities are just so ubiquitous and varied that it becomes hard to be exhaustive in our definitions. But for our purposes right here, let's assume there are about ten different presentation situations that I personally confront on a regular basis. This list is derived from those areas that my corporate clients consistently tell me require mastery in order to achieve exponential improvement throughout their organizations. I've modified it here to illustrate some of my personal presentation opportunities and have included abbreviated definitions, along with examples of how these opportunities arise in my own life (see table on pages 80–81).

Some of these categories are more about the *ways* we present and others are more about the *message*. That doesn't matter for our purpose, though. Right now we simply want to sample the kinds of opportunities we face in order to evaluate our performance in these venues to date. Make a photocopy of the form on pages 82–83 (or obtain an electronic file at www.tonyjeary.com/presentationtypes), then jot down some of the specific opportunities you have in your daily life to deliver all different types of presentations. I've left some blanks for you to create your own presentation opportunity definitions. My list tends to skew toward business because I spend so much of my time pursuing my profession. Your list may not have many business or professional opportunities (if you don't work outside the home). It may skew more in other directions, which is fine. For example, you may not have any media appearances at all, but you might have other opportunities that don't often appear in my life. Of course, your personal objectives and the medium of your presentations (whether live or taped, in intimate settings or public halls) might also differ from mine. This is a personal analysis. Be open-minded and liberal in how you fill out your list (see table on pages 82–83).

Now comes the moment of truth. Ask yourself whether the presentations you make on a regular basis completely have the impact that you desire. Are you comfortable in your own skin when you're making these presentations? Do you plan the content of these presentations ahead of time—even the impromptu ones? Are you capable of devoting 100 percent of your attention to the *content* of your presentations, rather than becoming distracted by the *process*? Do you achieve rapport with your audience, whether it consists of one person or a dozen? Do you get the desired outcome almost 100 percent of the time?

While you're thinking about these issues, let me tell you the story of a guy who has thrived after honestly evaluating his level of Presentation Mastery and deciding to increase his competency.

I met Michael Pleumer when he was about twenty-four years old. He was working for a brokerage firm in Dallas that I had a contract with for coaching, consulting, and training. One of my assignments was to coach the phone representatives in presentation skills, and Michael was one employee among many. Michael and I really hit it off, and he seemed to be genuinely and deeply affected by the training that he was receiving alongside his colleagues. I should note that the nature of training—like any form of teaching, whether received in person or from a book such as the one you're currently reading—is that its effectiveness depends as much on the receptivity of the student as it does on the ability of the trainer. Since I move among many companies, sometimes I don't get the chance to see in person how well a student has embraced the training. So getting to know Michael Pleumer was a joy and a privilege.

He not only absorbed the details of the training with utmost seriousness, he reflected on the role of presentations in every aspect of his life, professional and personal. Then he worked assiduously to put what he had learned into practice with existing customers, while cold-calling, with his friends, and with his colleagues. Lo and behold! Within a short time, Michael started skyrocketing at his company and in his personal life. Soon he had been promoted to become a mutual funds wholesaler, and within five years his income had increased by some 500 percent. By becoming a manager, he then went from presenting to customers as a rep

Business Presentation Type	Personal Presentation Type	How They Apply to My Life
Sales Presentations: Business development pitches in person or over the phone, as well as attempts to sell a product.	**Influence or Persuasion:** Any attempt to win someone over to your point of view.	Like any businessperson, I must continually sell my products and services. In my case, my customers are individuals and decision makers at companies large and small. Of course, I also have to sell my wife and kids on my home-life ideas.
Training Sessions: Communicating information for audience self-improvement.	**Teaching Sessions:** Opportunities to impart skills and information to others, from Little League to Continuing Education.	It is a big part of my livelihood to do this at seminars, in informal groups, and one-on-one with executives, so I do it often at work. But everybody trains or teaches. I find myself teaching all the time, at my church group, for example, and with my kids.
Speeches: Talks to groups with the purpose of entertaining or inspiring.	Same.	Often I am asked to speak in formal large-group settings, such as at a school or church function.
Meetings: Organizational attempts to move an effort from Point A to Point B. This could be a phone meeting, an in-person meeting, a video broadcast meeting, etc.	Same, but don't forget family meetings, volunteer meetings, etc.	I have very few scheduled staff meetings a week, but often I am called upon to meet with individuals or small groups to address issues involving the conduct of our business. We also have regular family meetings.
Media: Appearances in front of reporters, cameras, on the phone, radio interviews, etc., to communicate a message.	Same.	When conducting these kinds of presentations, I am usually working to get a message across about my business in general or some specific aspect of it.

Business Presentation Type	Personal Presentation Type	How They Apply to My Life
E-Presentations: Communicating or influencing via fax, e-mail, PowerPoint, etc.	Same.	These include opportunities to inspire and communicate with my colleagues, but also with family, friends, and neighbors via email.
Branding Messages: Efforts to communicate a consistent message about what we stand for as an organization or as a person.	Same. Remember that how you present yourself will have an impact on your success. Also, volunteer efforts can benefit greatly from branding.	These involve business cards, brochures, and handouts, but also include the way I dress, the car I drive, and my web site. Disseminating information about a fund-raiser is another example of a branding message.
Facilitated Events: Helping people communicate with, inspire, and work effectively with one another.	Same.	Many times I get paid to do this, but these opportunities also arise within my immediate and extended family, at church groups, and in the office. Planning family vacations is one example.
Seminars: In-person training event of 10 to 100 people.	**Group Instruction:** Teaching others how to pursue a craft or hobby, religious studies, sports, etc.	I do this professionally, but I am occasionally called upon to do it on a volunteer basis.
One-on-One: Any individualized presentation opportunity, whether in person or over the phone.	Same.	Besides business and family dealings, I'm always mindful that interactions with neighborhood merchants or hotel reservation clerks, for example, are presentation opportunities.

Business Presentation Type	Personal Presentation Type	How They Apply to My Life
Sales Presentations: Business development pitches in person or over the phone, as well as attempts to sell a product.	**Influence or Persuasion:** Any attempt to win someone over to your point of view.	
Training Sessions: Communicating information for audience self-improvement.	**Teaching Sessions:** Opportunities to impart skills and information to others, from Little League to Continuing Education.	
Speeches: Talks to groups with the purpose of entertaining or inspiring.	Same.	
Meetings: Organizational attempts to move an effort from Point A to Point B. This could be a phone meeting, an in-person meeting, a video broadcast meeting, etc.	Same, but don't forget family meetings, volunteer meetings, etc.	
Media: Appearances in front of reporters, cameras, on the phone, radio interviews, etc., to communicate a message.	Same.	
E-Presentations: Communicating or influencing via fax, e-mail, PowerPoint, etc.	Same.	
Branding Messages: Efforts to communicate a consistent message about what we stand for as an organization or as a person.	Same. Remember that how you present yourself will have an impact on your success. Also, volunteer efforts can benefit greatly from branding.	

Business Presentation Type	Personal Presentation Type	How They Apply to My Life
Facilitated Events: Helping people communicate with, inspire, and work effectively with one another.	Same.	
Seminars: In-person training event of 10 to 100 people.	**Group Instruction:** Teaching others how to pursue a craft or hobby, religious studies, sports, etc.	
One-on-One: Any individualized presentation opportunity, whether in person or over the phone.	Same.	

to recruiting and coaching other reps himself. Sure he worked hard, but he also lived and breathed the lessons he learned from ongoing training and self-education in the art of presentation. As a result, being a Master Presenter has impacted everything Michael touches. He even met a beautiful woman at work, and she agreed to marry him. In part due to the seriousness with which he committed himself to Presentation Mastery, in ten years Michael built a very nice life for himself.

Michael Pleumer is not a composite or a fictional character. He is a very real human being who has seen enormous results in many areas of his life by applying our practices toward achieving strategic effectiveness and Presentation Mastery. And he appreciates what, in some ways, is the most significant point of all: Presentation Mastery is not a destination, but a journey. Applying the discipline required to retain that mastery is a challenge that Michael and the rest of us face every day.

So, ask yourself one more time: Are your presentations so masterful in every instance that Level III of the Presentation Impact Curve has kicked in for you? In other words, are you seeing exponential results from your presentation strategy? If so, I hope you took my advice and made that photocopy of the previous chart, because if you didn't write in your book you can still return it to the store. As a Presentation Master, maybe you can teach me a thing or two. But if you're not *completely* satisfied with how you're performing during your presentation opportunities—the small ones as well as the big ones—then please read on.

Nobody's Perfect

When an adulteress was brought to Jesus and her accusers reminded Him that the biblical punishment was stoning, He said: "He that is without sin among you, let him first cast a stone at her."

You don't have to be a Christian believer to appreciate the point Jesus was making. It is easy to forget, sometimes, that no human is without flaws. But when it comes to self-improvement, only those who truly acknowledge their shortcomings have an opportunity to fix them. Having accepted the challenge of achieving Presentation Mastery, we must take one more careful look in the mirror before proceeding to build our skills.

My coauthor Kim coaches authors and other personalities on how to speak in public and on television. Kim makes the case to her clients that our greatest insecurities become magnified when we have to make a presentation. This is particularly true on television, which can "amplify our essence," so to speak, making the audience acutely aware of the most dominant (or submissive) parts of our personality. No matter the presentation scenario, however, these insecurities stand in the way of our best work—they *inhibit* us.

Henry Kissinger said, "The strong grow weak through inhibition." Inhibitors are a form of self-sabotage. They take control away from us and obscure what we really want to say. While an Inhibitor is in force, we become unable to present our information effectively. Worse, we end up presenting that most unattractive part of our personality: that insecurity we would have preferred to have kept locked in a closet. As a result, we talk too fast or we act too smug or we don't make eye contact with our audience or we seem distracted or we exhibit any number of behaviors that defeat all the other good efforts we have made to ace the presentation.

We cannot achieve mastery so long as our Inhibitors are ruling the day. The more you see your real self for the person you are, the better grasp of the master's art you will have. So in many ways the first step toward becoming a winning presenter is to confront these Inhibitors and put them into perspective. More specifically, we first need to be able to identify the Inhibitor, then to understand how it affects us, then to accept it as part of who we are, and finally to learn how to do our best work in its presence. Dealing with an Inhibitor is much like dealing with a regional accent. It's fine to have that region in your background—and we never want to pretend to be someone we're not—but it's also a good idea when speaking in public venues to be able to soften the accent so that people focus on your message, not on the way you speak. Until we acknowledge that our own source of insecurity is not unique to us and then take steps to overcome that weakness, we cannot perform at our best—either for an audience of one or one thousand.

Personality has as much to do with a successful presentation as the skills we employ or the information we give while we are presenting. Recall again Dr. Cialdini's observation on the power of Liking. If you come across to your audience as odd or uncomfortable, they will simply be less receptive to your message, no matter how well you execute other aspects of your presentation. *A good presentation leverages our most likable personality traits with our polished skills to invigorate the content of our message.* But even the most fascinating information can be lost when it becomes clouded by unwanted personality quirks.

The most important thing, then, is to recognize and identify what our Inhibitors are, to understand them, and to accept them as part of ourselves. If we can't necessarily learn how to get rid of them permanently, we can at least learn how to make them less visible while we're presenting, so that our best self can truly come out and our audience will not be distracted by the Inhibitor. (Interestingly, in Kim's experience, we may also find that as we make more presentations without these Inhibitors they will eventually start to regress in our own personality.)

Unless you're a born presenter—and, remember, like me most of us are not—your presentation personality is probably dominated by one of nine Inhibitors. Most of these Inhibitors have their roots in our own self-doubt, our inability to accept that we are qualified to be making the presentation we're making. Depending upon our personality type, these insecurities manifest themselves in various ways. One way to overcome your Inhibitors is to be completely prepared for your presentation, since that in itself builds confidence. The less prepared you are, the more that negative aspect of your personality will emerge.

Primarily, however, the best way to deal with Inhibitors is to acknowledge that they are a form of energy—negative energy. We must take the nervousness and insecurity that feed Inhibitors and turn them into something good—passion or excitement, for example. We must transform that negative force into a positive one.

When Sandy called Kim she was desperate for an appointment. A promising chef at a trendy Los Angeles restaurant, Sandy was a budding entrepreneur with wonderful ideas for cookbooks and dreams of starting her own catering business. She had dozens of contacts from working at the restaurant, had well-placed friends, and Los Angeles offered generous opportunities for caterers.

Where was the problem? As Sandy so simply put it when she called Kim's office, "When I talk, everyone thinks I sound like an idiot!" She couldn't have been more straightforward, and as she continued to try to describe her various ideas for cookbooks and businesses, Kim could see why Sandy's friends and potential business-backers did not take her seriously. She interrupted herself. She went on and on about irrelevant things. And though she was engaging, very nice and funny, Kim had a hard time discovering what Sandy wanted from the phone call. Kim decided to offer her a two-hour session to help focus her and get her to be clearer and more precise about what she wanted to present, both as a cookbook author and a possible business owner.

Kim and her colleagues were surprised when Sandy came to the door. Her "look" did not match the way she spoke on the phone. Sandy's speaking style on the phone had been all over the place but her appearance conveyed a very different personality. Sandy was completely put together: petite and fit, her long, straight, dark hair neatly in place, with a matching outfit from top to bottom. She was the perfect picture of someone you would want to discuss business with. Yet when she started to talk, everything changed. She sat down on the couch, and Kim pretended to be a prospective investor. As soon as Sandy began speaking, she became like a teenager on a first date. She looked away, blushed, played with her hair, flipped her head back and forth, and flailed her arms all around. The more energetic and excited she got, the more ideas she spewed forth and the more her hands seemed to move. Kim could immediately see why no one would take her seriously and why she had come for help.

When we have distracting physical gestures, they are there for a reason. They have relaxed us and shielded us from discomfort in the past, so we hold on to them. But what worked when we were younger may not necessarily continue to work as we age and want to be taken more seriously. With all Sandy's gesturing, Kim couldn't concentrate on or make sense of what Sandy was saying. Her words and gestures were fighting each other for attention.

First, Kim pointed out to Sandy how wonderfully put together she was, and that her careful appearance contradicted her careless presentation. She told her that, physically, she knew how to be concise and trim and to the point—in fact, she looked like someone who would stick to the facts, but do it with style. Now she had to make her presentation style consistent with that image. Kim and her colleagues helped Sandy control her hand gestures—flicking her hair, pushing up her glasses, etc.—by having her take her hands more to the center of her body. They started by having her clasp her hands and try to talk while holding them together. She seemed to become more comfortable and composed and stopped playing with her hair. Then they allowed her to unclasp her hands, but she still had to keep them centered in the middle of her body. This brought all of that energy to the center, and she was capable of talking—

still in an animated fashion—while keeping her hands and all of that live-liness centered and balanced. She practiced this for a few minutes until she grew accustomed to the feeling.

Also out of nervousness, Sandy would turn and look around the room when answering a question. She would just find an object and start talk-ing about it: "That is a really interesting clock! Where did you get that clock? Did you get it out of the country? Because I've never seen any-thing like that, it looks very European . . ."

This was after she had been asked to describe one of the projects she was working on. Kim suspected this Inhibitor was not going to disappear overnight, and she couldn't just tell Sandy not to do it. Sandy didn't even realize that she was avoiding the questions this way until Kim pointed it out to her. So the first step was just making her conscious of the distract-ing things she did while she was talking. Next, she had to accept that these mannerisms would never go away completely, so Kim tried to teach her how to deal with them when they came up.

Remember that she came to Kim because people thought she sounded "like an idiot" when they were talking to her, and part of this was because she was constantly distracted by her own speech. Kim told her that when she felt herself slipping away from a question and focusing on other things, she had to quickly snap herself back. It would be all right for her—and almost charming the way she did it—to interrupt herself, look around, and comment. She would need, however, to know she was doing that and bring herself right back to the question: "Where did you get that clock? It's really interesting; it almost looks European . . . I'm sorry. I'm not focusing. You've just got so many interesting things in this room . . ."

The key was for Sandy to realize what she was doing (playing with her hair, adjusting her clothes, flailing her hands, looking around the room) and nip it in the bud. But she had to allow enough of this behavior so as not to become too self-conscious. You don't want to *change* your person-ality. You just want to be aware of the gestures and habits you have that might take away from your message.

It turned out that Sandy's father had told her for years to stop doing this and stop doing that when she was talking. It became such a negative message that she blocked him out. Kim pointed out that what Sandy did was energetic, fun, and charming, but that she did it to such an extent that it was hard to pay attention to what she was saying. When she heard it that way, she was instantly much more interested in trying to change it.

For all of us, self-awareness is the first step, followed by a redirection of our energy. Within each of the Inhibitors lies its own "solution." Do any of the following describe you?

- **Pleasing.** People who have the strong need to please will talk too fast and will be excessively solicitous of their audience because they are so eager to make sure the audience likes them and what they are saying. **Solution:** Convert this instinct into a pledge to make the audience enjoy your presentation. Incorporate that pleasing instinct that you have and turn it into a positive. This will satisfy the pleasing aspect of your personality, but it will no longer manifest itself as an insecurity.

- **Impostor Syndrome.** This is a well-documented psychological state that often haunts even the most well-qualified experts: the deep-down belief that they are somehow not worthy of the task at hand. They simply don't trust that they know what they know. **Solution:** Write out all your qualifications for making the presentation and then review this résumé objectively as if it were someone else's. In a business setting, this résumé may look like a job résumé or a work biography, though it doesn't have to. If the presentation involves something more personal, create a curriculum vitae (literally a "course" of your life's accomplishments) that is weighted for relevancy to the presentation at hand. Even if you're talking to your kids this can be a great help.

- **Perfectionism.** The person who never believes her presentation is good enough will often have the sweatiest palms and the fastest-beating heart. She also tends to choose the wrong information to impart because she can never make up her mind about exactly what information is good enough. **Solution:** Again, take a negative and turn it into a positive. Use all the time you need to prepare (which will probably be more time than the non-perfectionist feels she needs) and then don't look back. Always build into your presentation ways to get confirmation of your thoroughness from the audience: "Did I leave anything out?" "Does anyone have any questions?"

- **Egomania.** Many high-level executives or others of great achievement never hear criticism from their colleagues. After a while, they may begin to believe that they are always the most interesting person in the room. These people never know when to close their presentation or pause for questions. They are a constant "wall of talk." **Solution:** The worst thing about the egomaniac is his lack of a sense of humor. Force yourself to develop a sense of humor about the fact that you think you know it all. Leave room for others to get a word in. Ask someone you know in the audience if they think you're going on too long. Ask the audience, too.

- **Peter Pan Syndrome.** This personality type finds it so difficult to believe he can be articulate and professional that he lapses into immaturity, never rising to the challenge and never taking himself seriously. The unfortunate consequence, of course, is that no one else will be able to take him seriously either. Keep in mind that Peter Pan Syndrome is often reflected as much in the way a person dresses as in the way he presents. Sandy was an exception to this rule. **Solution:** This is a tough one to tackle because people acquire this Inhibitor by having received a lot of positive feedback in the past for acting young. It has always worked for them, so they keep doing it. The key to its resolution, then, is not to seek to remove all aspects of Peter Pan Syndrome but to *add* to your personality—to acknowledge that you are older and wiser today than you were yesterday and to add in some of those more mature aspects of your personality that have been lurking in the background.

- **Defensiveness.** This person, out of fear of nervousness, acts almost annoyed to be in front of the room. He gets easily distracted, looks around the room too much, and swallows the ends of his sentences. He is so afraid of failing that he pushes his audience away. **Solution:** Defensiveness is largely a way people express their anger about the fear and uncertainty that presentations provoke. This sense is so visceral that you can literally feel it coming on, which gives you plenty of opportunity to redirect your energy in a positive way. Tell the audience a joke or even make fun of yourself. This will have the effect of dropping your defenses.

- **Aloofness.** A cousin to defensiveness, the aloof personality is such that the insecurity manifests itself by making a presenter act like he or she doesn't care. It's a way to deal with our anxiety by keeping ourselves separate. This person will make no effort to connect with his audience. **Solution:** Force yourself to lock eyes with someone in the audience. This creates some personal attachment, which should begin to pull you out of your own world. Even better, once you've made that eye contact, pretend you're talking to someone you know and love who wants to hear what you're saying.

- **Good Student Syndrome.** In interview situations, these folks are so anxious to answer the question "right" that they don't answer it well. **Solution:** The Good Student is a combination of the perfectionist and the pleaser. Tell your audience what you're going to give them, and then do it.

- **Tenseness.** In explaining the success of his 2000 World Champion Yankees, manager Joe Torre once said, "My players are *intense* without being *tense*." Many people are afraid to be spontaneous, as if they view their true personality as a liability and do not wish for it to come out. Nobody can perform at his best under such conditions. These people tend to be stiff and humorless when the chips are down. **Solution:** Tenseness is like defensiveness on steroids. As it is the most physical of Inhibitors, the best correction is also a physical one. Exercise before your presentation, squeezing out that excess energy. If you don't have the opportunity to do that (or even if you do), breath work can also be a great aid. Try to concentrate on relaxing physically by breathing through your diaphragm, not your upper chest. You can check this by resting a hand below your rib cage. Diaphragmatic breathing prevents the tenseness from coming out of your throat.

If you're still not sure which of these Inhibitors describes you, the following little test will help you get an idea. Simply take a look at the way you say "thank you" and the way you feel when you say it. There are all different kinds of thank yous that we proffer throughout the day. Think about a thank you that means something. A colleague offers kudos for a job well done. Your spouse says something nice about the way you look. Your boss praises your recent work. An old friend from college tells you she had a great time with you on a recent visit. Someone you don't know comes up and compliments what you're wearing.

Be honest with yourself about the ways you respond in these situations. (Perhaps ask someone close to you what they have observed in this regard—but don't get defensive if you don't like what you hear!) The way people say thank you can be a window into their personality. Here's what your thank you may be telling you:

- If you say *Thank you thank you thank you* over and over again really fast, chances are you are *Pleasing*. Your natural tendency when presenting will come from that pleasing place. We'll never forget Sally Field getting the Academy Award, when she thanked everyone a million times and blurted out, "You like me! You really like me!"

- Do you ever feel uncomfortable or awkward when thanking people? Do you feel shy? Do you keep your head down and not want to look at the person you're thanking? Chances are your Inhibitor is the *Impostor Syndrome*. You never feel quite like you mean what you're saying, and your natural tendency is not even to believe yourself when you're thanking someone sincerely.

- After you thank someone, do you pause, then thank them again—maybe do it a different way? Do you get a gnawing feeling in your chest, like you hadn't expressed yourself as clearly as you wanted to? If so, your Inhibitor is *Perfectionism*. Your thank you will never be good enough in your own mind, and neither will your presentation.

- When you say thank you to someone for a compliment about work, for example, do you almost harbor a grudge when you say it? Do you feel near-annoyance? Do you think, "*They* should be thanking *me*"? There's a good chance your Inhibitor is *Egomania*. Even though you might be a totally nice person, there is a part of you that resents having to thank somebody. An attitude like that will come out in your presentation style. You are the person who never stops talking because you think people are so interested in everything you say.

- When you say thank you, do you feel almost silly and embarrassed to be saying it? Do you think to yourself, "Nobody cares if I say it," or "It doesn't matter," or "What's the point?" You are probably suffering from *Peter Pan Syndrome*. You find it impossible to believe that something you say might have an effect, so a simple thank you makes you feel like you're being shallow or insincere.

- When you say thank you, do you say it with a chip on your shoulder? Do you behave not exactly like the egomaniac who thinks the other person should be thanking him, but as if you have plenty else to be concerned with, or as if you don't even really mean what you're saying? If so, your Inhibitor is *Defensiveness*.

- When you say thank you, do you feel like you really just don't care? Could you just as easily be saying "Who are you?" instead of "Thank you"? Perhaps you don't feel like you've connected at all? You'd be suffering from the Inhibitor *Aloofness*. If you can't make a connection while saying thank you, chances are you can't make one with your audience either.

- When you say thank you, do you feel like you've never really said it correctly? Unlike the Pleaser who keeps thinking of different ways to say it at that time, yours will come out okay, but later you feel as if you failed in some way. Your Inhibitor is the *Good Student Syndrome*, because although you answered the question right, you didn't answer it well, and you're constantly second-guessing yourself.

- When someone compliments you, do you feel your body actually get tense all over, just to get the words "thank you" out? Can you feel it in your shoulders? Your stomach? This is not nerves, but a real lock in your muscles before saying thank you. Your Inhibitor is *Tension*, and you will demonstrate it during a presentation.

The term "thank you" is itself a very tiny presentation. We are connecting with someone who is either giving us something or complimenting us. What they're doing naturally begs a response, so we go into a form of mini-presentation behavior. When we are able to look someone in the eyes directly and say, "Thank you! I appreciate that," shaking his hand and holding that eye contact for a few seconds, we have positively connected with our tone and body language. But when the thank you comes out in any of these other ways, it is a good indication your Inhibitors are too strong.

Remember that, to some extent, all of us have similar issues with Inhibitors. Tackle yours by practicing your thank yous with the Solutions in mind until you feel the barriers breaking down. *Pledging to address your insecurities head-on will empower you to fully employ all the tools and practices of the successful presenter.*

Your Own Little World

In his book *Mindshift* Price Pritchett notes that, "In an over-capacity world, speed is a basic survival skill." The way we achieve speed in life is through preparation and training. And it follows that one of the most important questions we can ask ourselves is, "What exactly am I training for?"

Here we return to the importance of discovering a definition of success for ourselves. For some, success is simply finding a happier, more peaceful course in life. For others, it's building an organization or getting to the top of a major corporation. For still others, it's the independence of running a profitable small business. In order to know how to apply the material in the chapters to come, you'll need to decide how you will define what I call your **Presentation Universe**. The Presentation Universe is your personal context for achieving success with all the information that follows in this book. It provides the framework upon which all your other presentation-related organizational efforts will hang.

The idea that life is a series of presentations can seem a little overwhelming to the person just setting out to craft a personal presentation strategy. While you may have as many opportunities during the course of a day to influence local shopkeepers as you do to influence colleagues or family members, you must acknowledge that these opportunities are of relative value. If you choose to define a narrower Presentation Universe for yourself, the task at hand will be more manageable. So *define your Presentation Universe conservatively at first by focusing on those presentation opportunities that will create the greatest impact on your life.* (Of course, you can always expand your parameters later.) In what circumstances specifically do you want to be a Master Presenter? When do you need to achieve your intended objectives nearly all the time?

Review the worksheet that you filled out on pages 82–83. In what kind of context do most of your most important presentation opportunities fall? Are they mostly business or personal? Do they typically involve audiences of one hundred or one? What do you hope to accomplish with the majority of your presentations? Are you usually in selling mode or do you spend more of your time facilitating communication among other parties? Do you need to inspire the troops—whether they be family members, employees, or enlisted men and women—or are you more often called upon to communicate information? Do you wish to become the leader of your company or the leader of your community? Are most of your presentation opportunities in person, over the phone, or by some other means?

In the next section of the book you will learn specific techniques for turning yourself into a Master Presenter. By absorbing and employing these Essentials and practices in the context of your own Presentation Universe, you will reap maximum benefits where it counts most—during your most life-affecting presentations.

✓
Very Important Points

- "Leadership is the ability to teach people and organizations to surpass themselves."

- Most of the time, stuff doesn't just happen to us—we make it happen by what we do and by the way we are.

- Our goal as presenters ought to be unconscious competence—or to be operating in automatic mode.

- Marginally competent presenters don't fully appreciate the critical impact that presentation effectiveness can have on their success or that of their business.

- Presentation Mastery results in a disciplined user of advanced processes and techniques that are effective virtually 100 percent of the time.

- A good presentation leverages our most likable personality traits with our polished skills to invigorate the content of our message.

- Pledging to address your insecurities head-on will empower you to fully employ all the tools and practices of the successful presenter.

- Define your Presentation Universe conservatively at first by focusing on those presentation opportunities that will create the greatest impact on your life.

PART II

HOW IT WORKS

Everyday Essentials of Successful Interaction

CHAPTER 5

Essential #1: Know Thy Audience

To Exceed Expectations, You Must Understand Personality Types, Character Identities, and How to Uncover Them

Many years ago a local television news anchorman visited a public high school in suburban New York. He was there to speak to an auditorium full of seniors nearing graduation. As you'll soon learn, it is unlikely that anyone who attended that day recalls the substance of his talk.

Then only in his forties, the anchorman in some ways had already led a more interesting life than most people twice his age. He had begun his career as a reporter in the Midwest and had risen through the ranks of his network to become the top gun at a major-market affiliate very early in life—and he had spent much of that time reporting from the most diverse city in America. It seemed only natural for the principal of the school to invite this man to share his wisdom with the soon-to-be graduates.

The students eagerly awaited the anchorman's visit. Unlike most of the assemblies they had been asked to attend over the course of twelve grades and kindergarten, this one had the potential to rivet their attention. The media age wasn't yet in full blossom: The world of 500 television channels had just begun, neither the Internet nor cell phones existed in public awareness, and everyone didn't get to be famous for fifteen minutes. So a guy who many students saw on the television every night, now visiting in the flesh, had a chance to make a real impression on these kids.

As you might expect, they sat at first in rapt attention, acclimating themselves to the familiar voice now amplified over the auditorium's

PA system. Soon the anchorman had launched into a story that he had culled from his vast experience as a reporter. It was a sort of shaggy dog story, one of those that goes on and on—and no one has any sense what the point will be until the end. Some of the students started checking their watches when the story had lasted ten minutes and showed no sign of letup.

It was a beautiful spring day outside, the kind of day that tempts even the best students to cut class and sneak out to the lawn chair. After a while the 400 or so students, who had begun the assembly in courteous silence, began to stir. Fifteen minutes passed and the story was still going—fifteen minutes is like a lifetime to a bored eighteen year old. Yet the anchorman droned on, still in the midst of the same tale after nearly twenty minutes had elapsed.

A steady murmur eventually began to work its way through the audience. They had started to fidget, then to whisper to their friends. Soon, many of the students took to speaking to one another at half-volume. Magnified by dozens of voices, the talking became a bit raucous. So when the speaker stopped and peered into the crowd, many of the students didn't even notice. The anchorman had to call for quiet, but the calls went largely ignored. This lack of response rattled him visibly. Those in the nearer rows could see that his face had gone red. He pleaded for quiet again and again, in increasingly strident tones, then tried to go on with his prepared remarks. But by this time he had completely lost the majority of his audience, which now demonstrated about as much open rebellion as one might ever expect from seniors of that era at an upper-middle-class high school. They were blatantly talking among themselves in normal voices, which, joined together, became something of a roar, drowning out even the amplified stentorian voice of this professional speaker. A half an hour earlier than planned, the anchorman brought his speech to an abrupt and uneasy conclusion.

My coauthor Kim might diagnose the anchorman, who surely had come to expect a certain degree of deference when he spoke, as suffering from a severe case of egomania. This Inhibitor blinded him to the fact that his pretty face and the sound of his own voice alone would not carry the attention of twenty-score high school seniors crammed into an auditorium on a sunny day in spring. If egomania was the root cause of his failure to achieve rapport, however, the proximate cause was something much easier to address: failure to know one's audience.

It may be hard to believe that an intelligent person who has already achieved great success and who, in a certain sense, speaks professionally would not have paused to reflect on the fact that a teenager's attention span is not the same as an adult's. Yet this is a true story, and the real-life anchorman did make this fatal mistake. The fact is, anyone might have been the victim of this story. Failure to know one's audience is among the most common and avoidable mistakes that presenters make—and among the most inexcusable, when you think about it.

I wonder what thoughts went through the anchorman's mind when he went to work later that day. Did he examine his own presentation and ask himself where he went off the tracks? Or did he attribute his bad experience to a rude bunch of kids who showed him disrespect? If the latter, I wonder how he reconciled their misbehavior in the last fifteen minutes with their exemplary behavior during the first fifteen. Because the reality is that the anchorman had started out with a receptive audience. His own lack of preparation lost them.

Imagine for a moment that we have to take a common-sense quiz that requires only yes/no answers. Does a three-year-old child have the same attention span as a sixty-year-old adult? Does mathematics interest a group of English professors as much as it interests a group of engineers? Is an individual who was born blind more receptive to visual descriptions than to aural ones? Will an appeal to personal loyalty work better on a stranger than on a friend? Is a fragile person likely to be won over by shouting? No, no, no, no, no. Congratulations. I bet you got 100 percent!

Amazingly, we instinctively know the answers to these questions, but when the time comes to make a presentation we rarely pause to reflect on the nature of our audience—even when it's the person we're married to or in a relationship with. Kim has a friend who knows that her husband likes to hear "the bottom line" of a story before listening to all the details. Yet her friend begins with every minor detail and can be halfway through an explanation of how something happened before mentioning why she's telling the story. Her husband gets irritated, and she complains that he's difficult to talk to. But the truth is that her husband would be a better listener if she would accept what kind of audience he is and give him the punch line first, followed by the meat of the story.

We may think for hours about what we want to say, but we often devote mere seconds to considering who we plan to say it to. This oversight can have professional and personal consequences. Just ask Al Gore. He talked to adult Americans as if they were children, and he lost the most important election of his life largely as a result.

Every person to whom we make a presentation is unique. The Master Presenter understands this statement not as an abstraction, but as a challenge to be met. Recall two of the most important points from our study of NLP: Everyone receives and processes information differently. And those who appreciate this and are flexible enough to respond to it will control the situation, rather than lose control as the anchorman did. Master Presenters never make the same exact presentation twice. They *learn the composition of their audience before the presentation begins, then prepare accordingly.*

Who's Driving the Bus?

Most people who never thought much about the issue find that their most successful presentations come before people they know and love—family members and very close friends. This is no accident. Like the fictional barista from Chapter 1 when talking to her sister, we often have a lifetime of practice presenting to the people closest to us. Through years of trial and error we have learned how to push their buttons (and which buttons not ever to push). We just know these people so well that when we present to them we truly do not have to think about what kind of person our audience is.

The problems arise when we must present to those whose personalities we do not know as thoroughly, either from lack of exposure to them or because we have never taken control of our presentations to them. Frequently—as when we communicate to our superiors at work—we're so worried about what we're going to say that we never really stop to think about who we're saying it to. Sure, we know she's our boss, but what kind of personality does our boss fundamentally have?

Based upon a model that has been around for many years, a colleague of mine, Dr. Michael O'Connor, has sketched a simple way to help us determine the basis of people's personality types. It may be represented by a diagram* that looks like this:

---

*Go to http://www.tonyjeary.com/DISC for a free electronic copy of this diagram.

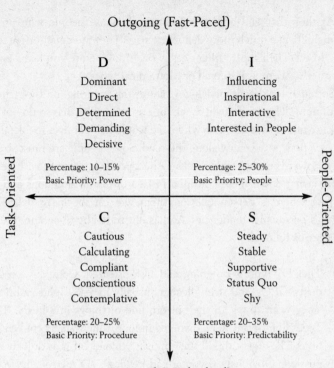

Outgoing (Fast-Paced)

D
Dominant
Direct
Determined
Demanding
Decisive

Percentage: 10–15%
Basic Priority: Power

I
Influencing
Inspirational
Interactive
Interested in People

Percentage: 25–30%
Basic Priority: People

Task-Oriented

People-Oriented

C
Cautious
Calculating
Compliant
Conscientious
Contemplative

Percentage: 20–25%
Basic Priority: Procedure

S
Steady
Stable
Supportive
Status Quo
Shy

Percentage: 20–35%
Basic Priority: Predictability

Reserved (Methodical)

We call this the **DISC Profiler,** an acronym for the initials of each personality type. The DISC illustrates the fact that two major forces act within each of us—forces that can roughly be plotted on a continuum. Think of yourself as a bus driver going down the road. How are you going to get from one place to another? Of course, by stepping on the gas pedal and turning the steering wheel. These two factors combined, with variations in intensity, will determine how and when you arrive at a given point, and two major personality factors will do the same for us in an analogous way.

Along one axis an internal motor drives us. Some people, as you know, are inclined to go through life at a very fast clip, always in a hurry and never stopping long to smell the proverbial roses. They like to make quick decisions and never look back. These folks always seem to have their foot on the gas pedal. They abhor the brake. We might call them Outgoing or say they live life in a Fast-Paced way.

At the other end of the continuum lie those people who proceed through life at a much more deliberate pace. They are detail-oriented and slow to act. Their motto might easily be, "Look before you leap," and we can refer to them as Reserved or Methodical types.

So much for the gas pedal; how about the "steering" on the right–left continuum? The other main aspect of our personality has to do not with the pace of our lives but with where we would like our lives to take us and the experiences we enjoy along the road. Some people are most strongly drawn toward accomplishing tasks. Others prefer interacting with people.

By laying down these continua in two different directions and then plotting where a person falls on them, we can begin to define that person's personality tendencies. And as illustrated by the graph, the four types are as follows:

- The "D" Type is outgoing and task-oriented. Company presidents, CEOs, and strong leaders usually have "D" personalities. They want to get to the bottom line of things in a hurry. "D" Types don't want to be involved in long, touchy-feely conversations. They want to kill the cow, skin it, and eat it as quickly as possible. Obviously, if you are addressing a "D" personality you don't want to waste a lot of time before getting to the core of your message.

- The "I" Type is outgoing and people-oriented. These are the folks who love to talk and talk, and they never meet a person they don't like. "I" personalities tend to become salespeople, trainers, or speakers—or they enter other careers that afford them the opportunity to spend most of their time with people. "I" personalities want to feel good about themselves, and they don't want to hear a lot of bad news or too much detail. If you are addressing an "I" Type, you need to get him or her involved with you. Since they love to participate, they will gladly do anything you ask them to do in a group presentation . . . so long as it's fun and exciting.

- The "S" Type is reserved yet still people-oriented. These folks are sympathetic to the needs of others and have a high degree of empathy. Counselors and people who love to teach have "S" personalities. An "S" personality will gladly make sacrifices to help another person in need. If you suspect you are addressing a group of "S" personalities, let them know how they can help you. They will be eager to do so.

- The "C" Type is reserved and task-oriented. These people want to know all the nitty-gritty details, and they are willing to spend as much time as it takes to get them. Accountants, auditors, and investigators have "C" personalities. If you are addressing a roomful of "C" Types, bring a lot of charts, graphs, and statistics. The "C" personality wants to know the tasks that lie ahead and each step necessary to accomplish those tasks.

As you might expect, many people show combinations of these personality types. As a presenter, you are most interested in which factor dominates your audience's personality. If you are presenting to a single person, ask yourself where that person's tendencies lie and tailor your presentation accordingly. If you have never met the person, consider the facts that you do know about him or her. In a work-related presentation or one that involves an errand around town, you will probably know what kind of job this person has, which may offer a clue. For an important presentation, it may be worth asking someone who knows your audience better about the salient elements of their personality.

If you are presenting to a group, consider the common elements of your audience members. For example, you can assume that a roomful of nurses is dominated by "S" Types, but a roomful of hospital directors is probably dominated by "D" Types. Another thing to consider is how the general subject of your presentation combines with the reason your audience is attending. For example, if you are hosting a party that was positioned as a networking opportunity, you might readily assume that a majority of those in attendance possess people-oriented personalities. *Once you grasp the composition of your audience with regard to personality type, you are in a better position to plan your presentation to suit their preferences.*

What Are They Carrying?

The moment someone walks into a room I begin to formulate a sense of who they are based upon the baggage they're carrying. Sometimes this is literally so. The "D" Type personality tends to travel light, while the "C" Type often carries one or more bags or briefcases so stuffed that you'd think they expected Monte Hall to walk up at any moment and offer them $100 for a scientific calculator and an Indian head penny.

Of course, even those who do not carry any bags are going through life with emotional and intellectual baggage. Their unique outlook on life and their consequent preferences for absorbing information will affect how well my message gets through. While I can't do anything to change the prejudices they carry—at least, not often in a single presentation—an awareness of those prejudices will enable me to make a more effective presentation and achieve my goals.

Think about all the different aspects of one's life that might have an impact on a person's receptivity to your message. What part of the country or the world are these people from? Was English their first language? Did they grow up rich or poor? What level of education have they achieved and with what kind of specialization? What is their religion and are they observant? How old are they? What sex are they? Do they have a family or are they single? Are they well traveled or have they stuck close to home? Are they adept at competitive sports or do they prefer non-competitive? Do they drive a car or rely on public transportation?

The list of questions you might ask about what influences a person's prejudices and preferences is endless. But we usually approach a presentation opportunity with some foreknowledge of that person. Anything we know will help us narrow down the field of possibilities and begin to achieve some understanding of where our audience is coming from. And it's important to remember that we are not looking to undertake a deep psychological analysis of our audience, just to learn some obvious likes and dislikes that will enable us to customize our delivery style and thus enhance our presentation effectiveness. For example, when I deliver training to new Ford engineers who are right out of college, I know they may have a prejudice against low-tech. So the use of audiotapes, flip charts, and white boards will not be congruent with their expectations. Instead they prefer CDs, DVDs, and animated PowerPoint visuals.

Another kind of baggage that people carry into a presentation has to do with their likes and dislikes in relation to presentation experiences they've had in the past. We'll talk about preconceived notions that your audience might have about a given presentation in the next section. For now, let's keep in mind that people do enter the room with biases that arise less from life experience than from prior presentation experience. For instance, children walk into a new classroom remembering the experiences they had the year before. Were they bored, picked on, stimulated, embarrassed? Was the room sticky and hot? Was the teacher often in a bad mood? Similarly, some of your colleagues at work may have sat through too many meetings where the person leading the meeting did not often request feedback from the group. Perhaps they've built up resentment on that point. If people like that are not engaged early on, they may turn themselves off during the meeting that you are leading. To take another example, a friend of yours may have bad associations from one-to-one presentations where she was asked to sit down in a chair to hear grave news. It may be better to deliver a serious presentation to this person while walking in the park. Like the psychological triggers that Dr. Cialdini observed, these biases could otherwise set off an automatic response in your audience that will interfere with her ability to receive your presentation favorably.

When he was a literary agent, my coauthor Joel represented a person who explicitly made his living by understanding and catering to the expectations of a specific audience type. Adam Christing was working as a stand-up comic and magician when he learned that many audiences were offended by the profanity they often heard from performers. Mr. Christing received many favorable comments about how entertaining people thought his act was. That flattered him, but what struck him most was how often audience members said they found his lack of profanity refreshing. His material was adult, he realized, but it was also clean—and this combination had great appeal for such venues as religious group and business conferences. So he founded a talent agency that he branded Clean Comedians, with the motto "It Doesn't Have to Be Filthy to Be Funny." And Mr. Christing knew his audience. Many organizations booked his performers based upon the name of his company alone.

Like Mr. Christing, all presenters should endeavor to determine the motivations, goals, and objectives of their audience. Sometimes the best approach is simply to ask them what they expect from your presentation before you prepare it. If that's not possible ahead of time, you might make an effort (in a business setting) to gain insights into their goals by studying the organization's philosophy. For a personal or professional presentation, you can ask questions of friends and colleagues about the motivations and objectives of your audience. Often you can glean these things by observing externally communicated values, such as the way a person dresses, what kind of car he drives and how he keeps it, the appearance of his or her home or office, and the words she chooses when speaking or writing. If you have an opportunity to observe behavior, noting how members of your audience react to different kinds of people can provide great insights. How do they treat people who serve them or work for them? How do they treat their peers or people they seem to admire? Under what circumstances do they seem most receptive to a convincing argument? How do they respond to different personal styles?

In one-on-one presentations it is especially important to appreciate the most immediate motivations of your audience. It's pretty obvious that if a person is standing with his briefcase in his hand and keeps checking his watch at six in the evening, his main goal is not to hear your presentation but to catch his train. But often the clues are much more subtle than that. I approach all phone conversations with my radar attuned to the tone of the other person's voice. Often I will begin the conversation with an innocuous question just to gauge their mood: "What's been happening in your world?" "How was vacation?" "Do you have ten minutes or two?" If the person seems relaxed, it may be a good time to launch into a presentation that will take some time and require a good deal of audience participation. If she is rushed and abrupt, I might confine myself to a "just the facts" presentation or postpone the discussion for another time. If she is on a cell phone, I might suggest we hook up at a time when we are less likely to be cut off.

It's always best to ask the other person whether it's a good time for a conversation or presentation. Doing so puts people at ease and keeps them from feeling ambushed or bombarded. It makes people feel in control of their own time. My coauthor Kim pitches stories to the media all day but always begins her phone calls by asking, "Are you on deadline?" or "Is this a good time to talk?" If the answer is no, she lets them right off the phone. Even with a spouse, it's always better to ask when would be a good time to talk rather than to launch into a serious conversation when you have no idea what kind of mood he or she is in. I have a friend who seems to come alive at 10 P.M. and wants to talk about his day just when his wife is starting to fall asleep. He gets hurt because she seems not to care, but she's just exhausted and would rather hear his stories in the morning over a cup of coffee.

It is also useful to determine whether your audience has any preconceptions about the subject on which you will be speaking. One of the most difficult presentations anyone has to make in business occurs when a new leader comes into a company turnaround situation. The audience of employees in that case is worried about whether they'll have a job next month and may have a notion that the leader was brought in to wield the hatchet. Until you address those concerns—which you might learn by polling a few key employees before calling a staff meeting—your presentation on other aspects of the turnaround will never get through.

In many settings, you may have an opportunity to send a short survey prior to the presentation, via mail or e-mail. This might work well before a business meeting or phone appointment, but it's even more effective in a situation where the presentation has been planned well in advance—a charity function, say, or a community meeting. Again, you can also ask the audience directly about their preconception of the subject of your presentation. Or, if it's a subject you have presented on before, reflect upon the potential audience similarities and recall how aspects of your other presentations were previously received.

Similarly, you can find out what your audience liked or disliked about previous presentations of yours and of others. At a neighborhood meeting or public forum or when calling in to a radio program, for instance, watch and listen to how other speakers are received. Observe not only what they say but how they deliver it. Then adjust your presentation to be consistent with the most successful ones in delivery style. This level of awareness will serve you as well at the Thanksgiving table as it does in the boardroom.

Finally, it is important to understand the strengths and constraints both of our audience and the environment in which we are called upon to present. I have watched presenters falter by trying to use slide projectors in sky-lit rooms. And I have heard people struggling to present too-complicated subjects to an audience with no basic knowledge of the subject matter. Kim tells me this is often the case when an author goes on a book tour and forgets that he or she is an expert on a subject that the general audience is hearing about for the first time. Sometimes people simply do not have the capability to receive the presentation that you wish to deliver. Don't offer too many statistics to a person who is math-averse, for example. You will lose him. The anchorman, of course, failed to appreciate that his audience did not have the attention span required to follow a story that stretched on for half an hour. Apparently, for that presentation, he never looked beyond the thoughts in his own head. We must always *remember that the success of your presentation is not primarily determined by you. It is primarily decided by the person or persons who constitute your audience.*

These practices will not only help you perform better for the presentation in question, they will broaden your understanding of human nature, which will undoubtedly result in greater presentation success in the future. *The more you know about people, the better your presentations will be!*

You're Such a Character!

Across the back wall of my presentation studio is a series of caricatures that an artist friend painted for me. Anyone standing up at the stage can survey these painted people as well as those who happen to be sitting in the live audience. In a manner of speaking, however, the slightly exaggerated portraits are the same audience members we are likely to face in many presentation opportunities.

In addition to the personality types that we all carry with us every day, we also enter situations in different frames of mind, depending upon our mood, the circumstances of the presentation, and any number of factors. If our personality type is the operating system of our mind, our attitude at any given moment is the software program we're working in. The result of these elements is the character type we represent as members of an audience. As presenters we tend to have greater awareness of personality types when dealing one-on-one and greater awareness of character types when presenting to a roomful of people. If you've ever done the latter, tell me if any of the following people sound familiar:

- *Fast Freddie.* This is the extrovert. He wants your speech to go quickly so he can get back to doing some of the talking himself. Watch out for this guy in meetings you're leading. He can create a major distraction and undermine your sense of purpose.

- *Methodical Mary.* She thinks about things very carefully before she does them. She listens closely to the presenter to determine what course of action she should take in response. Don't allow her to make you self-conscious. Be prepared to expect that she's hanging on to every word.

- *Detail Dan.* He likes to write down everything and loves the lists and charts you may use in your presentation. Handouts will give Dan a more fulfilling experience, since they will enable him to write less and listen more.

- *Friendly Fran.* She loves people and is the opposite of Detail Dan. She would rather chitchat with those around her than take notes, and she may very well do so during your presentation. Short of asking her to be quiet, you may want to put her to work distributing handouts or involve her in some of the ways we'll discuss in Chapter 11.

- *Greg the Graduate.* He is the know-it-all and considers himself already an expert on all you have to say. He may as well be sitting in the room wearing a mortarboard. Look for frowns, smug looks, and rolling eyes. Giving a nod to his perceptiveness during the presentation will turn him from a rival to an ally.

- *Prisoner Pete.* He is the guy who does not want to be at the presentation, but felt like he had to come (or, worse, was made to come). We don't like to see this person in the audience, but let's face it: We've all been in the situation of being forced to sit through a presentation that we didn't really want to attend. Prisoner Pete often has his arms crossed in a "pouting defense" posture. Recently at a presentation on the East Coast, a woman asked me to sign a book to "my friend who made me come and didn't show up herself." Rarely will a prisoner announce herself that blatantly, of course. I was thrilled to hear it, though, because she sat through a six-hour seminar, returning after three breaks that she easily could have used as a means of escape.

- *Student Steve.* With a roomful of these guys you're golden. He has a pen behind his ear and is taking thoughtful notes on his laptop computer. He has come to learn and is really listening to the speaker. With just a few more Steves in your presentation world, life would be a bowl of cherries.

- *Vacationing Virginia.* She is the person who acts like she's sipping a pineapple drink with an umbrella in it. To Virginia you are a form of entertainment—or at least a terrific excuse for her to play hooky from her other chores. She's just happy to be there instead of working, and you'll find her overly relaxed to the point of tuning out. She won't disrupt your presentation, but if you can get her to learn something it will be a real accomplishment.

- *Champion Charlotte.* She is the cheerleader for the speaker's ideas and will stand up and give testimony about why she believes in the concepts. She can validate your statements with personal experience, no matter what they are. Beware of Charlotte: She may give you a short-term ego boost, but if she starts sounding like a shill she can alienate your audience.

- *Sniper Sid.* The opposite of Charlotte, he is the guy who intends to shoot down your ideas no matter what they are. Unlike a heckler, whose very purpose is disruption, Sid is just a cynic who thinks he's got something to prove. To look at Sid on my studio wall is to stare down the barrel of a gun. Disarm him with humor.

These character types are derived from a list of four shared with me by my friend David Freeborn (originally: Prisoner, Vacationer, Graduate,

Student) and expanded by me based upon my own experiences and those of my students. There's not a one that I haven't witnessed firsthand over the years. In fact, in any group of twenty or more audience members, you're likely to find the majority of these characters. And these folks don't just show up for group events. Since people often demonstrate combinations of these characteristics at the same time, several of these characters might attend when you're presenting to an audience of one!

The first key to coping with character types is simply to remember that *your audience is not a monolith.* Forewarned is forearmed. When presenting to a large group, expect that all or most of these characters will be present and do not allow it to rattle you. The fact is that they are sometimes manifesting preconceived behaviors that will not yield readily to a presentation intended to reach the rest of your audience. If a guy has a fight with his wife in the morning and comes directly to your presentation acting like Sniper Sid, don't take it personally. Remember to assume that everyone is doing the best they can at any given moment. *Getting a handle on the majority of your audience is your most potent defense against one or two disruptive forces.* A willingness to adjust is equally important.

Unless you're a warden or facing an extremely unusual situation, most of your audience will not be prisoners and will not want to resist your message. They are there because they want to be and they are rooting for you to succeed because they don't want to be wasting their time any more than you do.

The achievement of our goals always requires two things: preparation and delivery. The first essential step on the road to becoming a Master Presenter is to know what to expect from the audience and to respond accordingly. We can certainly gather information about our audience the moment we walk into a room, but we will be much more thoroughly prepared if we have done our homework beforehand, making an effort to discover the types of personalities to expect, their prejudices, likes and dislikes, strengths and constraints, preconceptions, and motivations. With your presentation modified to address the features that make your audience unique, you can then cope with whatever mood—in the form of character types—they happen to throw at you.

We will return to our focus on the audience in Chapter 8. In the next two chapters, however, we direct our attention to the content of our presentations.

✓
Very Important Points

- Every person to whom we make a presentation is unique.

- Master Presenters learn the composition of their audience before the presentation begins, then prepare accordingly.

- Once you grasp the composition of your audience with regard to personality type, you are in a better position to plan your presentation to suit their preferences.

- Remember that the success of your presentation is not primarily determined by you. It is primarily decided by the person or persons who constitute your audience.

- The more you know about people, the better your presentations will be!

- Your audience is not a monolith.

- Getting a handle on the majority of your audience is your most potent defense against one or two disruptive forces.

CHAPTER 6

Essential #2:
Explain "Why" Before Planning How

*The No. 1 Question Most Presenters
Forget to Ask Themselves*

You and a colleague are going to a meeting. She could swear she told you a month ago what this meeting is about, so she doesn't mention it again when you call the night before to ask her how you should dress. "Wear a conservative suit," she says. Wanting to impress, you show up the next morning looking your best in a three-piece job with pinstripes, a red foulard tie, and lizard shoes. Problem is: The purpose of the meeting was to meet a client at his beach club and schmooze by the pool. When your colleague told you to wear a suit, she meant a conservative bathing suit!

Sound ridiculous? Yeah, okay. But what's equally absurd is the fact that many people make presentations without any consideration of *why* they are doing so (because the boss or your spouse said you have to is not a valid reason why). As a result, they show up unprepared or, proverbially speaking, wearing the wrong kind of suit.

The single most powerful thing you can do to convince your audience of something is to provide a compelling reason why they should do what you suggest (or believe what you say). I was reminded of this fact just recently when my wife and I paid a visit to our family counselor's office. We consider our marriage to be very strong, but we regularly attend sessions with a counselor because we believe so sincerely in the power of coaching to better one's life. I never underestimate the ability of outside experts to help me improve, which is why I don't only consult, I *use* consultants, and

I don't only coach, I've had the same business coach (Mark Pantak) for more than sixteen years.

As Tammy and I were walking out of the office, we bumped into the following situation. The family counselor poked his head out his door to greet the next clients and found *two* couples expecting to be seen at the next appointment. Oops. Someone had made a mistake and double-booked the therapist.

What would you do as a person expecting to see someone and confronted with this circumstance? Of course, both couples feverishly launched into presentations of their respective points of view. Both said they were sure the receptionist had told them that specific time and day. Both noted that they had booked well in advance and had been patiently waiting in the reception area for some time. Both claimed that they *really* had to see the counselor, like, NOW! Then half of one couple, a young woman, stepped a little closer to the counselor. "The thing is," she said softly, "we're getting married this weekend. So we can't wait for next week. It's imperative that we see you *this* week." Bingo!

I can't tell you whether that couple's wedding went forward without a hitch, but I do know that the young woman's provision of a convincing "why" proved to be the decisive factor in her presentation. The other couple? They rode the elevator down with us, frowning all the way.

Recall from Chapter 2 that a psychologist named Robin Langer discovered years ago that the word "because" is an automatic trigger of compliance. Being told a "why" by a presenter is not the same thing exactly, but its power is related. Simply hearing a why will not trigger an automatic response in your audience. More palpably, though, it will satisfy the basic human need we all have to understand the purpose of our actions. And, interestingly, I have found that the presenter can reap significant value not only by posing this question with regard to her audience, but also with regard to herself and why she is making a specific presentation (whatever it is) the way that she is (whatever that way is).

The key to the success of asking why is that it forces us to dig into something fundamental that we all share, which is the fact that we only perform tasks because we are motivated to do them. *Sometimes our motivation comes from outside ourselves and sometimes it comes from within.* That's just about the only thing the world of psychology seems to agree on when it comes to this subject. Plato, William James, Sigmund Freud, Carl Jung, Alfred Adler, Erik Erikson, B. F. Skinner, and a host of other famous shrinks and philosophers have opined on the subject of human motivation, and they've all drawn somewhat different conclusions. Two of the more convincing arguments, in my opinion, come from well-known psychologist Abraham Maslow and a less famous chap named Steven Reiss, who teaches and conducts research at the Ohio State University.

What Do *You* Want?

Abraham Maslow, who lived from 1908 to 1970, observed that human beings always want something, and these desires motivate all our behavior. Then, in an effort to create a universally applicable theory, he concluded that everyone's deepest desires correspond roughly to sequential stages or phases of our lives. At first, he argued, people must satisfy their most basic biological desires: the need for food, sex, and shelter. It has been observed, for example, that all social revolutions originate with the middle class because the poorest people are so busy struggling to meet their most basic needs that they cannot strive to improve their lot through rebellion.

In Stage 2 of Maslow's famous **Hierarchy of Needs,** once a person's basic biological requirements are met he prioritizes his own feeling of safety before all other desires. In Stage 3 a person seeks to satisfy his need for belonging or social contact. In Stage 4 his need for esteem and status takes precedence. Finally, in Stage 5, if he ever reaches it, a person's greatest desire is to achieve self-fulfillment.

One way to explore the why behind your presentation is to find your place and the place of your audience on Maslow's hierarchy. For example, are you or your audience at the point of longing for social contact, or are you most keenly in search of status? But knowledge of Maslow can only take you so far. The main problem with his hierarchy, as I believe he freely acknowledged, is that, while it has the ring of truth, it has never been scientifically verified. Also, it tends to be inherently judgmental, as if the person who never gets past Stage 3 is somehow living on a lesser plane of existence than the person who exists in Stage 5. But the shortcoming from our perspective as presenters is that Maslow paints all humanity with such a broad brush that his observations become difficult to employ as a useful tool when dealing with individuals in our audience.

In an effort to overcome this handicap, for years I have successfully coached clients to evaluate their audience's why through the prism of what I call **Seven Subconscious Desires.** Every audience member wants to belong, to be respected, to be liked, to be safe, to succeed, to find romance, and to be inspired or enthused. Every part of your presentation, I have instructed, should have as its purpose the satisfaction of one or more of these desires. Thousands of my clients, when they remember to focus the whys of their presentation on these desires, have had great success connecting with their audience.

Recently, I learned about a study that offers a scientific basis for the results my clients have achieved by keeping in mind the audience's subconscious desires. A psychologist named Dr. Steven Reiss managed to take Maslow quite a step further. Dr. Reiss agreed with the premise that human beings are creatures of desire, but he found Maslow's hierarchy too rigid. Instead, he set out to define a different set of fundamental desires that all people have in common, and to do it scientifically. Using surveys of more than 6,000 people and sophisticated computer models, Reiss and his graduate student, Susan Havercamp, arrived at the conclusion that sixteen basic desires constitute all our personalities and form the foundation for all our behavior. They defined these desires, in no particular order, as follows:

- *Power:* the desire to influence others
- *Independence:* the desire for self-reliance
- *Curiosity:* the desire for knowledge
- *Acceptance:* the desire for inclusion
- *Order:* the desire for organization
- *Saving:* the desire to collect things
- *Honor:* the desire to be loyal to one's parents and heritage
- *Idealism:* the desire for social justice
- *Social Contact:* the desire for companionship
- *Family:* the desire to raise one's own children
- *Status:* the desire for social standing
- *Vengeance:* the desire to get even

- *Romance:* the desire for sex and beauty
- *Eating:* the desire to consume food
- *Physical Activity:* the desire for exercise of muscles
- *Tranquility:* the desire for emotional calm

Writing in the book *Who Am I?: The 16 Basic Desires That Motivate Our Behavior and Define Our Personality,* Dr. Reiss asserts that, "The relative importance we place on each desire is what makes us individuals. In other words, every human being places a different level of importance on each desire. . . . What this means is that individuals differ to a greater extent than psychologists have previously realized." Amazingly, he continues, "There are more than 43 million possible combinations of the sixteen basic desires that can be produced by answering the questions [in the Reiss Profile survey]. More than 2 trillion different profiles can be assessed by the Reiss Profile." So if you've ever faced an audience of more than one and thought of them as a monolith, you are guaranteed to have been mistaken!

Dr. Reiss believes the relative proportion of the **16 Basic Desires** in each of us derives largely—but not entirely—from our genetic makeup. So, for example, a person might be born with a predisposition toward strong desires for Physical Activity, Romance, and Social Contact, and with weak desires for Eating, Idealism, and Saving. His other desires may be average. This sounds to me like a person who might enjoy working as a fitness coach.

What happens when the fitness coach runs across a person who rates highly for his desire toward Eating, Independence, and Tranquility? Say this other person rates very low in his desire toward Physical Activity, Social Contact, and Acceptance, and average for all other desires. Once we begin to see people through the prism of the Reiss Profile, we can conclude that these two people will almost never agree on the merits of regular exercise. In fact, as Dr. Reiss observes, "Your desire profile affects how you communicate with other people. You may find that you communicate instinctively and fluidly with people whose desire profiles are similar to yours. But your desires can also create an invisible wall that leads to miscommunication between you and those whose desire profiles are discordant with yours."

The result of head-on clashes of basic desire profiles can be what he calls "not getting it," which occurs when people talk past one another or simply cannot understand the other person's perspective on a certain subject. " 'Not getting it,' " writes Dr. Reiss, "is part of our everyday lives. Although some examples are amusing, 'not getting it' can be serious business. Every so often it breaks out into a cultural war, but even when that does not happen, it is a major factor in what people do not like about each other. It is so basic to human thinking that people do not realize when it is occurring, and how it biases their attitude toward other people.

"Interestingly," he continues, " 'not getting it' primarily occurs when people have significantly different desire profiles (motives, pleasures, and values). It usually does not occur between people who have different abilities, opinions, personalities, or habits. People can learn to appreciate others who are different from them in many regards; it is only when it comes to pleasures, values, and desires that 'not getting it' is seen.

"If we want to know what people will do," he concludes, "we should find out what they desire and predict that they will try to satisfy their desires. Desire may not tell us everything we want to know about ourselves and others, but what it tells us is very important for understanding behavior and happiness."

Keeping track of all sixteen basic desires might seem like a lot for you to do. If so, you can fall back on my original seven. And if that seems too much, focus your energy on the more important point here: *Your audience, like all human beings, is driven by basic subconscious wants. In order to reach them most effectively, you must tailor your presentation in a way that addresses those desires.*

Don't Plan in Two Dimensions

Clara has been an active member of her gardening club for years, but never a leader of it. She enjoys digging in the dirt with the other ladies from around town, improving the appearance of her neighborhood, and learning about new cultivars, but in ten years as a member she has never asserted herself successfully. Now the group is considering tackling a new project in an area that she has strong feelings about, and she would like to have a great degree of influence on the final result. The garden club decided at the last meeting to consider making their next project the traffic island just a block from Clara's house. Clara has driven past this site eight times a day for more than half her life, and over that period she has secretly planned improvements to the island a thousand times in her head. She would like at least some of her ideas to prevail.

But Clara has a problem. Perhaps because she never has approached her presentations to the group with confidence, Clara believes that most of her fellow members don't take her opinions seriously. Furthermore, she knows that some of the other ladies have very specific ideas about what to do in the traffic island, and these ideas do not at all agree with her own. She thinks back in frustration to the last presentation she made to the garden club. That time, she had wanted to convince them that they should create a demonstration garden at the town park. She prepared a beautiful handout with pictures of the current state of the park, with plant lists and with photos of similar gardens in other settings. After passing this around, she began to explain that they could do the project inexpensively and that she would even agree to pay for the plant markers herself to help get it all off the ground. You would have thought from the reaction of the other ladies, though, that she had proposed to drive an excavating machine through each of their front lawns.

Mrs. Hatfield pointedly observed that the rules of the garden club prohibit individual contributions like the one Clara had proposed, as all their resources were always to be pooled at the beginning of each quarter, according to the bylaws. Mrs. Capobianco said the town just spent a million dollars of taxpayer money on the park and she didn't think they'd appreciate ripping up the fresh sod for a bunch of old ladies. Mrs. Leander noted that the park was in such an out-of-the-way place that nobody in the group even drove by it with any regularity. Mrs. Morris pictured flying baseballs crushing all the flowers.

Clara just stood there flabbergasted. She knew her subject, knew exactly what she wanted to communicate, and had expressed herself pretty well, she thought. She had used Social Proof to show how other communities had done similar things. She had even proposed that they sleep on their decision until the next meeting, hoping to appeal to all the Methodical Marys in the club. Yet, astonishingly, all her friends had rejected her demonstration garden idea outright.

This time, Clara knew, her presentation for the traffic island had to be different. Now that she understood about the power of asking why, she began by probing her own desires. First, Clara honestly asked herself where she stood in Maslow's hierarchy at that moment in her life. As a method actor might melodramatically say: "But what is my motiv-*ay*-tion?" Clara was sixty-eight years old. She had long ago satisfied her needs for food, shelter, safety, and social contact, the first three stages of the hierarchy. She was involved in many town groups and had children and grandchildren who respected and admired her, too. So while Clara felt that she could use some more esteem from the members of the garden club, she also believed that she was pretty well advanced through Stage 4 and had at least rounded the corner to Stage 5: self-fulfillment. Why was Clara so interested in taking the lead on the traffic island project? She decided that it appealed partly to her need for more esteem from her friends in the garden club, but most important was the sense of fulfillment she thought it would bring her. She pictured herself driving by that island every day and feeling a deep inner peace, knowing that she had made that small patch of barren weeds into a more beautiful part of the world.

In short, this exercise allowed Clara to reflect on her own specific goals for the first time. Too many presenters are like careless people reading a map. They know they want to drive from Illinois to California, but they set out on their journey before they pause to consider what exact city they're going to. Then they're cruising along, wind in their hair, just allowing the inertia to carry them, and they only realize too late that they've ended up in San Francisco when they really wanted to be in L.A. In the past, Clara kind of knew which region she was hoping to head for, but because she didn't pause to reflect on her deepest motivations, she had no idea what her final destination really ought to be.

When a person is fully aware of what her primary motivators are as a human being, though, it gives her a huge advantage as a presenter, because it automatically gets her onto the right road. Personally, I am a little goal crazy. I have ninety-two *pages* of goals, which I study and tweak almost weekly. Whenever I set out to do anything—including, of course, making a presentation—these goals provide any additional motivation I might need to get me through to my destination with clarity. If you understand what your goals and desires are, it allows you to speak with more passion and conviction on the delivery side and gives you more motivation on the preparation side.

Having arrived at her own motivation for the importance of this new presentation in her life, Clara was ready to tackle an even more important set of whys—those that would lead to the satisfaction of her audience. Clara understood one of the most basic things a presenter has to remember: *Organizations (like the Garden Club) don't make decisions—people do.* Armed with her newfound knowledge of the significance of motivation, Clara began by reviewing the cool reception that her last presentation received. Now that she was detached from that event, she could see more clearly that she had not provided the whys that this particular group of ladies might be seeking. She now knew, for example, that Mrs. Capobianco was driven most by a desire for Tranquility. As a consequence, the potential of having to garden in a place where kids were running around and ball games were being played probably had biased her against the demonstration garden from the start. If Clara had just pointed out that the park was always quiet during the early morning weekdays, when the ladies preferred to do their work anyway, then the project may have held more appeal for Mrs. Capobianco.

Turning her thoughts to Mrs. Hatfield and Mrs. Leander, Clara realized that their objections to the demonstration garden masked opposition to the project that came from other motivations. These two ladies, Clara knew, were both mostly driven by Status. They looked at their membership in the garden club as a way to stay in touch with other women of social standing. Their families belonged to private clubs. The last thing they wanted was to spend their energy gardening in a park that they and their friends would never use.

Finally, Clara thought about Mrs. Penny Morris. Clara found her objection to the plan most disturbing of all, because she considered Penny one of her best friends. In fact, they didn't speak for a month about garden club business after Clara's unsuccessful presentation. Instead of avoiding the issue, she wished she would have taken that time to present to Penny in some other ways, because in retrospect she now realized that Penny's main motivator was the desire for Order. If Clara had only appealed to that need, she might have achieved a different outcome.

Ah, well, you live and you learn. Clara decided to direct her thoughts to the future. In the past, she would make an outline of her ideas, just the way she had learned in school a very long time ago, working through her presentation in linear fashion from Point 1 to point whatever, with a whole bunch of sub-points in between. Thus did Clara drive along the road of her presentation from beginning to middle to end, and thus did she often end up in San Francisco when she meant to go to L.A. Fortunately, besides Maslow and Reiss, she had now discovered a tool that would help her presentations correspond more closely to the multidimensional realities of her real-life audience. That tool is called a Three-Dimensional Outline.

About ten years ago, I created this mechanism for encouraging people to consider the why of their presentations before committing to the how. *I call this tool the 3-D Outline because it enables us to drill down into our own motivations and those of our audience as a means of taking our presentation where it ought to go.* The kind of outline we all learned in school and use every day primarily focuses on the whats—the one dimension that is very common. Most people miss the other dimensions of their presentation: the why and the how. My trademarked 3-D Outline goes a step further by calling upon you to make note of all the objectives you are striving to achieve in your presentation. By doing so, you will be forced to think through the specific techniques you must employ to touch your audience—not just focus narrowly on the information you're hoping to impart. The 3-D Outline will help Clara organize her thoughts and validate why she is saying what she is saying when she presents her views on the traffic island project.

Look at the blank 3-D Outline form on page 125. Clara (or you) can copy this form and fill it in, but for more flexibility she would be better off just using it as a guideline. The means by which you create the form are of no consequence. My company sells software (*Mr. Presentation Wizard*) that helps you fill in your 3-D Outline on a computer and comes with all sorts of bells and whistles. But you can almost just as easily take out a pencil and build a 3-D Outline on the back of an envelope, as I've also done many times. Or you can create your own template in some other computer program and repeatedly use it to build 3-D Outlines for all your presentations. On the other hand, you can do what Clara did: Take a legal pad and draw columns with a pen. It doesn't matter what mechanism you use. The important thing is to remember that—until the moment of your presentation—the 3-D Outline will be a living document. That means you need to be prepared not only to fill in the boxes, but to make changes by deleting, moving things around, adding, etc.

#	Time	What (Dimension 1)	Why (Dimension 2)	How (Dimension 3)

Presentation Title:
Audience:
Objectives:

Delivery Date:
Delivery Time:
Presentation Length:

#	Time	What (Dimension 1)	Why (Dimension 2)	How (Dimension 3)
1.				
2.				
3.				
4.				
5.				

* For a free sample of the above template, visit http://www.tonyjeary.com/3-DOutline.

Don't get into the habit, as some do, of presuming that the first thing you write down is an insight of such great genius that it may as well be carved in stone. Remember that there's always room for improvement.

Clara began her document, as we all should, by noting in the upper right-hand corner of her pad the number of attendees she expected at her presentation. This would help give her a picture of her audience and remind her of their complexity. Then she wrote down her three or four most important broad objectives, which are Clara's whys. She used action words toward the front of the statement (inspire, convince, and create). For the presentation on the traffic island project, her objectives were the following:

- To inspire the garden club members to make the traffic island project their next priority.

- To convince the group that I (Clara) should take the lead on the project.
- To create buy-in about my design plans and ideas.

Clara expected to make her presentation at the next meeting of the club, and she knew from past experience that she would have about half an hour to get her points across. Then there would be about fifteen minutes of questions and discussion. Including fifteen minutes of final preparation before the meeting, Clara figured on a total time of one hour, which she wrote down at the bottom of her outline.

In the "What" column, Clara's first entry was "Final Prep." For "Why" she wrote "To assure that everything is in place and working." She was referring specifically to the handouts she had prepared and to the slide projector she intended to use. Under "How" she simply noted, "Set up and test." The "Time," as mentioned above, was fifteen minutes.

Then she turned her attention to how she would begin. At first, she thought she would open with a statement about how much the traffic island meant to her personally. *Why* would she do that? Hmm. Upon asking herself that question, it dawned on Clara that her main reason for making such a statement was to satisfy one of her own desires, not those of the audience. So she scratched that entry out and tried again.

Under the "What" column Clara wrote the following:

Opening

- Welcome everyone as the friends of mine that they are.
- Remind them of how much fun we've all had on recent projects.
- Touch upon the prestige the club has achieved, with awards from the Garden Club of America and commendations from town leaders.
- Introduce the idea that the club can go on to even bigger and better things in the near future.

These elements made a lot more sense to Clara after she paused to consider the why. She planned in the beginning to subtly remind the other members of the bonds they have with one another, bonds based upon past friendship and shared experience. Then she would make them feel good about their accomplishments, so she could sell them on the idea that this next project would be congruent with their past efforts. She wrote this a little more succinctly in the "Why" column, and figured this piece would take about ten minutes.

Continuing, Clara moved to the heart of her presentation, the first part of which was a demonstration of the mess the traffic island looks like now. Under the "Why" column she wrote, "To deplore the ugly." She knew that every member of her audience loved beauty and despaired at public places that don't reflect well on their town. Under the "How" column she wrote, "Pictures of the current situation." These pictures honestly portrayed the state of the current traffic island as a mess of weeds, leaves, garbage, and abandoned hubcaps, with close-ups of some very ugly pieces of traffic island trash thrown into the mix. She expected to hear a lot of tut-tutting during this part of the presentation, which she believed would take about five minutes.

The building of Clara's 3-D Outline proceeded apace. In the course of this exercise she determined that her presentation would contain six parts, including Question and Discussion time (she didn't number Final Prep, which was not part of the presentation itself). She also clarified exactly *why* she was including each of the pieces in her talk. Some of her points were intended to appeal to the higher desires of her group: Maslow's Stage 5 self-fulfillment and Reiss's desires of Honor and Independence, for example. Other aspects of her presentation appealed to less altruistic desires, such as Maslow's Stage 4 need for esteem from others and Reiss's desires for Status and even Power. She also noted where the whys touched upon the Seven Subconscious Desires—most particularly, in this case, the desires to be respected and to be inspired or enthused. In the end, Clara's 3-D Outline looked like the one on page 128.

Clara, of course, is a figment of my imagination. I picture her getting up in front of that roomful of ladies and making a most convincing argument. It is effective first because she knows exactly what her objectives are and why she has those objectives. Most important, she achieves those goals because she appeals to the fundamental desires that her audience brought to the presentation.

While Clara is not real, her concerns and challenges may as well be. It continues to amaze me that the people I coach do not have the awareness

Presentation			
Title: Traffic Island Project		**Delivery Date:** April 26	
Audience: Fellow garden club members		**Delivery Time:** 9:00 a.m. **Presentation Length:** 45 mins	
Objectives: Inspire club to make traffic island project the next priority. Convince club to let me take the lead. Create buy-in about design plans/ideas.			

#	Time	What (Dimension 1)	Why (Dimension 2)	How (Dimension 3)
		Final Prep: Develop film Gather flower samples	To assure that everything is in place and working	Set up and test
1.	10	Opening Welcome Fun factor of past projects Club prestige, awards, commendations Future growth	To remind the club about their bonds & past experiences, and make them feel good about past & future projects	Present
2.	5	Current situation of traffic island	To deplore the ugly	Pictures of the current situation
3.	15	Design idea: Patriotic theme	To explain my ideas about what should be planted and how	Drawings & flower samples
4.	10	Question & discussion	To close any gaps	Facilitated discussion, HUHY cards
5.	5	Summarize & close	To recap and end the meeting	Present
	45			

they should that the audience always comes to the presentation with certain goals and motivations of their own. These presenters are so focused on what *they* want that they forget to think about what their audience wants. Couples do this to each other and parents do it with their children. We all have our own agendas and know what *we* want to accomplish or gain in a discussion without necessarily thinking about the needs that drive others.

I was recently coaching the folks in Wal-Mart's home office who oversee the entire construction process for new and refurbished stores. They observed that it sometimes takes more energy than they would like to convince their general contractors (who are all over the world) to do things according to the company's guidelines. My question for these executives was simple: *Are you telling them why they should follow these guidelines?* Not as much as they should, I learned. And it turns out that Wal-Mart, as a hugely successful company with decades of experience, has some very good reasons for their guidelines—reasons that benefit not just the company but their contractors, as well. The Wal-Mart executives walked away from our meeting with renewed determination to explain the company's past experiences, citing other general contractors who made more money and benefited in other ways by following the guidelines. Armed with the why (and with Social Proof), we all agreed that their presentations to the general contractors would be more effective—and would require less effort.

I know the 3-D Outline works because I use it nearly every day and because thousands of my clients and past seminar students have used it to great effect. Some years ago, my staff and I employed the 3-D Outline to launch three simultaneous cascading training initiatives in three different languages for Chrysler. We literally took flip charts and stuck them all over the walls and planned it down to the minute. This exercise forced us to look at why we were spending every moment of that training session the way we planned.

While all people want to know why they're being asked to do things, this becomes especially true for kids. At home, telling your teenager to clean up his room and throw the food out downstairs in the garbage is one thing. Telling him to clean it up and get rid of the food while explaining *why*—because, if he doesn't, those yucky bugs that he hates will come out—is another thing altogether.

As useful as the 3-D Outline can be, we must always remember that its utility derives most pointedly from the way it empowers us to ask ourselves the right questions about our presentations. Why would the audience members want to listen to you and potentially buy into your message? Why would you, the presenter, want to put effort into the presentation? Why would your audience members be influenced by someone outside the presentation (parent, child, religious or community leader, colleague, etc.)? Why would a particular audience member be receptive to you? Why would his or her organization support this receptivity? Why are you saying what you are saying? Why are you using the tools (flip charts, video clips, etc.) that you've chosen?

By writing down these whys, we force ourselves to address the fundamental desires of our audience. The result may seem miraculous: *We will get what we want from our presentation because we gave the audience what they wanted from our presentation.*

✓
Very Important Points

- The single most powerful thing you can do to convince your audience of something is to provide a compelling reason why they should do what you suggest (or believe what you say).

- Sometimes our motivation comes from outside ourselves and sometimes it comes from within.

- Your audience, like all human beings, is driven by basic sub-conscious wants. In order to reach them most effectively, you must tailor your presentation in a way that addresses those desires.

- Organizations don't make decisions—people do.

- The 3-D Outline enables us to drill down into our own motivations and those of our audience as a means of taking our presentation where it ought to go.

- We will get what *we* want from our presentation because we gave the audience what *they* wanted from our presentation.

CHAPTER 7

Essential #3:
Conquer the Sum of All Fears

*To Overcome Anxiety, Successful Presenters Eliminate
"Unknowns" by Turning Them into "Knowns"*

According to an entry I once saw in *The Book of Lists,* Americans rank heights, insects and bugs, financial problems, and deep water as their second, third, fourth, and fifth greatest fears. Sickness is number six. Death is number seven. Number one is the fear of speaking before a group.

From the perspective of the presenter, most of us are familiar with the symptoms of this fear: that pit in the bottom of our stomachs or the twitching lip or the tightening larynx or the trembling leg or increasing dryness in the mouth and throat. To our audience, this fear reveals itself as a quaking voice or inconsistent vocal tone, as negative or inappropriate body language, and ultimately as a failure to achieve rapport with the audience because we are so absorbed in our own anxiety that we disconnect. Even seasoned professionals can manifest this condition when they work under unfamiliar circumstances or enter a situation that presents unexpected distractions.

I believe that people's well-documented *nervousness with regard to public speaking derives from what Carl Jung concluded was the hard-wired mother of all fears: fear of the unknown.* If we only knew that we wouldn't mess up when we get up to talk in front of a group—if we only knew they would *like* us—then a great deal of the burden would be lifted from our shoulders. If we only knew what kind of experience we were going to have as presenters before we present, rather than having to set sail for uncharted, foreign waters; if we only knew how our spouse or our boss would react when we make an important presentation to them, then we could approach the situation with so much more confidence than we otherwise would. But we can never know all these things, of course. The great quarterback Jim Kelly used to go into the locker room toilet and throw up a few minutes before every game—not just in high school but as a professional. He did this year in and year out, in spite of the fact that he also consistently put up Hall of Fame numbers during that time.

Imagine! The inability to know how he would perform in front of a stadium full of people ran so deep that it actually made Kelly physically ill every week during the season. And it's not just football players who are throwing up. My sister-in-law decided not to become an athletic coach only because she feared having to deliver after-dinner talks and speak publicly. Many of my and Kim's clients have confided that they have terrible physical symptoms before giving their presentations. This is not an exclusive club; it includes teachers, executives, authors, actors, people going on job interviews, folks who need a special favor from someone, spouses dealing with marital tension, employees about to ask for a raise, people trying to get a refund—men and women who are facing any unfamiliar or uncomfortable situation you can name.

There's a famous prayer about not trying to control the things we can't control, making sure to control that which we can control, and having the wisdom to know the difference. While it certainly helps not to allow ourselves to become anxious about things we can't control, I believe it is also true that we *can* control more factors in our presentation's success than we may at first think. Furthermore, simply familiarizing ourselves with those factors we cannot control enables us to settle our anxiety and focus our minds, because the most difficult thing about the unknown is its ability to surprise us. When true surprises come, we risk getting thrown off our game. So *by reducing that surprise element we can have a significant impact on the smoothness of our delivery.* This boosts our confidence, which improves our chances of success even more, and on it goes, cascading forward toward a masterful presentation.

In the context of presentation opportunities, I focus on four "unknowns" that have the ability to vex us and consequently play upon our fears. First there is fear that we are delivering the wrong message to our audience or delivering a message that we are not qualified to present.

Second is fear that we are presenting to the wrong person or people. Third is fear of the variables in our environment. Last is that old standby, performance anxiety. By addressing these fears head-on, we come to an appreciation of the "unknowns" that are haunting us. And *by turning these unknown quantities into known quantities, we can overcome the anxieties and uncertainties that undermine any presentation.*

Like so many of the keys to achieving our presentation objectives, the techniques we apply to overcoming these destabilizing forces can be summed up in one word: preparation.

Say the Right Thing—To the Right Person

How many times in our lives do we wish we could have taken back something that we said? Commonly, we have an opportunity to make an impression by offering a quick-witted response or we have the chance to ask a question of someone we might rarely get to meet, and when the moment comes we blow it. If only we could rewind the video and play a second take, we think. If only we could do that, we would say the *best* thing. But, of course, there are no rewinds in life. We can only live it going forward. So we spend the rest of the day—or, sometimes, the rest of our lives—wishing in vain that we could relive that moment now that we've had time to reflect on what we should have said.

A woman I know who is very active in her community has always had a lot to say about politics. As she became more connected in the political community in her state, she began to realize that her fantasy of meeting the governor might one day become a reality. And, sure enough, one afternoon she attended a brunch where the governor was the guest of honor, and she found herself standing next to him at the omelet station. Miraculously, he wasn't talking to anybody else, so she realized that her long-dreamed-for opportunity had finally arisen. Now, this is a woman who cares deeply about her neighborhood and has very strong opinions regarding many of the political issues in her state. Yet for all the times she had pictured herself speaking to the governor, she never once planned exactly what she would say. So when the opportunity arose, she became so intimidated by the situation that she stammered something about the food and missed her chance to get a substantive message to the governor or to impress him with her political insights. Her fear of not saying the right thing was borne out because she went into that situation unprepared.

When my friend told me about her disappointment, I made some suggestions that would put her in a better position to make an impression next time. The first thing I communicated was my faith that there *would* be a next time for her. After all, the conversation with the governor was not a blunder, just a lost opportunity. That is, she didn't say anything wrong or embarrassing at the time, she just missed a chance to engage the governor in a substantive conversation. So, undoubtedly, if he remembered her at all, the memory is likely to be benign.

What might she have done differently? Most obviously, she could have planned long in advance what she would say if she ever had a chance to meet the governor. Upon learning that the governor would be present at the brunch reception that afternoon, she should have revisited that plan and refreshed her presentation for the current situation, enabling her to say something charming about the host or to reference something the governor had recently accomplished. By planning what she would say *if* she met the governor, my friend would have been better prepared *when* she met the governor. She would have turned the "unknown" of what to say into "knowing" exactly what she would say if the opportunity arose. As Louis Pasteur said, "Chance favors the prepared mind."

How often do we go into a situation without having thoroughly thought through what the content of our presentation might be? Perhaps it's most common for us not to be ready for impromptu opportunities like a fortuitous meeting with someone we admire, but it certainly is not uncommon for people to enter even planned presentations without a complete grasp of what it is they are there to communicate. Typically in such a case, this inadequacy dawns on presenters when they are standing in front of their audience. You begin to present, and a voice in the back of your head says, "Where am I going with this?" When that happens, it can shake your emotional foundation to its core because *the effectiveness of any presentation depends greatly upon our confidence in the quality and appropriateness of that presentation's content.*

For any of us the first order of business is having a grasp of what we are going to say when we make our presentation and knowing that we are delivering the message that we want to be delivering. If you have chosen to use the 3-D Outline to prepare your material—and I hope you always will—then you should feel confident that you have control of that material. Next, remember to ask yourself exactly who you hope to reach with this specific presentation. Is it the right presentation for that audience at that time? If you don't ask yourself that question before your presentation—and answer it to your satisfaction—you may succumb to anxiety over it in the midst of your presentation.

Time and again I hear stories about people who casually decide to present to one group material that they had initially prepared for another. This might work if the two audiences are truly very similar, but you would feel more confident if you had taken a few moments to review that material in the context of a fresh 3-D Outline, to see whether you are addressing the whys for your new audience. There's a difference between assuming and knowing; it's easy to do the former, but the latter takes some work. On the other hand, when you don't do your homework, the inaccuracy of your assumptions may reveal itself at the worst possible moment—like in the middle of your presentation.

One significant aspect of all this is learning not just to know your audience but, if possible, to help constitute them. If you're conducting a meeting, for example, you may have a good deal of control over who the attendees will be. You can tackle the issue of who to invite by using a technique we call **Political Mapping.**

Political Mapping is a way of assessing the importance of various stakeholders in a meeting or other presentation and determining the impact they may have on your desired outcomes. The technique involves considering every individual's degree of potential influence on a decision or direction while also taking into account his or her existing position on the matter. This approach is especially valuable when you are dealing with emotional or highly controversial issues and need to anticipate specific positions or concerns in advance of the meeting. By knowing ahead of time which people will support or oppose your agenda and why, you will be able to better tailor your material and process. The cost of not knowing is that you may lose control of your presentation the moment someone responds negatively to something you say. By allowing your participants to remain "unknown," you open the door to fear of this kind of derailment. But you can build on the support you have and manage objections more professionally by being prepared.

To undertake a Political Map, start by jotting down the names of people who have a stake in the matter at hand or a strong opinion about it and noting their function. Then think about whom on the list you need to get on board to resolve the matter, and assess the influence each may have. You must consider both the individual's power or rank in the decision-making process and the influence that person may have on the content of the discussion as an expert on the subject matter. You also must take into account that person's probable impact on group dynamics, due to either her role in the organization or her personality. Anyone who has worked in the corporate world has seen how a meeting's direction can change in an instant when someone with authority or with a forceful personality speaks up. Eventually, you will want to anticipate that person's impact and plan for it.

Next, write down what you know about each individual's going-in position on the topic. A simple grid, such as that shown below, can be used to make your notes.* This is a hypothetical rundown on a meeting about launch timing for a new product, and your job as the meeting leader is to get a decision on whether or not to move the launch ahead.

Function/ Activity	Person	Power/ Influence	Going-In Position/ Issues	Implications
Marketing	Pete	High (VP rank)	Supports, not happy with timing	See in advance
Finance	Chris	Medium/High (holds "veto" power)	Neutral, needs to see business case	E-mail in advance
Sales	Sally	Medium	Will support VP Marketing	See in advance
PR	Pat	Low	Neutral, will support whatever outcome	See in advance
Production	Bill	High (vocal)	Supports, but needs funding to improve timing	Phone in advance

(continued on next page)

*Go to http://www.tonyjeary.com/politicalmap for a free Political Map electronic template.

Function/ Activity	Person	Power/ Influence	Going-In Position/ Issues	Implications
Engineering	Jane	Medium	Neutral, but needs direction on other priorities to improve timing	See in advance
Warehousing	Sylvia	Low	Negative (schedule changes again!), but will support VP	Don't invite

The point of this exercise is not only to anticipate the flow of the meeting but to influence it. Once you've thought over the perspectives of the members of your audience, it behooves you to manage their participation before the meeting starts. In anticipation of the meeting, reach out to key individuals by phone or e-mail. This is the time to elicit their opinions on the subject of the meeting, to begin to answer any thorny questions they may have, and to solicit their help in making the meeting a success. By using this form of the "Targeted Polling" that we'll discuss further in Chapter 13, you not only take some "unknowns" to "knowns," but you give these participants a greater stake in the meeting's success.

Although I'm illustrating this concept using a meeting, the technique of Political Mapping works equally well in other presentation circumstances. If in a business setting you are simply presenting a new program, launching a new initiative, or making a sales contact, knowing your audience better via Political Mapping can be a big help in achieving your objectives. If, like my friend, you are hoping to meet the governor and his cohorts, it would also benefit you to have used a Political Map to think about how he is likely to receive and respond to your presentation.

Where Wuz I?

Another friend of mine was anxious recently because her daughter had failed to land a part in the high school play for two years running and wanted desperately to get cast at least once before she graduated. The girl's mother knew she would have to approach the drama teacher on behalf of her daughter, but the whole scenario made her so uncomfortable that she feared she would fail miserably. I suggested she take some of the "unknowns" to "knowns" by talking to other parents and teachers who had had dealings with the drama teacher. Once she knew something about his personality, the issues in his frame of reference, and even the physical place where he was likely to meet with her, she could approach the presentation with a much greater comfort level—and be more likely to succeed.

Often we fail to take into account the environment in which we will be presenting, even though the wrong environment—or environmental surprises—could have an enormous impact on the success of our presentation. Sometimes, in fact, the environment can be the most important deciding variable of all. While nothing is more important than your message and your audience, those two things largely involve what happens between people's ears and therefore have a degree of abstractness. But though our perceptions are a big part of how we experience life, we of course do actually live in a physical world. To take an absurd example, if I'm making a presentation on the Scarcity principle to three people in a quiet classroom and I am prepared, I am likely to have a strong influence over that presentation's success. But if a hurricane is roaring outside and trees are crashing through the windows, then the environment will have asserted itself in a way that I simply cannot compete against. (If this ever happens to you, I suggest you abandon your presentation and run for cover!) But in most circumstances not involving acts of God or nature, you are likely to have more control of your environment than you at first may think. The first step is to be aware that this factor is part of the context of your presentation, whether you like it or not. Furthermore, understand that it forms one of the most intractable foundations of your subconscious fear of your presentation, especially if the location of your presentation is completely unfamiliar to you.

How to cope? One classic example of taking environmental "unknowns" to "knowns" is something most parents do when their preschoolers are about to start kindergarten. Oftentimes we first take them to spend a day in their new class weeks or even months before school will actually start. Educators and parents know that many of their children's anxieties and fears will dissolve after they see the new space, visit a little with the teachers, and get a peek at where they'll be eating lunch. *Once we can replace what we imagine the presentation environment is going to be with what we now see it will be, much of our stress subsides.*

That's why I instruct my clients to educate themselves about the setting and physical setup of their presentation before the time comes to deliver it. This level of preparation is essential for achieving Presentation Mastery, as I was reminded by a story that my coauthor Kim related— a story that illustrates that Bette Davis had much more going for her than just those famous eyes.

In the late 1980s, a couple of years before her death, Bette Davis wrote a book called *This 'N That*, and the publisher hired Kim to arrange a press conference for the launch in Los Angeles. If you have the right contacts, are well organized, and have a subject whom people would like to interview, arranging a press conference can be a straightforward matter of logistics: hire a room, invite the reporters, and have the author make a few statements about the publication of the book. Kim decided to stage the press conference at the Hollywood Roosevelt Hotel, near where Ms. Davis's star was embedded in the Walk of Fame on Hollywood Boulevard. Then she planned to take the author across the street to the B. Dalton bookstore, where she would meet the public and sign copies of *This 'N That* before departing. Kim made the arrangements and, without further ado, notified Ms. Davis's office that all was set. She expected to meet the star for the first time in person that morning, but it turned out that Bette Davis had other ideas.

About two weeks before the scheduled event, Kim received a call from Ms. Davis's personal assistant. She advised Kim that, being a consummate professional—and something of a perfectionist—Ms. Davis never "took on anything" until she performed a run-through. So Kim made an appointment to meet the two women at the Roosevelt, where Ms. Davis appeared with her assistant in tow, the latter carrying a Polaroid camera. Every few steps the assistant documented the plan, taking more than thirty shots in all as Kim showed them where she would disembark from the limousine, climb the steps to the hotel conference room, stand at the podium, depart the hotel, walk across the street to the bookstore, sit down, and sign the copies. Kim was so puzzled by this behavior at the time that only later did she realize what was going on: Bette Davis was familiarizing herself with every bit of the environment in which she would be making her presentation. In short, she was turning virtually every one of her "unknowns" into "knowns."

This story about Bette Davis is an undoubtedly extreme example—

I'm not suggesting that you need to shoot a roll of film and study the pictures every time you make a presentation. But I have little doubt that this kind of behavior on Ms. Davis's part was one of the secrets to her success in life, because people's anxieties are considerably lessened when they take control of their surroundings and know what to expect. And when their anxiety is reduced, they perform better.

One of my associates took this insight to heart in her approach to a blind date that a friend had set up for her. She knew she'd be nervous, so rather than allow the guy to choose the dinner location, she volunteered to make the reservation and chose a restaurant so familiar to her that she already knew most of the staff. Now, though she couldn't control all the "unknowns," she moved forward reasonably certain she would find comfort in her environment that night. That knowledge left her much less nervous, making it easier just to be herself on the date.

When I began my career as a presenter I didn't know about taking "unknowns" to the "knowns," and as a consequence I went into that hotel ballroom in Seattle like a man on a high wire without a net. I thought I was prepared because I had worked hard on my material and had my flow of thoughts down, having rehearsed the presentation multiple times in my hotel room. But like the man on the high wire, the second I became thrown off balance I started to flail, which does nothing to improve the situation. This began literally the moment I walked into the room, because it turned out that the seminar was overbooked and there were not enough chairs for everyone. The crush of people—many standing along the side walls as well as in back—unsettled me tremendously, I think because this surprise reminded me subconsciously that I had no idea how the audience would react since I had never practiced my presentation in front of an audience. Then, you may recall, I put the transparencies on upside down because I had not practiced with the equipment. And the cart was too small for me to rest my notes upon, forcing me to fumble with them. And the room, filled with all those people, began to get too hot—and felt even hotter as my face flushed with embarrassment—because I had never thought to plan for variables in my environment. In short, all these elements conspired against me. All made me nervous, which led to mistakes, which cascaded into an unsuccessful presentation.

It took me a long time to realize that I could have controlled all those things that had distracted me, if only I had made them known to myself *before* they happened. But at the time I didn't *know the what-ifs.*

Today I have a sort of system for taking control of my presentation environment. For formal presentations in front of large groups, I make sure there will be enough seats ahead of time. If it's a room or location I'm not familiar with, I quickly learn how to work the climate control system. Nothing can strangle a presentation more effectively than insidious changes in room temperature—it's axiomatic that people in physical discomfort cannot focus as well as they should on what you have to say. I also always arrange to have a six-foot-long table at the head of the room or on stage, where I can spread my notes out the way I like them for easy reference. You must remember that people who have asked you to make a presentation usually want you to succeed. It is in their interest to give you the tools you need to perform your best, so you shouldn't be shy about asking for them.

If there is an opportunity to do so, I will go to the location of my presentation hours or even days before to study the layout of the room. (If that's not possible, see if someone can send you a picture of it.) Where will I stand? Can everyone in the audience see me from there and can I see them? Is there the potential for distracting ambient noise, such as a busy hallway or neighboring room or a loud air handler? How is the lighting? What kind of equipment will I have to work with and does it suit my purposes? Is there an odor in the room that may distract people? How comfortable are the chairs?

A short time before the presentation, my crew and I check the air situation and test the equipment. How many times have you attended a presentation that includes a slide show that begins with technical problems? If lightning strikes or a bulb blows up halfway into your presentation, maybe your audience can accept the interruption—so long as you're ready with a fix. But to have a problem with the equipment from the get-go is inexcusable because it is entirely avoidable. And just because the equipment worked last week doesn't mean it will do so today. That's why we always test the day of the scheduled start—our "testing" including checking to make sure there are materials for the whiteboard, flip charts, etc. Then I do one other thing that is essential for anyone who may initially feel intimidated by the setting of their presentation: *I take owner-*

ship of my surroundings. Most people wouldn't spend two minutes at their office desk if the phone wasn't exactly where they like it and the files weren't just so, yet they walk to the head of the room to make a presentation and they're afraid to touch anything. Even if it doesn't require it, I will adjust a tethered microphone, move a chair or two around, position the table just as I prefer it, and so on. Why shouldn't you have things as you want them—you're the one who has to deliver! But besides that, this is a great psychological technique for fooling yourself into feeling more comfortable. Now that you have taken control of your surroundings, it's a smaller step to take control of events in the room.

In less formal situations, of course, you can often control your presentation environment even more. Years ago a friend of Joel's called him in desperation. His girlfriend had dumped him weeks before, and he had just managed to convince her to join him on a dinner date, where he hoped to woo her back. Having completely exhausted himself in the effort to get her to see him again, however, he was at a loss for what to do next. Joel's advice was to take her for a candlelit dinner at the most romantic restaurant in New York, which in his opinion was One if by Land, Two if by Sea in Greenwich Village. Joel told his friend he must schedule the date after sunset and ask for a table by the window, which looked out on a romantically lit garden. His friend took his advice a step further: He told the maître d' the purpose of his dinner and enlisted his help, leading to even more impeccable service than he might already have expected. Having left little to chance, he made his presentation in this irresistible setting—and it worked. She agreed to resume their relationship that very evening.

What D'ya Know?

Joel's friend wanted to make his presentation in a perfect environment that night. Ms. Davis's assistant had told Kim that the lady was a perfectionist. So, in a sense, must be the Master Presenter. One of the practices we talk about at Tony Jeary High Performance Resources is approaching your presentation with a mind toward making it "bulletproof." The bulletproof presentation may not be perfect, but it should be unassailable by the forces of serendipity. As discussed above, we begin by overcoming our fear of the material and reviewing the outcomes we desire from this particular presentation. Next, using Political Mapping, we overcome our uncertainty with regard to the audience: Are we presenting the appropriate material for this individual or group? We reinforce this analysis by reviewing our 3-D Outline and test our confidence by asking ourselves a series of questions. These so-called **Reporter's Questions** will help us become satisfied that we have minimized the risk of failure and maximized our opportunity for success. Reporters are trained to cut to the heart of a matter by asking very simple questions and drilling down: who, what, when, where, why—over and over again. By emulating this technique we can put ourselves in the hot seat before we step in front of an audience. In other words, we can test our preparation intellectually while we're still in a position to plan out adjustments.

A chart of typical Reporter's Questions for a presentation might look like this:

Reporter's Question	Typical Presentation Plan Questions
Who?	Who am I trying to reach with my presentation? Who has been asked to attend?
What?	What am I trying to accomplish—both with this presentation and after this presentation? (What is my desired outcome?) What will success look like? What can go wrong that would ruin my day? What prework or prereading has been assigned (or should I assign) to participants? What could someone say that would trigger positive outcomes? What natural support do I have? What might someone say that would undermine progress? What known roadblocks do I need to overcome? What questions will be asked? What facts and data do I need to have on hand?
When?	When is the presentation? Is this the best time? (What is going on immediately before and after my presentation that could influence my key participants?)
Why?	Why would *each* participant want to support what I'm trying to accomplish? Why would specific participants want to derail my plan?

How?	How can I emphasize the positives? How, and in what order, should I present the plan or proposal? How can I demonstrate that all contingencies have been provided for?
How Much?	How much time do I have for the presentation? How much time do I have to prepare for the presentation? Do I have a budget?
Where?	Where is my presentation? Does the room layout support the degree and type of interaction needed? Does it make the participants comfortable? Does the room have the right equipment (A/V, flip charts, etc.)?

Follow-Up	Many of the above can be answered positively or negatively. For those that don't come out strongly positive, ask other "follow-up" questions such as the following:
	    If not, why not?
	    If not here, then where?
	    If not now, then when?
	    If not these people, then who?
	    If not this much, how much can I afford?

The gist of this exercise is that it forces you to review your preparation. Having thoroughly convinced yourself that you are ready to go, you will approach the presentation with infinitely more confidence than you otherwise might. If my friend had gone to these lengths for her meeting with the governor, I feel strongly that she would not have fallen back on lame comments about the food. Rather, she would have met the situation with enough self-possession to focus on the messages she really wanted to communicate to the leader of her state.

But even people who undergo this level of preparation can see less than stellar results if they succumb to performance anxiety. You can be confident that you are saying the right thing to the right audience in the right environment and still fear that you will trip on the way to the stage or flub your lines. Even with proper preparation my friend might yet have feared spilling her drink on the governor's jacket or not putting her words together articulately when the moment of truth arose.

To overcome this fundamental fear that we will fail to perform, Master Presenters take their level of preparation one step further by putting themselves through rehearsals. *Practice your presentation at every opportunity:* at home, in your car, or while you're engaged in any rote activity that doesn't require 100 percent mindshare. The more you rehearse, the closer you come to preempting the biggest anxiety question: Am I going to forget what to say? You may also ask a friend or colleague or family member to act as the audience. They can help you practice for the question and answer session that is often a part of so many formal presentations these days. Having a mock audience may further enable you to see how competent you already are to deliver the presentation. My friend Gary Revson observes that some especially talented people move so quickly from conscious incompetence to unconscious competence that they don't realize how capable they already have become. *Parrying with a mock audience may help you appreciate how advanced your skill level is and instill further self-confidence.*

One final way to conquer performance anxiety is to *give yourself support that you can carry into your presentation,* such as preprinted handouts, brochures, or slides on a laptop. These "positive crutches" need not be slick or technically sophisticated, though. Before an important phone presentation, for example, they can just be scribbled notes to yourself on a piece of paper. In one-on-one presentations, I'll often use a legal pad as a kind of miniature flip chart. Writing the points I want to make on the "flip chart" ahead of time frees me up so I don't have to have anxiety about whether I'll remember all I want to share. But, of course, the mere knowledge that I have the chart prepared usually gives me enough confidence to avoid tripping up.

If you have to make a team presentation, one of the ways to take the "unknown" of your partner's performance to a "known" for you is by instilling confidence in that other person. How are you going to do it? Of course, by turning his or her personal "unknowns" into "knowns." A few years ago I hosted a business conference with former senator Bob Dole. Before we made our team presentation to a roomful of 1,000 people in an auditorium in Dallas, I asked Senator Dole to do a walk-through, where I explained where we would stand, what we would say, and when we would say it. This gave us both more confidence in each other, and we nailed the presentation even though we had not seen each other for two years. Even the pros should prep.

All the steps we reviewed in this chapter may seem like a lot to do. As with many of the practices covered in this book, you must make qualitative decisions about whether these steps are worth your time. A starting point would be to examine the importance of your next presentation in the context of your Presentation Universe. How important is your next presentation to your personal goals? The answer to that question may help you gauge the level of preparation required. Then ask yourself what kind of nervousness is your worst enemy. Are you more worried about whether you know your stuff or about the unfamiliarity of the setting? Does the audience spook you or do you suffer from fear of making a misstep? Once you've identified and addressed this vulnerability, take the pertinent "unknowns" of that aspect of your presentation and work toward turning them into "knowns." Continue to do that in order of your own priorities. I guarantee you will feel more confident in your presentations before you know it!

✓
Very Important Points

- Nervousness with regard to public speaking derives from what Carl Jung concluded was the hard-wired mother of all fears: fear of the unknown.

- By reducing that surprise element we can have a significant impact on the smoothness of our delivery.

- By turning unknown quantities into known quantities, we can overcome the anxieties and uncertainties that undermine any presentation.

- The effectiveness of any presentation depends greatly upon our confidence in the quality and appropriateness of that presentation's content.

- Once we can replace what we *imagine* the presentation environment is going to be with what we now see it *will* be, much of our stress subsides.

- Know the what-ifs.

- Take ownership of your surroundings.

- Practice your presentation at every opportunity.

- Parrying with a mock audience may help you appreciate how advanced your skill level is and instill further self-confidence.

- Give yourself support that you can carry into your presentation.

- If you have to make a team presentation, one of the ways to take the "unknown" of your partner's performance to a "known" for you is by instilling confidence in that other person.

Chapter 8

Essential #4: Arm Yourself

*Successful Presenters Do Research to Load
and Organize Their Presentation Arsenals*

Some years ago, Jack Welch entered his Stamford, Connecticut, office early one morning to find a message that a business emergency had arisen at General Electric's jet engine division in Ohio. One advantage of running the biggest conglomerate in America is that you don't have to fly commercial: Welch hopped on the corporate jet and within two hours was addressing the troops in Cincinnati. What material do you suppose Mr. Welch used to get their attention? Year-over-year sales comparisons? The concerns of the division head? Gross profit statistics? Nope. He opened his presentation with . . . a story about his grandmother.

Welch made so many presentations a day during his tenure at GE that he often used to say that his main job was really to be a teacher. But while the man once known as the nation's greatest manager could certainly talk for hours about notions like Just-in-Time Inventory or Six Sigma, he often peppered his presentations with personal stories and sports metaphors. And, as Mr. Welch's visit to Cincinnati reveals, he always had a potent anecdote or two at his fingertips.

If life is a series of presentations, you could spend your life preparing each presentation in sequence—but then you wouldn't *have* a life. Nor would you be ready for the impromptu presentations that we are frequently called upon to make. Better to be prepared for any contingency by constantly keeping an eye out for stand-alone concepts, stories, or quotations that might bring value to given situations or audiences. That's exactly what Master Presenters like Jack Welch and my friend Zig Ziglar do. Years ago I got to know Zig and his son-in-law, Jim Norman, who then ran his entire organization. Jim observed that Zig carries in his head what he called a "mental jukebox" of about 1,500 stories that he can access at a moment's notice, the way a jukebox pulls a prerecorded song out of a slot at the press of a button. Undoubtedly this impressive reserve of material that is always nearly at the tip of his tongue has helped him become one of the most successful presenters of all time. And, though Zig Ziglar is a professional speaker of supreme accomplishment, there is a lesson for all of us in his use of the mental jukebox. When I train people on how to improve their presentations, I apply Zig's mental jukebox more broadly to include all the ways we can arm ourselves ahead of time for the presentations in our lives. I call this battery of weapons the **Presentation Arsenal,** and *it includes not just quotes, stories, and statistics, but printed and other visual material, the way you dress, electronic files you keep, and anything of substance that can help you make future presentations more colorful and effective.*

Where does one find this material? Anywhere. One of my coauthors, Joel, is involved in land preservation issues near his home and sometimes has to speak on the subject at town meetings. While reading a magazine one day, he came across a quote on political activism from the playwright Tony Kushner and put it into his Presentation Arsenal. After trotting it out during a recent presentation, the secretary to the organization at which he spoke asked for a copy of the quote for herself. So now it is in *her* Presentation Arsenal, as well. As Milton Berle used to say, "I know a good joke when I steal one—I mean, hear one."

Those aspiring to become Master Presenters must not underestimate the importance of building and organizing their Presentation Arsenals, and if you don't have one, you had better start collecting material now. The good news is that you have probably already begun to build a **Mental Arsenal** simply by recalling interesting stories, facts, and figures that you've picked up over the years. Reflecting on this ongoing process ought to affirm that this is not something you do once and then refer to forever. Rather, *building one's Presentation Arsenal ought to be a habit of mind.* That way you will keep your stories fresh and always have increasing troves of material on which to draw. But you won't do this randomly.

The information you harvest will be those anecdotes and data points that are useful within the context of your Presentation Universe.

Imagine an armory loaded with weapons, perhaps one like the famous Seventh Regiment Armory on Park Avenue in the middle of Manhattan. The Park Avenue armory is known to most New Yorkers as a venue for large annual antique shows and other public events, and it has become so commonly put to this use that most New Yorkers were startled after September 11, 2001, when the big brick building suddenly was swarming with National Guard troops.

Fortunately, most of the time—even for years at a time—the majority of weapons in armories throughout America go untouched by human hands. An armory is essentially a stockpile, after all. It's meant to be there for you when you need it because when the moment of crisis arises you may not have the time to build or collect those weapons on the spot. But when you do need them, you must immediately know both *where* they are (which requires organization) and *how* to use them (which requires training). So it is with *your Presentation Arsenal, which generally contains four kinds of ammunition: Mental, Hard Copy, Electronic, and, for lack of a better word, Material.*

The **Mental Arsenal** is most familiar to all of us because, obviously, it consists of the things we carry around in our own heads. If you're in the middle of an impromptu presentation, tapping your Mental Arsenal is a way to freshen up your mind and change the pace for your audience. The content of your Mental Arsenal may include instructive or entertaining stories, insightful anecdotes, good ways to do things, interesting statistics, and other pieces of information that you can apply to a variety of subjects. Though most of us have Mental Arsenals, too few seek to apply them proactively toward their quest for presentation excellence. You should always be on the lookout for stories or bits of information that pertain to subjects within your Presentation Universe. When you hear a good story or learn an interesting fact for the first time, try to file it away in your mind within the context of a subject that you are often called upon to present about. Periodically re-file these weapons by creating or reemphasizing associations in your head whenever you recall them. By doing this regularly, you may find that they free-associate into your presentations at the most opportune moments.

We can't retain everything in our brains, of course. Some things are too complicated. And sometimes we just don't have the time to commit things to memory. Often, too, we're not sure how something applies to us, though we know we find it intriguing and might have an opportunity to use it one day. These are a few of the reasons why we build a **Hard Copy Arsenal.**

How many times have you read an interesting article in a magazine and thought there was something special in it that you wished you had time to commit to memory or to share with another person? Most people have had this experience while flipping through printed material—books, magazines, brochures, training manuals, what have you. And most people do nothing more than turn the page and move on. We get lazy. We procrastinate. We tell ourselves we'll tear it out later or tomorrow or we'll ask our assistant to do it—whatever. Then we forget about it. As a result, in all likelihood, we never have the opportunity to use that information in our presentations because we never took the trouble to capture it. The Master Presenter doesn't make this mistake. She sees every interesting tidbit as potential fodder for a future presentation—even if she does not yet know what those presentations will be. She clips the articles and files them according to a system that makes her comfortable. Personally, I go to the extent of keeping binders of printed material for future use. Others choose to employ different types of filing systems. It doesn't matter whether you use an off-the-shelf organizer or a system you've designed yourself. You have to organize in a way that fits your personal style, routine, and the way you live. The simplest thing is to write the relevant theme or subject across the top of the clipping and file it accordingly. When you have a presentation coming up, seek out those clips based upon the content of your talk or meeting.

As you might expect, the **Electronic Arsenal** is analogous to the Hard Copy one: It is a collection of virtual weapons. As with magazines and other printed matter, too frequently we allow relevant electronic information to melt away by skipping off interesting web pages without recalling the address, by deleting e-mails too quickly, or by failing to file things in our computers in a way that allows us to easily reach them again. There was a time when hard disk space was expensive and floppy disks were fragile and limited in volume. But today we have burnable CDs and inexpensive hard drives that hold enormous amounts of information. Sometimes, people treat this capacity cavalierly by doing things like never deleting e-mail messages from their in-box, other than spam. On the contrary, I believe the e-mail in-box should be like the mailbox in front of your house.* Even if you had the capacity to store your mail by the curb, it would soon become an unwieldy pile, nearly impossible to find the gem buried in all the dross. So, generally speaking, a person sorts the mail on his desk by throwing away the junk and putting the rest where he can find it according to his own way of dealing with the world. Incoming e-mails should get the same treatment: Read 'em, zap 'em, or file 'em. The last part pertains to your Electronic Arsenal. Take advantage of all that cheap disk space the right way: by *creating files based upon the subject matters in your Presentation Universe and directing e-mails containing relevant information into their respective places.* In just a few clicks a day you will have created one foundation for a robust Electronic Arsenal. Then, when the time comes, you not only can browse through the appropriate file, you can search for pertinent words or names to quickly locate otherwise buried material for your next presentation. Similarly, you should organize your old electronic notes, 3-D Outlines, slide decks, and other documents with the presumption that you may one day need them again. (You can do this most easily by using one of the products my company produces, the *Mr. Presentation Wizard*.) And you can take your preparedness a step further by forwarding particularly juicy stories and visuals to your PDA, laptop, or cell phone for easy impromptu recall.

A final set of weapons fits into your **Material Arsenal,** which I use as a catchall for the physical elements of a presentation that people too frequently overlook. If you think of your clothing as a part of your Material Arsenal, you won't be wringing your hands hours before an important presentation wondering what to wear. Rather, you will have thought through and loaded your Arsenal ahead of time with the appropriate outfit for the occasion. Other aspects of your Material Arsenal may include props or tools you need to maximize use of equipment. I carry extra whiteboard markers in my briefcase, for example, in case I'm in a room with a whiteboard and feel that using it can enhance my impact. Never take for granted that this material will be available. That's like rolling the dice on your presentation.

---

*For a more in-depth treatment of my philosophy on e-mail management go to http://www.tonyjeary.com/emails for a free copy of my e-booklet *TOO Many E-mails*.

These four Arsenals—Mental, Hard Copy, Electronic, and Material—can be brought to bear in ways that at first might not be obvious to you. Benefits of having a good Arsenal include its impact on your confidence, the smoothness of your delivery, and the overall professionalism of your presentation. Well-prepared Presentation Arsenals will also enhance your ability to break down barriers between you and your audience, leading to quicker buy-in to your message; will improve your preparation-time efficiency; and, if shared in a company setting, will yield economic benefits to the entire organization. We'll look at all of these possibilities in the rest of this chapter.

Be Quick Without Hurrying

Think about the life of a person who works in sales. Many salespeople have a scant few minutes to describe each of the products in their lineup and attempt to generate an order. Or imagine that you are Under-secretary of Education and may have half an hour per month to brief the president on all the current issues in your department. In some respects, the president of the United States, the prospective customer sitting before the salesman, and most adults in *your* audience, whatever the subject, have something important in common: They are all being called upon daily to process a great deal of information, and to do it very quickly. As members of the audience, we may all feel at times like the emperor of Egypt in those old movies, with a line out the door of people who all want to step up and receive our attention. The difference is that in modern society so many more things than ever before are competing for our attention and throwing information at us, from friends on the phone to ads on the radio, that we often don't even know where to turn. In self-defense our audience must tune some of it out, of course, but it's your job as a presenter to be the one whose message gets tuned in.

What will get the attention of our audience? A great story? An incisive statistic? A cut to the bottom line? As we've learned in earlier chapters, the impact of your strategy will depend not upon some cookie-cutter formula but largely upon the personality and attitude of your audience. What's for certain is that presenting a series of products or ideas in the form of a laundry list will not get us to our desired objectives.

Think of your presentation as a feature movie. The stuff you *have* to say is the script, largely arrived at through your 3-D Outline process. The tone of your voice, which you've adjusted to the situation, is the sound. The venue of your presentation provides the scenery. All the rest, I might argue, involves the weapons in your Presentation Arsenal. The visuals and music are elements drawn from your Electronic and Hard Copy Arsenals. The costumes and props come from your Material Arsenal. What about the acting? In a manner of speaking, since the script of your presentation is unlikely to have been written word for word, the acting is an ad lib that draws from the most important reservoir of all: your Mental Arsenal. As always, this element must never be phony or manipulative and must always come from a position of sincerity and genuineness. What weapons will you choose to complete the scene?

The incompetent may not know because she may not have full command of her Presentation Arsenal. She will be like the private who has never before set foot in the armory and has just been informed that the barbarians are at the gate. This person will run higgledy-piggledy from one room of the armory to the next, hoping to trip over the right ammunition. She will be scurrying about, making a big show of respecting the time limitations, but operating inefficiently in reality. *The masterful presenter, on the other hand, is quick without hurrying because she knows what is stored in her Presentation Arsenal and knows where to find it.*

So, if he, too, is a Master Presenter, the salesman who needs to impress the benefits of his product upon a customer in half a minute need not panic. Having already determined the inclinations of his audience and written the script, he reaches into his Presentation Arsenal and extracts a weapon that will make an impression in the allotted time. Maybe it's a story he read in this book that inspired him greatly. Maybe it's a statistic he heard years ago that suddenly has relevance to what he needs to accomplish now. Whatever he conjures, if he has command of his Presentation Arsenal this morsel will be relevant and polished. It will move his presentation along in a way that breaks up monotony and reflects well upon his own professionalism. It will simply make his presentation better and more natural, because it will be *interesting.* How do I know it will be interesting? Because there would be no point otherwise. The smart presenter will have loaded his Arsenal only with interesting material; otherwise he'd be firing blanks!

Let's take a more concrete example. I suggest that everyone carry a surprising prop or two in their bag or briefcase, something they can whip out at any time to enhance their presentation. Inexpensive children's toys (such as a LEGO, a toy tank, or a toy doll) or novelty items (such as a Chinese puzzle or a snow globe) will often do the trick—anything that may benefit the way your presentation is received. Using such props can introduce an entertainment factor to your presentation and take some of the pressure off you. Like many elements of your Arsenal, the more you use props the more they build your confidence and smoothness because you already have a good sense of how they will be received.

There's a further benefit that can accrue from the use of props or of visually oriented Arsenal items: They help break down barriers. There is almost always some kind of psychological barrier between you and your audience. Sometimes it's a barrier that was erected by you, as when you decide to present from up on a stage. Sometimes it's a barrier that was erected by your audience, such as a desk that that person is sitting behind or a counter he or she is standing behind. At other times, it may be something as fundamental as a significant age difference between you and your audience. Let's see how a prop or visual Arsenal element might overcome these three situations.

If you are making a presentation to a large group, you might have no choice but to present from a stagelike setting, which immediately sends the message of *Us* v. *Them*. I have to do this a great deal, and I often break down this barrier with the pad of newly printed dollar bills that I told you about earlier. I know the dollar bills are always good for a laugh, so using them helps my confidence level, but they also serve another purpose. They give me a chance to step down into the audience and make physical contact by peeling off a few bills and passing them out as "rewards" for an interesting contribution to the presentation. That increases the audience's comfort level and makes them more receptive to my message.

In the second scenario, you may have to make a presentation to your boss while she sits behind a desk or across a table. Similarly, if you are having a problem in a retail store the manager or cashier may be standing behind a counter. I have an Arsenal of funny videos that I've transferred to CDs. If I have to present to someone who is sitting across a table, I might load an appropriate video into my laptop and ask permission to come around to their side so that we can view it together. Now, by employing this element of my Electronic Arsenal, I have managed to connect with my audience at a human level that goes well beyond the status issues that may have formed a barrier between us.

It may be fairly obvious how the third example of breaking down age barriers would work. Certainly if I have to present to a five year old, a toy or cartoon clip would help me get through. But what's more interesting to note is the effect of these same props or visuals when used between adults. A toy or a funny audio might also help me break down the barrier between myself and an audience composed of ninety year olds, because we can all relate to the lowest common denominator. Toys conjure fond memories for all of us, putting us in a better frame of mind to receive almost any message. Then, too, we were all kids once, so the use of toys can remind our audience that we're not that different from them—and if we're *like* them, they're more likely to *like* us. The same logic applies to any prop that taps into our common humanity.

One further barrier worth noting is the one that may exist *among* members of your audience. We'll talk about all the ways to attack those barriers in Chapter 9. For now, be aware that a brief game passed from hand to hand can help make all your audience members more comfortable with those around them and thus more receptive to your message.

The Color of Funny

Gray is sad. Envy is green. Purity is white. What color is funny? Try telling a little kid that an orangutan is blue and he will probably laugh at you. Blue orangutans are funny. Show her the red hair and nose of a circus clown and she'll laugh with you. Redheaded clowns are funny. Watch the tape of Sam Walton dancing a jig in a tan hula skirt on the floor of the New York Stock Exchange when his company went public. Tan hula skirts on middle-aged men in motion on the floor of the exchange are funny.

The point is that we don't associate any single color with funny. It's all about the context. So, too, with the elements of your Presentation Arsenal. A field biologist for The Nature Conservancy once showed up to a presentation wearing a suit and tie when everyone in the audience was dressed casually. If you know anything about field biologists, then you know they spend a lot of time crouched in forests or up to their knees in mud. On the job they wear jeans or chinos or shorts a lot. So the field biologist making this presentation in the seminar room of a prep school found himself in the unusual position of being overdressed. He looked down at his tie and looked up at the audience and returned his gaze to his tie and lifted his eyes again to his audience and said, "Those of you who know me may be a little surprised to learn something my mother has always been proud of: I clean up well." Everyone in his audience laughed. In the context of his presentation, a plain suit and tie were funny.

I'm not a wardrobe expert, but I do encourage my clients to appreciate that the clothes in your closet are part of your Presentation Arsenal. Generally speaking, people who are supposed to know these things have argued that a presenter should dress one notch above the expected level of his audience. So, these folks would say, if you think your audience will be wearing sport jackets, you ought to wear a suit. Perhaps they're correct, but the passage of time may be changing this assumption. These days, I tend to believe that in most circumstances you should consider dressing similarly to your audience in order to invoke the Liking principle, which is an instant rapport builder. The more important point, however, is to remember that *the clothes you wear can help communicate your message.* Image does count. If you're a surgeon who needs to impress upon his audience the urgency of a matter, you should consider keeping your scrubs on. If you're a businessperson who wants to shake your employees out of their complacency, consider wearing something that will startle them. If, on the other hand, you need to break up with your boyfriend or girlfriend, don't wear something sexy if you want to present a consistent message. All these considerations fall within the context of your Material Arsenal.

One of my neighbors, call him Randy, is a very successful commercial real estate developer and builder. Recently, an old friend from his college days phoned Randy out of the blue looking for some business support. Though they had not seen each other in twenty years, he had read about Randy's success and decided to solicit his help in raising money for a new venture. Randy decided to invite his friend to make a presentation for funds in front of a number of potential investors whom Randy would gather at his house. Though he hadn't seen this man for decades, he felt comfortable taking this step because he knew his old friend had become a successful heart surgeon and had always been an honest man. But once

Randy had everyone in one room, his part was done. The heart surgeon's presentation would be crucial if he wanted to raise the money for himself.

The appointed hour came and Randy's friends and associates gathered in anticipation of the surgeon's investment presentation. When the doctor walked through the door, however, he was dressed in a slovenly manner, with his shirt coming untucked and his pants wrinkled. Randy couldn't believe his eyes.

A couple weeks later Randy's friend called to ask whether anyone was interested in investing in his project. Randy told him they were not and offered a little friendly advice. "I told these people you were a successful heart surgeon, which I know you to be," said Randy. "But the guy who showed up at my house didn't look the part. I'm going to be honest because we're old friends. You might have demonstrated how to spin hay into gold and those people would not have invested in you. Next time you're presenting to a roomful of strangers to ask for their money, you had better not just be able to *say* that you're a successful heart surgeon— you had better *dress like* a successful heart surgeon." An opportunity missed because a very smart person failed to consider this element of his Material Arsenal.

Branding Is a Presentation

There are other natural opportunities to leverage your Arsenal into your overall presentation strategy. For example, if you're an entrepreneur or business owner your business card is part of your Hard Copy Arsenal. My friend Peter Montoya, coauthor of *The Brand Called You*, says he is "constantly astounded how people do not have business cards on their person in professional settings. My advice: Never leave home without a business card." If your ammunition is sitting in your desk drawer and you're on the road, what good is it?

When you do remember to employ your card during *branding presentation* opportunities, keep in mind that that card is a reflection of you. So many times people put too little thought into their business card's design and use. Many people have a Plain Jane business card that doesn't communicate anything beyond their phone number and address. As Peter observes, others too often forget to keep their cards on their person. I'm always ready for my next impromptu presentation with business cards in my pocket, in my wallet, in my car, and in my briefcase. I've even snuck cards into my wife's pocketbooks and glove compartment. If I run out at a crucial moment I know I can turn to her.

One of the biggest lost presentation opportunities comes when a person's business cards do not have details of what they're offering. Most glaringly, people generally leave the back of their cards blank. But I view my business card as an essential element in my Hard Copy Arsenal. In one of my training manuals called *Presenting Your Business Visually* I teach people that the title of your company should say what you do, and a second piece of the puzzle is a by-line. So my company is not Tony Jeary Enterprises, which would mean nothing to anybody who doesn't already know me. Rather, we call ourselves Tony Jeary High Performance Resources. This captures the idea that I'm the driving force behind the company while also communicating that we improve people's performance and that we are here as a resource for them. And the by-line on my business cards is "The presentation strategy experts," which communicates specifically what makes us unique.

I also believe that if you can use texture and graphics on your card people will respond to it better. First of all, colors and graphics, in and of themselves, can be very communicative. If you're running a conservative children's clothing store, your card should show traditional baby colors. But if you're the president of a lollipop factory I'd expect bright colors, maybe even polka dots. A former client of both Kim's and Joel's, Howard Schultz, who turned Starbucks into one of the most recognizable brands in the world, once commissioned a group of artists to create entire books filled just with shapes and symbols that would be compatible with the company's image. All their packaging and advertising would then incorporate that look and feel. Similarly, all the physical qualities of your business card should be a reflection of what you stand for. The thickness, texture, sheen, color combinations, photos, graphics—all the physical qualities of the card are ammunition that can be employed in the service of your presentation. These things also have the ability to invoke some of the elements of Neurolinguistic Programming that we discussed in Chapter 3 and will revisit in Chapter 10 when we address Anchoring.

Road warriors should carry extra fax cover sheets in their briefcases. If you have to stop at a Mail Boxes Etc. or use the business office of a hotel, what good does it do you to be plugging their businesses by faxing around one of their cover sheets? Your fax cover sheets are yet another opportunity for you to present what you're about. And all these things contribute to the professionalism of both you and your presentation.

To Be Sure, Insure

Remember that companies are people too. That's why we advise our corporate clients to create centralized Presentation Arsenals electronically. These Arsenals contain stories, facts, phrases, and images that speak to the values of the company. So if anyone needs to make a presentation on behalf of the organization, she can tap into that reservoir of information and know that all the material is congruent with the company's position. We call *the consistent filtering down of messages throughout an organization or group* **cascading messages.**

A company is a collection of like-minded individuals trying to get to a goal. Doesn't this also possibly describe your religious congregation, your nonprofit organization, or your family? A shared Presentation Arsenal may serve the same purposes for any of these groups as it does for a company like Chrysler, for whom we set up a Presentation Arsenal in a centralized database. Say your family's values prioritize hard work and study before play. Naturally there will come a time when your kids are under peer pressure to compromise these values. Such pressure might leave them speechless if they're unprepared, but if they can turn to the family repository of instructive stories and examples, they might be in a better position to present the strength of these values. They might even manage to convert their ne'er-do-well friends into studiers, too!

Think of the Presentation Arsenal as a kind of insurance policy against which you can make claims at opportune moments. In the course of our lives, things sometimes happen that knock us off our plan. The way we respond to these surprises can be a major factor in our success and happiness.

What if you're making a formal presentation that is slated to go for two hours, but someone walks into the room halfway through? If you really care about that person's takeaway, the thought that he's missed half your talk may rattle you. But if you are prepared with a handout that reviews the most important points of your presentation (part of your Hard Copy Arsenal), then you can pass it down to him and proceed with confidence. This kind of thing can also serve as a *positive crutch*. If the big boss walks into a meeting that you're conducting, having prepared yourself with the proper elements of a Hard Copy Arsenal would enable you to have something to hand to him that might both inform and impress him with your professionalism. And you can do so without losing your train of thought.

It amazes me how many otherwise competent people are not aware enough to have their Arsenal prepared for the impromptu opportunities in their lives—and many of these "impromptu" presentations are very predictable if you take the time to think about them. For example, all the head buyers at a big retailer meet weekly like clockwork with the senior executives of the company. As you might expect, big retailers have lots of buyers, so this is a rather large meeting during which much territory is covered. Any given buyer may go weeks without being called upon to make an impromptu presentation, but then suddenly the chairman wants to know why the margins are slipping in Health and Beauty Aids—and that buyer is on the spot.

A little unsettled by this kind of pressure situation, one of the buyers for this particular organization asked me to help her perform better at crunch time. I suggested she add an item to her Hard Copy Arsenal that I call a **Critical Success Factor Sheet.** On this document we built a template of the kinds of questions she may be called upon to answer at the weekly meetings and the kinds of answers that would advance both her personal goals and the strategic objectives of her division. Her assistant updates her Critical Success Factor Sheet the day before the meeting, so when the buyer goes into the weekly meeting she is eminently prepared for any "impromptu" presentation she may be called upon to make to explain her department's issues and numbers. As a result of this single element in her Hard Copy Arsenal, the buyer is more confident in this high-pressure meeting. When she's called upon she refers to the sheet, and her presentations are so focused that they enable the meeting to proceed more efficiently.

Like a good presentation itself, your Presentation Arsenal can yield surprising benefits that accrue to third parties. One of the things I like to do is carry a tiny digital camera on my belt because you never know when the opportunity will arise to add an outstanding visual to your Electronic Arsenal. A few weeks ago, my gardener asked me to take a look at something in his truck. It was a garden bench that he thought might interest me, but it didn't suit my taste. I noticed, however, that the arms were horse heads, and I thought a friend of mine who is into horses might like it. So I took a picture of the bench with my handy camera and presented it to my friend at church the next day. Sure enough, he liked it. Soon my friend had some new outdoor furniture to consider, the gardener had an opportunity to make a future sale, and I was pleased to have facilitated the whole thing with a small piece of ammunition from my Presentation Arsenal.

If you accept the premise that life is a series of presentations, then you will stay on the lookout for opportunities to present. Furthermore, you will also be more aware of the way *others* present. Kim advises her authors a few weeks before they go out on their book tours to listen to the radio and watch television to see how other people do their interviews and to assess what they, as viewers and listeners, like to hear and see. She advises them to study people's styles and to be aware of whether they like or dislike something. When they get the impulse to change stations or switch channels, Kim asks them to write down why. Kim believes that her clients can learn a lot about how to give better interviews by studying the way others do it. It's important to remember, too, that—in between the presentations that you give—opportunities may arise to gather material for future use. Seize those chances and I guarantee that your presentations will benefit from the effort.

✓
Very Important Points

- The Presentation Arsenal includes not just quotes, stories, and statistics, but printed and other visual material, the way you dress, electronic files you keep, and anything of substance that can help you make future presentations more colorful and effective.

- Building one's Presentation Arsenal ought to be a habit of mind.

- The information you harvest will be those anecdotes and data points that are useful within the context of your Presentation Universe.

- Your Presentation Arsenal generally contains four kinds of ammunition: Mental, Hard Copy, Electronic, and Material.

- Create electronic files based upon the subject matters in your Presentation Universe and direct e-mails containing relevant information into their respective places.

- The masterful presenter is quick without hurrying because she knows what is stored in her Presentation Arsenal and knows where to find it.

- The clothes you wear can help communicate your message.

CHAPTER 9

Essential #5: Build Bridges

Successful Presenters Prepare Their Audience

When I was a kid, the dad of a friend of mine bought him a tropical fish kit for Christmas. His father had really gone all out, providing everything my friend needed: a wooden stand and giant tank, chemicals, pebbles, a heater, a deluxe filter, and all the appurtenances, including a certificate for live fish from the pet store. My friend's father warned him to get the kit set up and to follow the instructions on how to condition the water before introducing the fish, but you know how kids are—they always expect that they can take a short cut. So my friend did things a little out of order. He went and bought the fish first, then set them aside while he madly raced to get the tank ready. And when he realized he was running out of time, he dumped the fish in the unprepared water and hoped for the best. I don't have to tell you what happened after that, except to say that my friend was saving his pennies for a long time before he had the dough to replace those fish.

Unless you're a little kid with no patience, you wouldn't introduce a tropical fish into a tank that wasn't ready for it. So why do so many people make presentations without laying the groundwork with their audience? Everyone wants a receptive audience, but in my experience few people take the time to prepare the audience to receive their message.

It has been said that success is the place where preparation and opportunity intersect. Having come to understand your audience with the practices we discussed in Chapter 5 and prepared your material in the ways we've highlighted in other chapters, you must now take steps to influence how your audience will receive your presentation. This begins with a renewed appreciation of the fact that these people (or this person) have minds of their own. They have come to your presentation with their own biases, opinions, and agendas, which may predispose them in favor of your message or against it. To a degree, your understanding of the particular prejudices of your audience may affect the time, place, and content of your presentation. But at some point, the show must go on. That's why *it is so essential to direct some of your effort toward creating the necessary receptivity to your message.*

While my friend was playing with his fish, I was playing a card game called bridge, which I learned when I was around nine years old. Derived from whist, which was a diversion for many of America's founding fathers, bridge is a game of endless fascination and complexity that has appealed to thoughtful people of all stripes, from regular folks all over the world to the actor Omar Sharif to businessmen Bill Gates and Warren Buffett. Even several current members of the U.S. Supreme Court play. I believe one of the reasons bridge has come to interest these people is that, unlike most card games, you are not pitted against all the other players. Instead, you are in partnership with the person across the table, opposed to the other partnership (it's always a game for exactly four players). Good bridge players never for a second forget that they are playing with a partner. They communicate to their partner, via a bidding process, what's in their hand. Then one player in the partnership that won the bidding plays both hands. It's called bridge because the key to success is how well you communicate with your partner and then how well the contract winner *bridges* the two hands of his partnership.

Any presentation is a lot like a bridge game in my view. Each party to the presentation—the presenter and her audience—arrives with the hand life has dealt her. Meanwhile, certain outside forces (your opponents in bridge—other factors in life) have the potential to disrupt your communication and stymie your success. One way to overcome these forces is by keeping in mind that you and your audience are coming to the table with different cards that reflect relative strengths, weaknesses, and inclinations. Having made this acknowledgment, the other means of insuring your audience's receptivity is by taking steps to prepare them for the presentation to come.

The possible actions to prepare your audience fall into three places in the timeline of your presentation: What you can do long before the presentation, what you can do moments before the presentation, and what you can do during the presentation. Let's look at these in sequence.

The Long View

It's easy to make the mistake of believing that the first substantive contact you have with your audience comes when you begin your presentation. In reality, though, you probably have made some kind of contact at least once before—and possibly on several occasions. First of all, if it's a meeting or a formal presentation or even a chat with a friend, you had to invite that person to the presentation. This might have happened with a formal printed invitation, an e-mail, a phone call, or just a mention in the hallway or on the street. However you got that person to your presentation, if you didn't then take the time to manage expectations, you missed an opportunity to build rapport later. By creating an early expectation on the part of your audience, you can tease people on the value your presentation will provide, making them more receptive to your message and— not coincidentally—tempting them to be more likely to attend your presentation in the first place. In essence, you are instilling in them a vision of the value and outcome of your presentation.

Once you've made the invitation, keep in mind this most important point about the preparation of your audience: *Don't think of your presentation as an isolated event.* Reach out to your audience again with a technique we call **Pre-Contact**. This approach usually involves touching base by phone, e-mail, or in person with selected individuals in your audience (if it's a large audience) or even with everyone in your audience if it will consist of a handful or fewer people. Instances of Pre-Contact outreach might involve any of the following:

- **Surveying for content.** Use formal or informal surveys to find out where members of your audience stand on issues that may arise in your presentation and on techniques that you may be inclined to use. By hinting at the kinds of things you plan to communicate later, you can preliminarily gauge reactions now. This creates multiple effects. If your ideas are well received, knowing so will give you confidence during your more formal presentation. If the surveyed person raises objections, you will have an opportunity to change your content before the presentation or at least know how to react when the objection arises again later. Furthermore, even if your audience objects to the content during surveying and you decide not to change for the formal presentation, he or she will be less shocked the second time around and therefore might be more inclined to listen on the merits. But a word of caution: If your surveying concludes that there will be major resistance to your message, you must find a way to constructively respond during your formal presentation. Don't ignore negativity. Find a way to turn it into a positive.

- **Surveying for technique.** Learn the preferences of your audience by asking ahead of time. If they want to interact with other members of the audience, for example, having them sit in the dark for an hour looking at slides wouldn't be a good idea. By finding out their likes and dislikes with regard to props, presentation tools, handouts, presentation techniques, and even venue, you can gather intelligence for adjustments you might want to make while, at the same time, managing expectations.

- **Lobbying.** If you expect your presentation to address a controversial subject or a matter of high importance to you or the group, don't leave the outcome to chance. Take steps to establish support ahead of time with specific e-mails or phone calls. This is particularly important when a few individuals have concerns that may not be of interest to the majority of participants but that would threaten to derail the session if not handled properly.

- **Aligning.** Simple "get to know you" contacts can be extremely helpful when the work of the session will involve a lot of interaction among people who haven't met or don't know one another very well. Take pains to introduce fellow participants beforehand. Make sure that they understand why each of the participants was specifically invited and appreciate common perspectives with regard to the subject of the presentation.

The best way to give your audience a stake in the outcome of your presentation is to assign what I call **Pre-Work.** As the phrase implies, however, Pre-Work asks more of your audience than any other form of preparation. As such, you must be very careful about the context in which you venture to assign it. The good news is that Pre-Work can build involvement *before* the event, allow accelerated pacing within the session, and drive higher-quality results. Pre-Work is task-related. It usually entails distributing materials ahead of time for review by participants. These materials can be as simple as background data or prior meeting notes. Yet, alternatively, the Pre-Work request can include "real" work assignments such as the following:

- Asking your audience to study a problem and prepare potential solutions.

- Asking your audience to carefully review proposed solutions to a problem (drafted by you or by others) and to identify issues that may have an effect on the plan.

- Requiring your audience to undertake an experience, such as visiting a relevant person or place before a meeting; running through "Process A" before a session so they will be ready to learn "Process B"; or developing or practicing skills that you have identified as prerequisites for work you will ask them to perform during your presentation.

- Requesting that your audience provide a list of people or processes to review during the meeting, such as a sales prospect list, a list of potential donors, a list of potential venues for a future event—whatever is relevant to the purpose of your meeting or presentation.

This list could go on and on. The important thing to remember is that Pre-Work should not be too onerous unless you are simply asking people to do things that they would already have to do anyway. Nobody wants to feel like they're doing all the work so you can stroll through your own presentation. At the same time, though, if the Pre-Work is congruent with the goals of your audience, fun for them, and relatively easy to carry out, you will have engaged your audience before even opening your mouth.

How does long-run audience preparation work in real-life situations? For example, if you are making a presentation at a business meeting, you might appeal to your colleagues' desire to belong by sending an announcement e-mail including the agenda and who is expected to attend. If a person knows that her boss's boss will be at the meeting, you can bet she'll show up and be prepared to focus. Even without that incentive, simply knowing who the other players will be can help a person understand how to prepare themselves for your meeting, which will make it flow more efficiently.

Here's another scenario in which the kind of audience preparation that I'm talking about can make a big difference. People who organize fund-raisers might mention in the invitation that there will be a charity auction after dinner. Then they'll seat you next to people you're already connected with, whom they know are likely to bid in the auction. When the auctioneer takes to the stage, you'll be primed for the auctioneer's presentation, and you might find it difficult to abstain from bidding when your neighbors' paddles go up. Masterful presenters always look for opportunities to cascade their audience preparation in this way.

The Eleventh Hour

You have already learned that one essential means of taking "unknowns" to "knowns" is to show up early to your presentation in order to scope out the scene and make final preparations. One of the steps we talked about was taking ownership of your presentation space. With the proper planning, in fact, you can go even further by, in a sense, taking ownership of your audience.

The first few minutes before your presentation afford a crucial opportunity to begin to build rapport by breaking down the invisible wall between you and your audience. Smart entertainers are always trying to break down that wall, which is why lounge singers often wander with their microphone into the audience and rock 'n roll stars sometimes dive right into the crowd. When Jay Leno was losing the late-night wars to David Letterman, he and his producers decided to do over the set. One element of their redesign was to bring some members of the audience closer to the stage so that Leno could shake their hands before beginning his monologue. Along with the other changes they made, this element added energy to the set and helped the comedian soar back into contention.

If Jay Leno, who gets paid millions of dollars, can shake hands with some of his audience, why can't you reach out and touch someone? While it should go without saying that shaking the hand of everyone in a small group is just polite, don't let the sheer numbers of a larger group intimidate you from reaching out. Mill about the audience while they're still coming in. Shake hands, hug when appropriate, put a hand on a shoulder, thank them for coming, instigate smiles. This kind of contact is easy to execute on your part, and it can make people feel special. Those who are happy and feeling good about themselves will undoubtedly be more receptive to your message.

You can take this kind of initiative a step further with a little extra planning. Especially when I'm making a presentation in a venue I'm unfamiliar with or to a type of audience I don't know well, I often invite a few of the attendees to arrive early if possible. Then I conduct a little meet and greet session where I learn a few names and do a little schmoozing. This is a great last-minute way to get a read on your audience in order to know what subtle adjustments to your presentation will help you get through to them. It will also make you less nervous—now you're presenting to people you *know*—and you can even ask them to participate later in some ways we'll address in Chapter 11. But, equally important, this is a chance to build a bridge to some audience members, to let them know that you are a real person like them. Simply having met and greeted them will likely have a positive effect on their receptivity and begin turning them into champions of your presentation (we call them **Audience Champions**). The result of this effort? When you take the stage you might just find that you have a fan base in a crowd that was completely unknown to you just minutes before.

Other kinds of introductions lend considerable weight to your efforts to prepare the audience for your presentation, as well. *A basic element of work with groups, often overlooked, is the simple matter of introducing people to one another and to the meeting leader.* In our hurry to get on with things, we sometimes forget this essential element, or we assume that everyone already knows everyone else. The "Who are these people?" problem occurs countless times every day. It's easy to fix by including a "Participant Introduction" element in every session you conduct.

A main reason people are brought together for meetings, training, and sales contacts is to *leverage human interaction* to solve problems and to gain results. Basic interaction starts with knowing the names of the people with whom you are working. Added background on other people lends deeper understanding and richness to the interaction. Introductions allow each person a chance to tell who they are and to provide some context—something that can give them credibility when the work begins. Introductions allow all participants to learn who is in the room in order to help understand the potential power of the group, as well as to know the limitations that may become apparent if key stakeholders aren't represented. The right introduction also helps eliminate the tensions that can arise when people are expending psychic energy asking themselves, "Who is that?"

Depending on the size of the group and the layout of the room, a variety of practices may be used. For really small groups (fewer than six), informal introductions as people arrive can get the job done. For slightly larger sessions where you know everyone but they don't all know one another, you can do the introductions and place emphasis on potential contributions (for example: "Sue has budget approval authority and Pete will be implementing whatever the group develops.").

For sessions with up to twenty-five participants, a quick "round robin" of self-introductions can work. As part of your agenda review, ask participants to very quickly give their names and a few key points, such as company or division name at a business presentation, or the length of time they've been interested in the subject of the meeting in a more social situation, or their role in the organization in a nonprofit or community scenario. If you have time, you can use this moment to build engagement by asking the participants to answer a fun question that can be related or unrelated to the work for the session—a favorite vacation destination, for example, best TV program over the weekend, favorite sports team, best web site for some purpose, or one or two words about expectations for the meeting. Make sure you provide the time required for this in your agenda and tell the group your time limitation for this exercise.

In still larger groups with table seating, you may prefer to use the round-robin approach at individual tables. If desired, you can have someone from each table "report out" the attendance in summary form. In much larger groups with theater seating, you can have people introduce themselves to the person on their left and right. From the front of the room, you may choose to take a few callouts to get words about expectations. Place cards (or tent cards) are a good tool for interactive sessions with people seated at tables. Name tags work well for groups of all sizes and are essential for large groups. If you're going to use place cards or name tags, remember that preprinted cards or tags are best, using large fonts for legibility. If you use do-it-yourself materials, supply appropriate markers (neither too fine nor too blunt) and provide examples printed large and bold for legibility. Put emphasis on first names, making them bigger so they can easily be seen at a distance.

Those are some guidelines for getting members of your audience to become familiar with one another, but what about you as the presenter? Even when you're presenting to an audience of one, the **Host Introduction** is an indispensable tool because often the best person to build a bridge is someone already familiar with both sides of the river. Think about what happens when you meet a total stranger for the first time. You often begin by talking about things you know you're sure to have in common. You talk about the weather. You discuss your surroundings. If you're in transit, you may talk about your destination. This feeling-out process can go on for a long time, and you might easily walk away from the conversation without realizing that you both shared an uncommon interest in progressive jazz. But rewind the tape and imagine that you and the stranger have a mutual friend in the room. If this person is thoughtful, he might say something early on like: "I'm so glad you two are finally getting a chance to meet. Did you know that Bob here is a huge fan of Wynton Marsalis?" You don't have to grope for the commonality because the person introducing you already has a handle on it.

In more formal situations, people often make the mistake of leaving the Host Introduction to chance. Often a person known to the audience (or, at least, with some kind of special credibility with the audience) is called upon to introduce your presentation. In my experience, merely competent presenters assume they have no input into the content of this introduction. Usually, they're standing off to the side, absorbed in their nerves or the final mental rehearsal of their presentation. Wrong!

The Host Introduction is an integral part of your presentation. First of all, it saves you valuable time because when following a proper Host Introduction you don't have to waste minutes explaining who you are. Second, it lends authority to what you will have to say by transferring the audience's trust in the host over to you. Having someone else note your credentials is always more credible than blowing your own horn. Third, an appropriate Host Introduction puts your upcoming presentation in context and helps establish the audience's expectations for what is about to come. Finally, a well-executed Host Introduction "warms up" the audience, helping set a mood that will make them more open to receiving your message. For all these reasons, Master Presenters never leave the Host Introduction to chance. If given the opportunity, suggest the person by whom you would like to be introduced, choosing someone who already has credibility with the audience. Then ask the Host to emphasize those things that will help break down barriers between you and the audience. This might include your prior credentials, a brief rundown of the work you did in preparation for this presentation, a "tease" about what they are about to hear, or even a relevant joke to get the audience smiling.

For large presentations the Host is also the ideal person to deal with "housekeeping" issues, such as when breaks will come, locations of fire exits, or whether to hold questions until the end. Having the Host deal with procedural things helps you and the audience focus on your own message and performance. The last words that leave the presenter's mouth should never have to relate to the choice of sandwich or the location of the restrooms!

Don't confine your thinking about the Host Introduction to formal presentations. This concept is relevant to all aspects of our lives. For example, we may want to get our children into a certain preschool with a long waiting list. Perhaps we know someone who is a good friend of the person who runs the school. We might ask for a Host Introduction by having our friend call on our behalf. Anytime we want something and need to break down a barrier to get it, whether it's renting a time-share house, getting a job interview, or having someone endorse one of our products, there is an opportunity for a Host Introduction.

The Moment of Truth

A bridge, of course, is something that connects. If we need to build a bridge to our audience, it follows that the two parties begin in a disconnected state. What does it mean for your audience to be disconnected from you? In the simplest sense, it means they are not inclined to be moved by what you have to say.

All humans with possession of their faculties are paying attention to something all the time. It may be an artificial stimulus like a radio or television. It may be a visual stimulus like something moving within their field of view. Or it could just be the thoughts in their own head. Naturally, as the presenter, you want them to focus on you and your words. But in order to make that happen, you have to overcome four **Subconscious Tensions** that inevitably exist in any presentation scenario. These tensions are like a force field that is keeping your audience from getting too close to you, the way similar magnetic poles repel each other. The Subconscious Tensions that could interfere with your attempt to establish rapport are as follows:

1. **Tension between each member of your audience and other audience members.** Depending upon the circumstances, this tension can manifest itself two ways. If audience members are sitting next to people they know but haven't seen in a while, they will tend to want to catch up on each other's lives. If, on the other hand, they are surrounded by total strangers, the natural inclination is to wonder who these people are. In either case they are not giving the presenter maximum mindshare.

2. **Tension between audience members and you, the presenter.** Nobody wants to be confronted by a negative experience, and all unknown things have the potential to disappoint us. So from the moment a person learns of your presentation—whether it's min-

utes before or months before—he or she begins to engage in self-talk. "Am I going to enjoy this experience? Is it going to be worthwhile? Can it help me get ahead? Is there a better use of my time?" These questions reside in the back of every audience member's mind, whether they are aware of them or not, and they represent a point of resistance to the presentation.

3. **Tension created by the materials you've given your audience.** Handouts are a great tool when used properly, but you must be aware that they are also a potential distraction for your audience. If they're flipping through your printed material, they can't be listening completely to you.

4. **Tension between audience members and their environment.** This tension is twofold. First, we have undoubtedly been hard-wired to be suspicious of any unfamiliar environment, and the more foreign it feels, the more we will have our hackles up. Second, there are always potential environmental distractions competing for the attention of our audience, whether it's the bird outside the window or the honking of a horn.

Audience members feel these tensions mostly because they are unsure what to expect from any given presentation. Pre-Contact conditioning, in the forms discussed earlier, provides one way to complete the picture for them. The Host Introduction and peer-to-peer introductions are additional practices that help break the force of Subconscious Tensions. As for the tension created by your handout material, we advise people not to let their handouts turn from powerful tools into equally powerful distractions. Do not overwhelm your audience with printed material. If you are using handouts, control their potential to distract by parceling them out during the course of your presentation, and never just leave the whole set within reach of your audience from the get-go; you're serving up a ten-course meal, not a buffet. Also, as we mentioned in some detail in Chapter 7, taking control of your environment is the best way to insure it will not create tension for you or your audience.

But there are more elegant connecting tools available to the presenter who is looking to increase the receptivity of his audience. One of the most important things you can do is to prove that you sincerely care about the people or person who is sitting in front of you or on the other end of the phone line. If you don't really care about them, you had better *make* yourself care or find a way to avoid the presentation, because any audience will see through insincerity in a flash, and then it'll be like you're talking to the heads on Mount Rushmore. While they may never articulate it, the whole time they will be thinking: "Why should I care about what you have to say if you don't care about me?"

You must control or manage the self-talk of your audience or you will be fighting it the whole way through your presentation. Generally speaking, it is less likely that your problem is not caring and more likely that your problem is not knowing how to *show* your concern. Inexperienced presenters—like the conscious competent overthinking how to tie his shoes—are often so busy concentrating on the substance of their presentation that they lose sight of the importance of connecting. Prove that you care, first, by making yourself accessible to your audience before, during, and after your presentation. Don't hide behind the podium or behave as if you would never deign to walk among the "cheap seats." Second, give away something of value. This could be a small promotional item, but the best giveaway is something that adds to the takeaway of your presentation, such as a short pamphlet, a book, or a wallet card. Finally, don't ever allow yourself to sound canned. Communicate early on in your presentation that you have done your homework specifically for the presentation at hand.

Most audiences spend the first three minutes of the presentation sizing up the presenter. So don't ease into your presentation. Open with impact. Demonstrate immediately that what you have to say directly relates to the concerns of your audience and benefits their world. This will negate their self-talk, alleviate tension, and make them want to listen to what you have to say. First impressions do count!

One effective technique for building bridges early on is to let your audience know that you are aware of the doubts that they are carrying inside them. Share their thoughts and express their doubts. They will appreciate your empathy and return it to you in spades.

About ten years ago, a major publishing house in New York was going through a very difficult time. The president of the company, who had been hired with great fanfare a couple of years before by the head of the conglomerate, had lost her luster. The company was hemorrhaging money and had squandered the respect it once commanded in the industry. Morale was so low that the company's employees were having trouble doing their jobs. The editors spent more time talking to one another about the next rumor than they did talking to agents about their next project. Mercifully, the ineffectual president finally got the ax, but word of her replacement only caused greater anxiety. Few of the employees knew the new president by anything other than his no-nonsense reputation. To make matters worse, he had a stern, red face that always made him look like he was on the verge of exploding at any moment.

After a few days of small closed-door meetings, the new president attended his first weekly editorial meeting knowing that everyone was on edge. Fresh rumors were flying. People wondered when he was going to bring the hammer down and whether it would fall on them. When the staff sat around the large conference table for the first time with the new president at its head, you could cut the air with a knife. But rather than berate anyone for the poor performance of the past, the new president began his presentation by saying he didn't know exactly what to expect when he arrived and relating his pleasant surprise that there were so many talented people working at the company. You could almost hear the sigh of relief across Manhattan, and the bad news that followed—there was bound to be some bad news in this situation—was all the more palatable because everyone present was basking in the glow of the compliment. With one opening observation, the feared new president had made his anxious audience receptive to his message.

So should you.

✓
Very Important Points

- It is essential to direct some of your effort toward creating the necessary receptivity to your message.

- Don't think of your presentation as an isolated event.

- A basic element of work with groups, often overlooked, is the simple matter of introducing people to one another and to the meeting leader.

- The Host Introduction is an integral part of your presentation.

- You must control or manage the self-talk of your audience or you will be fighting it the whole way through your presentation.

- Most audiences spend the first three minutes of the presentation sizing up the presenter.

CHAPTER 10

Essential #6: Feel Good, Do Well

Manage Mental States—Yours and Your Audience's

Though I've cut back on some of my travel lately, there have been times in my life when I was away from home literally more than two-thirds of the year. Since I always made an effort to get back to the proverbial ranch on weekends, which are by most definitions 28 percent of the year, that means I spent the vast majority of my work week in cars, airports, airplanes, and hotel rooms. Have you ever lived out of a suitcase like that? If you have, then you know it can make you more tired than a bear on the last day of summer. Some people stumble into meetings so low-energy that they want to cry when they're supposed to be generating smiles.

It doesn't take a PhD in presentation skills to know that *the mental state of the successful presenter absolutely must be congruent with the message being delivered.* People don't want to hear sermons from clowns at funerals, and they don't need Mr. Gloom and Doom warming up the crowd at the *Late Show with David Letterman.*

That's why almost two decades ago I began studying and pondering techniques for reaching the peak state of mind at the right time. There's a reason, I think, that we use the expression *frame of mind.* In order to take our emotional and mental attitude where we require it to go at a point in time, we need to give it a context, a set of parameters that will guide us to the spot. For example, wearing clothes that make you feel good about yourself will help you get up for a big presentation. We all choose our outfit carefully before a hot date. The need for confidence is just as important whether you're preparing for your first encounter with someone special or you're getting ready to make a presentation in front of an important client. There are reasons why feeling good about our appearance helps us perform better. One of these reasons is that the body can actually "fool" the mind into feeling more confident. When Kim is doing media training she shows her clients how the way they sit and carry themselves will actually alter the energy they feel. Posture is key to performing well. If you're slumped down in your chair while you're engaged in an interview you will look and feel tired and sluggish. You will be drained before the interview begins! But if you sit erect and imagine a string holding your head up high and if you breathe from your diaphragm instead of your throat, you will obtain energy and confidence—merely by having changed certain physical properties.

You can also create what is called an *Anchoring Stimulus* by donning cologne or perfume that gives you confidence or that brings to mind a certain positive association. Or you may choose to listen to appropriate music in preparation for a presentation—music that lends you its energy before an inspirational presentation or that mellows you for a more somber occasion.

No matter what the event or your personality type, whenever presenting before a group (or even preparing for a one-on-one presentation) you must get it into your head that *you are the one in charge*. Erin Brockovich, whose story of going from down-and-out housewife to the leader of a major environmental lawsuit against PG&E became a hit movie starring Julia Roberts, talks in her book about the moment she faced the realization that she had to take control of her own life. In *Take It From Me: Life's a Struggle But You Can Win*, she recalls her epiphany this way: "There are some things you just have to do. There is no choice, there is no decision, there is no avoidance. Life is filled with certain obligations and responsibilities, but none more basic, primal, or important than the responsibilities we have to *ourselves*. I realized that up until that day I had been continually letting myself down. I had squandered so much energy, I had looked away rather than inside, I had ignored my inner strength rather than calling upon it. I had been living my life as if I were my car, blindsided by events that hurt me rather than helped me. I may have been behind the steering wheel, but I was not in control of what I never saw coming and even if I did wouldn't know how to avoid it."

If you're going to become a Master Presenter, you must confront every opportunity with a sense of command, which will always translate into a sense of well-being. How do you achieve that state? First and foremost, by understanding what modern science has taught us: that what we do to our physical world and our physical selves can have a huge impact upon our frame of mind. And once we have learned to attain top psychological states for our presentations, we can employ the same practices in order to enhance our audience's receptivity even beyond what we achieved in the last chapter. We can also be guaranteed that our everyday interactions with people will be more productive and satisfying.

What's for Lunch?

In a wonderful short story entitled "USFS 1919: The Ranger, the Cook and a Hole in the Sky" Norman Maclean (author of *A River Runs Through It*) relates the adventures of a brash young man who is spending the summer working for the forest service in Montana. The work is physically taxing, the men are tough, and it all goes on in a remote corner of pristine western forest. Naturally, like many men his age, the narrator believes he knows a lot about the world and is tempted by the slightest provocation to set out to prove it. In that spirit, he decides to take an ill-advised solo hike through the summer heat to the nearest town. The kid is tough, but so is the terrain. He makes it into town barely able to walk a step farther, sits down in the ice cream parlor, and quickly inhales two ice-cold ice-cream sodas. Feeling rejuvenated, he then proceeds to a Chinese restaurant where he tries to impress the waitress—the first woman he has seen all summer. But suddenly, the young man is not feeling so well. When he tries to stand up to leave, he gets dizzy, passes out on the floor, and a doctor has to be called. After reviving his patient, and in front of the waitress, the doctor pronounces judgment: Those ice-cream sodas did our hero in.

Undoubtedly in this story Mr. Maclean is saying something about the almost comical arrogance of young men. But we can draw a more modest conclusion: Don't walk twenty-odd miles across the mountains in the heat, drink two ice-cream sodas, and expect to make a successful presentation to a potential love interest. You'll only embarrass yourself!

Too many of us allow our presentation performance to become slave to our physical and mental condition, when it should be the other way around. If we are going to achieve peak presentation performance, we must begin with an acknowledgment that the body and the physical world have an influence on our psychological state. This is something that was suspected as long ago as when William James wrote that "the sovereign voluntary path to cheerfulness, if our cheerfulness be lost, is to sit up cheerfully and to act and speak as if cheerfulness were already there."

The work of Dr. Andrew Weil, sports psychologist Dr. Jim Loehr, Dr. Herbert Benson, and a host of other writers and scientists has argued persuasively that we ignore the power of the mind-body connection at our peril. Dr. Robert Arnot, the chief medical correspondent for NBC News, summarizes much of the current thinking on this subject in an intriguing book called *The Biology of Success*. He observes that "Mental energy is both the currency of success and its most basic biological underpinning." His book is a primer on how to achieve the patterns of positive thought that—not coincidentally—I also advocate for maximizing your presentation performance.

Applying his observations to the presenter's art, we might summarize the relevant steps toward peak psychological readiness as follows:

1. **Act like you want to feel.** "Affect"—with the emphasis on the first syllable—is our visible mood. Dr. Arnot recaps an important study from the 1980s as follows: "Positive affect encompasses feelings related to energy; negative affect encompasses feelings relating to tension." In other words, happiness is as happiness does. If you smile, you will be happier than if you did not smile. If you are happier, you will think more clearly. If you think more clearly, you will perform better.

2. **Arrange your physical world for positive reinforcement.** We talked in Chapter 7 about the confidence-building value of taking control of your presentation space. There are other benefits to controlling your environment. "Just like the CEO in his [private] jet," writes Dr. Arnot, "you'll want to build your own phys-

ical and psychological work 'cocoon.' General Patton brought his best linen, crystal, and china to war. You'll want to create a personal space you feel confident in, then bring that confidence and sense of calm into the world." For the "work" of your presentation, too, you'll want to build your own environment.

3. **Use music to set your moods.** "Because music accesses so many different parts of the brain," Dr. Arnot observes, "its effect is profound on our emotional and physical lives and therefore on our quest for success." It follows naturally that you can use music to set the appropriate mood for your presentation.

4. **Dress the part.** We discussed in Chapter 9 how the way you dress can affect your audience's receptivity to your message. Dr. Arnot further notes that your dress is another element of your physical world that can have an impact on your mood and your self-confidence. As he puts it, "Always try to be appropriately dressed so that you're transmitting a consistent message. You don't want to look one way and speak another, or feel one way and look another."

5. **Choose appropriate foods.** It is clear today that the foods you eat can have a measurable effect on such things as mood, body rhythm, and alertness. By observing a few basic rules we can make sure that—unlike Norman Maclean's hero—our most recent meal does not frustrate our presentation ambitions.

6. **Exercise for focus.** "Exercise is the magic bullet for creating mental energy," writes Dr. Arnot. "The immediate effect of exercise is increased energy, so tactically it can be used at any point of a flagging day to get you up and going." Consider the positive effects of exercise on mood when planning your presentation day.

7. **Rely on ritual.** Much of the underlying explanation for the power of Dr. Robert Cialdini's six Weapons of Influence of Chapter 2 was the way fixed behavior patterns allow us to func-

tion more efficiently. A certain kind of fixed behavior, the ritual, can help us focus on the big picture without, as the expression goes, "getting lost in the weeds." "During high stress," Dr. Arnot writes, "rituals are like landing pads in a storm." There's a reason why successful baseball hitters always step up to the plate and perform the same motions before each pitch. As Dr. Arnot observes, "Dr. Loehr emphasizes that in every single arena of high stress, whether in sports, the military, medicine, or business, the more demanding the performance, the more people rely on ritual to do the job." Using your own pre-presentation rituals will similarly help you focus on the unique parts of your presentation.

8. **Reduce anxiety.** When it comes to performing at one's best, we might define anxiety as misdirected, out-of-focus energy. Anxiety is energy that is absorbed into the body as tension, rather than projected out into the world. In terms of getting your message out, anxiety has the effect of static on the radio—a little bit and the message still gets through, but a lot and it drowns out what you're trying to communicate. We talked in Chapter 7 about reducing nervousness by taking "unknowns" to "knowns." But you can also reduce presentation anxiety by using meditation and prayer. As Dr. Arnot points out, these ancient approaches have recently been scientifically validated as effective in reducing stress, which often affects performance.

How might we explicitly integrate Dr. Arnot's eight steps into our quest for Presentation Mastery? (For the record, Dr. Arnot has nine steps for creating mental energy, but I think the eight that I've adapted above are most relevant to the presenter.) We begin by recognizing the potential of these steps to bring both ourselves and our audience into the proper emotional state to achieve rapport. Then let's think creatively about how we might employ these insights to the fullest advantage.

Begin by reminding yourself that genuineness is the key to effective action. As the author Mark Victor Hansen has said: "Your belief determines your action and your action determines your results, but first you have to believe." Then set about creating an affect that is congruent with the content of your presentation. If you're going to break up with your boyfriend and you want to do it sensitively, don't spend the fifteen minutes before the meeting watching *Seinfeld* and yukking it up. If you need to give a motivational talk or cheer up a friend, on the other hand, get yourself smiling at least fifteen minutes before the presentation. Watch a funny TV show, phone someone who you know is always good for a laugh, or simply try to recall something happy or funny that happened to you once. If none of these avenues is available to you, force yourself to smile. Forming the muscles of the face into a smile has been shown to release natural chemicals in your body that engender happiness. Make yourself smile while looking in the mirror. That's usually a sure way to crack oneself up.

The space around you can also have a huge influence on your mood. Don't make anything other than somber presentations in dimly lit or physically uncomfortable locations. Dr. Arnot further notes that, "Some experts believe that intellectual thought is greatly hampered when the temperature is much more than 70°F." When possible, in order to be your sharpest, present in a room that's cool (not so cold as to be a distraction, of course), well ventilated, and not too humid. Lighting is also a major factor in a person's performance, since it is the main cue to our body's circadian (that is, daily) rhythms. A dim space will tell our biological clock that the day is winding down and it's time to start shutting off the systems. A bright space, on the other hand, will keep us alert.

Two often overlooked aspects of our environment can have an enormous impact on our presenting capabilities: sound and smell. "Noise demands a series of cognitive decisions that take us away from the task at hand," writes Dr. Arnot. "There are three steps in hearing noise: detect it, identify it, and interpret it. Only then can you suppress it. Distracting sounds undermine your concentration and allow your thoughts to drift." So it follows that, if you have control over the venue of your presentation, you should locate it in a place without significant noise distractions. If you cannot pick the place, look for ways to mitigate the impact of ambient noise, such as closing windows and turning on the air conditioning, if necessary.

We should pay attention to the ability of odors to affect our mood and concentration, since they take the most direct path to the brain of all stimuli perceived by our senses. Bad odors could obviously cause inattention. But also remember that positive odors such as the smell of flowers, of your favorite perfume or cologne, or of fresh baking can help set a positive mood.

The most obvious external stimulus for mood setting is music, which besides soothing the savage beast can also pull his heart strings or get his adrenalin pumping. When it comes to unique ideas for capturing people's attention and influencing their state, one worth examining is called the **JukeBox Journey.** It was developed by Al Lucia and Donna Long, both experts in the field of learning. The idea is simple but profound: Employ music (Lucia and Long use classic rock) to create memory anchors and to inspire action. Start with any musical piece or song that can be easily remembered by a majority of the audience, and then send the associated message while the music is playing. Once the idea is demonstrated, people on the receiving end can run with it on their own, creating connections that add the aspect of participation to memory and inspiration. More than just a theory, this idea has been utilized by organizations including Southwest Airlines, McDonald's, Caterpillar, Daytona Speedway, Wal-Mart, and many others. It's a fun way to learn and to help insure the retention of that learning. By the way, there are also some benefits to the presenter, who is vitalized by the reaction of the audience.

But, of course, you can also set moods without using something as involved as the JukeBox Journey method. When my wife and I host small group meetings with fellow church parishioners in our home, we simply light candles and tune to the Soundscapes channel of our satellite television. The mellow background music puts people in a receptive frame of mind, as does the smell of candles. Once again, in order to make your mood congruent with the content of your presentation you will want to choose appropriate tunes. I use music in two ways: to help set my mood before going to my biggest presentations and—if there is an available sound system on site—to air to the entire room, which influences the audience's mood as well as my own. If you have the latter opportunity, do what I do: Bring to your presentation a few tapes, CDs, or DVDs appropriate to the mood you want to instill. When in doubt, always presume there will be an opportunity to play music before the presentation. But do not assume someone else can provide the content. That's your job, and you must assure that the music you select will have the intended impact on the audience. Choose your selections with care.

The final external mood stimulator consists of the clothes you wear. My clients often ask me what they should don for presentations. First and foremost, you should wear clothes that make you feel confident. This is a very personal thing. Some people feel more comfortable in heavier fabrics while others prefer lighter ones. Some folks require comfortable shoes and others feel better in stylish ones. You should certainly dress appropriately to your message, as we discussed in an earlier chapter, but within that context remember to wear clothing that makes you feel good about yourself. Usually, however, this should also involve dressing in a way that shows respect for your audience and for your message.

It is important to do all this while maintaining authenticity. An executive used to wearing expensive business suits most of the time might wish to dress down a bit more than usual when addressing a roomful of twenty-something computer programmers, but if he shows up looking self-conscious in a torn T-shirt and sandals, that may hurt his credibility and he won't feel comfortable. *Anything that diminishes authenticity is self-defeating.*

Sometimes you can go so far as to use your clothing as a kind of visual vocabulary. A powerful example of this, noted by my friend Orvel R. Wilson in *Guerrilla Negotiating,* is strategically choosing the moment to take off your jacket and roll up your sleeves. This sends the message that you are ready to get down to business.

You Are What You Eat

The second half of the list that I've adapted from Dr. Arnot involves what I would call internal mood stimuli: eating, exercise, ritualization, and anxiety modification. Volumes have been written about these methods of affecting our moods and maximizing our mental acuity. Generally speaking, Dr. Arnot suggests eating protein in order to improve alertness and eating high-carbohydrate foods when you need to achieve a calming effect. If this aspect of physiological preparation interests you, I would suggest that you do some independent reading and then experiment to find out what works best for your own body. The important thing is to be aware that what you eat can affect how you will perform in any situation, including during your presentation opportunities. I usually eat a high-protein breakfast and skip lunch on days when I have a big afternoon presentation that requires high levels of energy, for example. Consider what kind of presentation you're making and when, then try to eat appropriately in anticipation of that event.

Sadly, I rarely find time to undertake formal exercise, though I do walk around a great deal during business hours. I naturally happen to be a high-energy individual, so I don't feel like I need the "rush" from physical exercise to get me psyched up for a presentation. But I know many professionals who cannot function at their peak without frequent exercise. If you're one of those types, time your exertion for the days of your biggest presentations. Any amount of time that you sacrifice by this move may be more than compensated for by greater focus and a more energetic presentation. And exercise can help you work off the excess energy that sometimes manifests itself as tension.

Similarly, living a life filled with prayer has helped me eliminate unease and fear, as well as energizing me for many a presentation. As Dr. Arnot points out, it has become well accepted among scientists that prayer and meditation also help dissipate tension and anxiety.

Another, more ecumenical approach to relieving tension should be on the agenda of anyone who hopes to achieve Presentation Mastery. That is to let go of any inclination you might have to want to achieve perfection—especially on the first try. One of the maxims that I live by is **Production Before Perfection.** Perfection is almost by definition an unattainable goal, because as you get better your standards rise as well, so perfection can be touched in just a momentary way, if at all. More to the point, when people hold themselves to an extreme standard, the most likely effect is to cripple their ability to act. It won't do you any good to focus on producing a perfect presentation if you are so hampered by the anxiety of your own outsized expectations that you miss the deadline or waste time chasing diminishing returns. In most instances, too, the quest for perfection sows self-doubt (as, ultimately, would the search for anything unattainable), which makes people less productive and often miserable. *Presentation Mastery is not about being perfect. It's about achieving your objectives.* And that should be good enough for anyone—so, relax!

The final element in creating a psychological state for peak presentation execution is the introduction of ritual into your presentation preparation. I mentioned above that professional baseball players often go through the same motions every time they step into the batter's box. It's worth pursuing the sports metaphor for a moment. The interesting thing about many ball sports is that all that really matters happens within a space of a couple inches and in a fraction of a second. Think about how different each batter's stance and swing appear to the casual observer. But all that positioning and motion is intended to maximize the number of times that a thin stick (the bat) will make contact with a fast moving object about four inches wide (the ball). If this were easy to do at the major league level, a few men wouldn't get paid millions of dollars to do it. In fact, it's hard to get to that sweet spot. Besides world-class skill and athleticism, it requires blocking almost everything out of your mind other than the task at hand. How do you do it? By constructing a ritual that will carry you to your comfort zone most of the time.

"If you create too much chaos in your life," writes Dr. Arnot, "you can't concentrate on being really creative in your work. . . . Routines simplify, clarify, and create order, symmetry, and familiarity in [moments of] chaos and high stress." That's one reason I advocate consistently undertaking steps like the 3-D Outline before every significant presentation. Other aspects of your presentation routine that I encourage you to include are: always arriving early, testing your equipment (if any), doing an audience "meet and greet," and arranging your presentation space before you begin. If you do these things—and take the other steps that are featured in this book—every time you present, then they will become automatic. They will get you into a comfort zone, calming your nerves. Most important, you won't have to think about them and can then concentrate only on the variables that make every presentation different.

Remember that you and your audience share, above all, your common humanity. That means *all the techniques you use to get yourself into the proper state of mind can also be used to influence the state of mind of your audience.* During phone presentations, tools that involve visual stimulation are unavailable to you, but you can still establish a pleasant tone with some brief opening chitchat and try to end the conversation in a way that leaves your audience smiling.

When planning a presentation where you'll be physically present, take into account all the elements that might keep your audience eager and alert: lighting, air temperature, time of day, even the food you may serve. By putting yourself and your audience into the same mental state, you will have made the situation most conducive to achieving rapport—which, for a presenter, is just like hitting the ball on the sweet spot.

It's All in Your Head

Have you ever been engaged in a conversation or presentation and suddenly come down with a case of the presentation yips? In golf, the yips happen when a person misses a short putt out of nervousness—almost like their neurons misfire and they lose their smoothness for that crucial split second. The presentation equivalent comes when our mouth is moving or we're pretending to be listening, but we begin to disconnect our thoughts from the task at hand and focus instead on our own self-consciousness—prompting self-talk like *how do I look, what does he think of me, what will I say next?* Everybody does this at one time or another, and it's a symptom of our failure to live in the moment. It's important to be conscious of what one is doing or saying, but when that becomes *self*-consciousness our presentation effectiveness is compromised.

The book *The Biology of Success* is not about making presentations or connecting with people per se, but Dr. Arnot does make an interesting observation that pertains directly to the presenter's art. "A great conversationalist," he writes, "is totally caught up in what you are saying, understands what it is you are communicating, feels your emotion, and then reacts in a natural and empathetic way. When someone is preparing his own rebuttal during the time you are talking, he escapes the moment and misses whatever you may be communicating."

Needless to say, in a case like this rapport has been lost, and that happens when people get caught up in worrying about results and don't allow themselves to enjoy the process. "When you relax in the moment," Dr. Arnot writes, "you are priming the most creative part of your brain, the visualization center. . . . What scientists believe happens is that when we live entirely in the moment, we free up the brain to think visually by turning off parts of the brain that drain energy away into neurotic and anxious thinking. . . . We believe we accomplish so much by constantly worrying, when in reality we are preventing ourselves from opening the most magnificent part of the brain, the center of visual thought."

One of the training manuals I coauthored for our clients is called *The*

Complete Guide to Effective Facilitation. When you think about it, "facilitation" is just a fancy word for encouraging people to focus their energies toward a positive result. One of the paradoxes I discuss in that work is that the facilitator must get people to allow themselves to be guided, yet to think for themselves at the same time. People can only do this well if they are "into" the process, not stressing over the outcome.

It is no accident that the word "present" forms the heart of the word "presentation." In order to make a presentation, you must be present in some way (even if, through various means, your presentation is viewed long after you're gone, you still had to be present at the time *you* delivered it). Most important, however, I believe *you must be mentally present to make a successful presentation.*

What might most likely prevent you from being present for your presentation? First, lack of preparation, which we work to overcome throughout this book. Second, the tyranny of perfectionism, which I addressed above. And the final thing that might prevent you from doing your best is that old bugaboo of failure: negative energy. Recall that negative affect comes from tension and produces tension. So does negative self-talk. If you've followed all the steps in this book, you must believe that your presentation will succeed and you must enter the situation anticipating that you will enjoy the process. That attitude will engender success. Your outcome will be assured.

The Future Is Now

Way back in Chapter 3 we introduced the concept of Neurolinguistic Programming, or NLP. It is difficult to talk thoroughly about directing your own mind or that of your audience to a particular state without addressing some of the techniques that NLP has to offer. As was the case when we first discussed this subject, our goal is not to use these practices for manipulation, but to heighten our awareness of how some less obvious forms of influence can come into play when we present.

My coauthor Joel heard an interesting story from a friend who always had an irrational fear of dogs. Recently she ran into her old family pediatrician, whom she hadn't seen in more than a decade. The doctor recalled the time when, as an eighteen month old, she had come into his office with a dog bite that required one or two stitches on her face, an event of which she had no memory. Lo and behold! Her fear of dogs suddenly became quite clear. It was what the psychologists call a conditioned response. Practitioners of NLP use a different term for this: **Anchoring.**

Anchoring works the same way as the conditioned response that Ivan Pavlov elicited from his famously salivating dog. We all manifest some conditioned behaviors, and sometimes we share the same exact ones. For example, our behavior when we see flashing red lights behind us in the car is conditioned. We see the lights and we get anxious. There is no clear link between flashing red lights and our anxiety level when we see them, except that life has taught all of us that flashing red lights often signify situations that produce anxiety.

Since we know that we can form anchors unconsciously, all that remains is to understand how to form, or set, an anchor at a conscious level. And since anchors can actually change the way we feel at any moment, it can be useful to set anchors to change our feelings or those of another person at any time. Imagine how much more easily you could communicate with a person if you always knew how to make that person feel wonderful. And imagine how little resistance to your ideas and suggestions people would have if you were able to make them associate your ideas with feeling great. This partly explains the success that trainers have had with the JukeBox Journey described earlier.

Here's how it works: When the person you wish to influence is at a peak emotional state that you hope to anchor, apply a unique stimulus. This might be a touch in a certain place on the arm or a particular sound or smell. Whatever it is, make sure it's unique. Don't use a common stimulus like a handshake, which will already have too many associations to be effective as an anchor. Once you have set the anchor, the next time you need to evoke that feeling in the person you will do so by repeating the stimulus.

Like all the practices we discuss in this chapter, you can use Anchoring on yourself as well as on others. When you're feeling particularly happy, for example, play an upbeat song that you recently purchased. Next time you need to feel the same way, play it for yourself again. It is likely to pick you up.

Another way to change a person's state of mind is through a process called **Chunking,** which leads your audience to a different way of thinking rather than a different mood. Did you ever hear the story of the three blind men and the elephant? One is touching the trunk, another is touching a leg, and the third is holding the tail. From this information, they draw completely different conclusions about the reality of the elephant. If your audience is focused on the tail while you're thinking of the essence of Babar, you both may be talking about an elephant, but you will be talking past one another.

We all are capable of focusing on details or abstractions, of course. Chunking helps us move from one to another in order to get ourselves and our audience onto the same wavelength. Moving from an abstract concept to some specific ways that concept can be put into action is called *Chunking Down*. Moving from the specific parts of a plan to the abstract concept of why that plan is important is called *Chunking Up*.

Imagine that you and your spouse are discussing the potential purchase of a new car. You ask, "What is the car for?" The answer might be for driving (duh!). Why drive? To get to work. And why get to work? So I can earn money to live. So you can now assert that on some higher level buying that new car allows you to earn a living. You Chunked Up from a tangible thing (a car) to an abstract concept (earning a living). The specific question to ask when Chunking Up is "For what purpose?"

Chunking Down, as you might imagine, works the same way, but in reverse. To Chunk Down from a car, we could ask ourselves, "What are some examples of cars?" Well, you have convertibles, sedans, minivans, SUVs . . . What are some examples of SUVs? Luxury SUVs like the Lincoln Navigator, say, or more entry-level ones like the Honda Element, etc. So we just Chunked Down to specific details about a car. The questions to ask when Chunking Down to details are "What are some examples of that?" or "What are some component parts of that?"

Chunking Up or Down has a variety of uses. It enables us to negotiate when we seem to be at an impasse, for example. It also allows us to understand the higher purpose behind plans or processes. And it encourages us to generate new ideas or options. Most important, if we and our audience are looking at something from different perspectives, it helps us get on the same page.

One of the advanced practices that I use most commonly to set an audience's frame of mind is a technique called **Future Pacing.** Future Pacing is a way to help others organize their responses to situations that have not yet occurred. For example, if you know your friend is going to the dentist and that she is a little worried that it is going to hurt, you might say, "You shouldn't be too concerned, since you are going to feel great when you get in the car to leave. Can you imagine how good that is going to feel, with all this behind you?" This has the effect of projecting your friend's mind past the unpleasant experience of the dentist and ahead to a happier event.

Future Pacing is a simple technique to employ. First, focus on those behaviors and feelings you want to encourage in the future. Then relate these feelings to the specific time in the future that you want your audience to feel them. When the other person physically gets to that point in the future, he or she will remember how he or she is "supposed" to feel. In effect you have conditioned that response.

One response that most of us have been conditioned to have is to relax our minds when we hear a story. So telling a story or using a metaphor is a much more subtle, elegant way to make a point than a lecture or diatribe. Especially if you are engaged with a resistant audience, you should turn to this technique. Many years ago Dale Carnegie wrote that ". . . I have come to the conclusion that there is only one way under heaven to get the best of an argument—and that is to avoid it. . . . Nine times out of ten, an argument ends with each of the contestants more firmly convinced than ever that he is absolutely right." Arguing head-on when the audience resists is like trying to push open a door that someone is leaning against. By using stories and metaphors, on the other hand, you relax the grip of your audience on the doorknob, and you may just find that you've been allowed to walk through without a fight. This occurs because the person hearing the story is now in a position to get the point without feeling threatened.

In similar fashion, we can do an end-run around our audience's defenses through an approach called **Creative Confusion.** When people's minds are in a state of confusion, they naturally search for some command or directive to break that confusion. For instance, the first person to speak up in a meeting that has gotten out of control can usually bring the discussion around to her point of view. Similarly, in the confusion of combat, soldiers and sailors usually obey directions from above without question because they are searching for some sort of order.

The master of Creative Confusion, of course, was the television character Columbo, who intentionally bumbled around until his suspect became so exasperated that he would let down his guard for the truly important question—the one pertaining to evidence of his guilt. Then, groping to break the confusion, the suspect would give himself away. Keep this in mind if you have to make a presentation that involves a lot of technical data. Knowing that your audience will be searching for order, you can follow this confusion with a directive that you want the audience to follow.

One final way to influence your audience's state of mind is by using a technique called **Looping,** which takes advantage of everyone's desire for completion. Since we typically listen to someone speak so that we may *understand*, the presenter's failure to complete a thought can be a tremendous attention grabber. In order to maintain another person's interest, the presenter starts a thought but leaves it incomplete. As he moves on to other subjects, the listener remains attentive, expecting the speaker eventually to finish his initial thought.

The best public speakers use this technique all the time. A good presenter might start a speech with, "Have you ever wondered what happened to Elvis?" Then she moves on to the body of the speech without ever answering the question. And the audience is left wondering about Elvis. The speaker doesn't give you the answer until the conclusion of the speech, of course, and in the meantime she has commanded rapt attention. In this way Looping is a very effective technique for increasing attention and keeping people focused on what you are saying.

When you combine the universally effective practices of this chapter with the understanding of your audience that you gleaned from the practices in Chapters 5 and 9, you have a most powerful set of tools for putting your audience in a receptive state. When you further apply these techniques to yourself, you will enter every presentation situation completely on your game, ready to attack the challenge before you with the confidence of knowing that your frame of mind is consistent with the message you want to convey. And you will notice, to your great delight, that the confidence you've acquired as a presenter will carry over to your relationships and interactions with anyone you encounter throughout your day.

✓
Very Important Points

- The mental state of the successful presenter absolutely must be congruent with the message being delivered.

- You are the one in charge.

- Anything that diminishes authenticity is self-defeating.

- Presentation Mastery is not about being perfect. It's about achieving your objectives.

- All the techniques you use to get yourself into the proper state of mind can also be used to influence the state of mind of your audience.

- You must be mentally present to make a successful presentation.

CHAPTER 11

Essential #7: Room to Breathe

Involve Your Audience for Maximum Buy-In

"I hit the wall."

"He walled me off."

"It's like talking to the wall."

"Throw up a firewall."

"I'm banging my head against the wall."

When it comes to protecting ourselves against the elements, walls are a great thing. They're also good for hanging pictures on, for keeping sound out, and for maintaining privacy. But, as the expressions above suggest, walls are not good for promoting communication. The old style of making presentations was to lecture at your audience. Today, we rightly criticize people who present that way for being a "wall of talk."

Whether you're presenting to your first cousin or your first customer, to a group of associates or a roomful of alumni, you will have an easier time maintaining rapport with your audience if you can make them feel vested in the presentation. We do this by creating audience involvement.

The relationship we have with our audience is like a living thing that requires nurturing, nutrition, and warmth. It may be able to survive under harsher conditions, but it will not thrive that way. At the same time, it will do us no good to smother the audience in unrequited attention, either. So, in other words, while in the past some have viewed presentations as being about what the presenter gives to the audience, the relationship really should be more about give and take. Even the well-nurtured being must eventually participate in its own growth.

Furthermore, throughout this book, where appropriate, we have addressed ways to relieve the anxiety that may arise from the presenter having to be "on stage." Even when you have taken your "unknowns" to "knowns," have prepared yourself for your particular audience, and have led yourself and them to the appropriate states for delivering and receiving your message, there is an inevitable stressor that you cannot have mitigated beforehand: the fact that by the very act of presenting you have made yourself into the center of attention.

Fortunately, there is a point where the benefit of involving your audience dovetails effectively with your natural desire to momentarily take some of the attention—therefore, the burden—off yourself as the presenter. This opportunity is called the **Breathing Space.**

The Power of Pause

The "staring contest" has to have been a fixture in every person's early life. At some point in our childhood, we all got into an eye-to-eye challenge with a friend or sibling, seeing who would blink or look away first. Who doesn't remember the uneasiness that creeps over a person in the midst of a staring contest? That feeling is so deeply ingrained in our mammalian genes that even wild animals, when they feel your eyes on them for too long, get the heebie-jeebies and may express that anxiety by becoming aggressive. Many people like to be the center of attention at one moment or another, but only the well-trained actor or the most incorrigible egomaniac wants to be the center of attention *all* the time.

Especially when we have to make a presentation in front of a group (or in front of a camera), we might find ourselves in a situation where it seems like the eyes don't ever leave us. And once that feeling insinuates itself into your neocortex, it can take a cataclysm to jar it loose. As we saw in the last chapter, it's good to be in the moment—but when the attention on us never pauses we sink too *deeply* into that moment. It's like a taut rope pulled ever tighter in a movie. The camera focuses in closer and closer until we're looking at a stretch of the rope, then at a small piece, then at the individual fibers, wondering when the next one will snap.

At my organization we regularly evaluate tapes of executives making presentations. On these tapes I have witnessed people under the gun visibly losing their train of thought. You can almost see on their faces the complete redirection of their focus to trivial flash points of self-consciousness: *What is my audience thinking? Do they notice how dry my mouth is? Did I just say something stupid? Is my leg beginning to tremble? Do they realize I have no idea where to go from here?* These people fail to appreciate one of the most useful techniques any presenter can employ: creating and leveraging Breathing Spaces.

The presenter is the center of attention, and needs to be, but that does not mean she ought to be the center of attention at every moment. Successful presenters know when and how to give themselves a break. And the most masterful among them can seamlessly change the direction of the energy in a room at any moment of their choosing by doing something other than just talking. Your relationship with the audience is like a contract where something is expected of both parties. Many people look at this relationship as if you are obliged to talk and the audience is obliged to listen, but there's something much more subtle and complex going on. The second you turn your attention to your audience—again, whether that's one person or a thousand people—you begin to build rapport. If, rather than expecting passive acceptance, you involve them in your presentation, then you will accomplish two things: You will give yourself time to regroup your thoughts at critical moments and you will enhance audience retention.

A friend of my coauthor Kim's was once trying to convince her husband that they should spend an expected windfall on an in-ground pool instead of the Jaguar he wanted to buy. She was making little progress and began to sense that her effort was fading when she remembered that her husband's friend had put in a pool and loved it. She picked up the phone while they were speaking—creating a Breathing Space that redirected attention away from her flagging argument—and called the friend. Now she had instantly changed the energy in the room and, as a bonus, inadvertently invoked the technique of **Peer-Trust Transference** that, as we addressed in Chapter 2, is also called Social Proof. The friend told her husband that he and his family soon would practically be living poolside, describing the potential scene in such detail that *he* inadvertently invoked Future Pacing, which we discussed in the last chapter. Now the husband couldn't help envisioning himself floating in the pure blue water with a planter's punch in one hand and the tanning lotion in the other. Needless to say, Kim's friend got her pool.

Another advantage to Breathing Spaces is that they give your audience an opportunity to reflect on what you've recently said, allowing it to sink in more deeply before you move on. Dr. Norman Vincent Peale once observed that the great orator William Jennings Bryan was a master of the strategic pause. After making an important point, Bryan would stop talking and slowly drain a glass of water while the audience waited. This gesture served almost like a rhetorical exclamation point during Bryan's speeches.

But a true Breathing Space is much more than a strategic pause. *It is often an opportunity to get your audience personally involved in the presentation by giving them something to do that supports your communications objectives while drawing attention away from you.* Research has shown definitively that when you engage people in doing something they retain more than when you just talk at them. So by involving your audience, you will achieve multiple purposes.

The average person speaks at approximately 200 words per minute but the average listener can effectively hear and process up to 800 words per minute. In the space between those two numbers lies a great deal of potential for your audience either to allow their minds to wander or to be engaged by you in some way beyond the spoken word. In fact, we know that some of that mind power is being devoted to subconsciously reading your body language, which is the single most well-perceived aspect of communication by any audience. If you are tense and it affects your posture, for example, the audience will read that tension and it will undercut your message. The ability to redirect their attention, of course, is a great asset in that situation, as well.

A few years ago, my friend Jeff Davidson wrote a book called *Breathing Space: Living and Working at a Comfortable Pace in a Sped-Up Society.* Jeff, who founded an organization dedicated to coping with modern time pressure that he calls the Breathing Space Institute, writes that we are "part of the most time-pressed population in history. From fast-food counter clerks, to high-powered executives, to retirees, few people today have what they consider to be breathing space—in which to reflect, unwind, truly relax, or simply *be*."

Even the person who has achieved presentation mastery may need to take a rest from time to time to regroup, collect her thoughts for the next phase of her presentation, or just diffuse the stress that inevitably comes from having to deliver a convincing message at a particular time and place. That's why, ever since learning about Jeff's work, I have been applying his ideas about Breathing Spaces to the particular circumstances of the presentation environment. All of my clients have benefited from this easily applied practice.

There are many ways to create a Breathing Space in your presentation. Some—like simply throwing a question out to your audience—may be executed in impromptu fashion, while others require more planning. A few ways to employ this concept follow:

Show a visual. When presenting to medium-sized or larger groups in appropriate settings, a video or a series of great still pictures can be a powerful Breathing Space tool. Well-selected videos can appeal to the emotions of your audience in ways that only the most moving speech or music might ever hope to do. A short clip can make your audience roar with laughter, begin to cry, or evoke any emotion in between. This helps set their mood for what's to follow and will certainly give you time to collect yourself for the next part of your presentation.

My good friend and presentation colleague Mark Magnacca recently showed me a video clip that he often uses to get his audience laughing. It's an excerpt from the old *Candid Camera* where a man gets on an elevator that is already occupied with several people. Unbeknownst to the subject, all the others are actors working for the show. When they turn in unison away from the door, he turns away from the door. When they remove their hats, he removes his hat. This video isn't just a riot that puts Mark's audience in a good mood. It's a brilliant illustration of the power of Social Proof.

Don't underestimate the strength of a visual Breathing Space creator in one-on-one presentations, either. Just by producing a picture from a magazine or portfolio and asking your audience to react to it, you can take their eyeballs off you and create a degree of engagement that you would not necessarily be able to achieve with words alone.

Use an Audience Champion. We talked in Chapter 9 about the value of an Audience Champion in helping you achieve rapport. *Having someone else speak not only helps direct attention away from you, it also changes the dynamic in the room by introducing the power of Authority or Social Proof,* depending upon who is doing the speaking. Hearing an authoritative voice in addition to (or even above) yours can reinforce your message by lending validation to your perspective. Similarly, the voice of a respected peer introduces Peer-Trust Transference and often helps relax the crowd, resulting in increased receptivity. By directing your own attention to the Audience Champion, you can stop looking inward, which should relax you, too.

Introduce a device or machine. *Sometimes getting the audience to hone in on an inanimate object is as good as having them focus on another person.* The potential objects will vary widely, of course, depending upon the context and content of your presentation. It may be a car or it may be a couch or it may be an egg beater. Who knows? The important thing is to direct your audience's attention to the device and invite their interaction with it. Besides creating a Breathing Space for you, this involves the audience in ways that can increase their buy-in to your message. For example, if you're in the store trying to convince your spouse to buy a certain brand of new computer, have the salesman conduct a hands-on demo. This will take the attention off of you while guiding your spouse a step closer to ownership of the right machine.

Conduct a game or quiz. In the seminars that I present to the public, I often include a printed twenty-part quiz that I ask the audience to fill out to the best of their abilities early on in the presentation. Then we go over it and I have them self-grade while I explain the correct answers. *Conducting a written quiz creates lots of Breathing Space and audience involvement,* and since there are a few joke answers mixed in, it also enables me to loosen the crowd up with some easy laughs. For example:

In the presentation environment, one of the best ways to reduce nervousness is

        a. Procrastination
        b. Preparation
        c. Avoidance
        d. Valium

While this more formal approach works best when presenting to groups and when planned ahead, there are plenty of opportunities to use games and quizzes in a more impromptu manner to get audience involvement and create Breathing Spaces. In social situations, for instance, you can ask a trivia question or two, which, if related to the message you want to present, forms a perfect opportunity to segue into a more in-depth discussion.

If you choose to do a quiz or game of any kind, keep in mind that the point is not to make the other person look dumb or foolish. Quite the opposite. As Dale Carnegie said, "Abilities wither under criticism. They blossom under encouragement." Your goal is to inspire people, not tear them down. People want to be winners. When you ask them to get involved they want to look smart. So don't make the questions so difficult that they will be made to feel inferior. Also, if I'm doing a written quiz for a large group, I don't start the "grading" process by asking who got 90 percent of the questions right and work down from there. If I did that, wouldn't the person who got 60 percent right feel pretty bad by the time I came to him? Instead, I begin by asking who got half the questions right and work my way *up* from there. That way everyone feels included and nobody feels stupid. I have also given the audience the sense that we have embarked, for this presentation, on a common enterprise. I have made them feel included rather than lectured to. I have given them a personal stake in the outcome of my presentation. *When possible, set your audience up to win.*

Pause to introduce an outsider. Kim's friend did this when she was pushing for the new pool. *Often when we're in the midst of a one-on-one presentation, opportunities arise to change the tenor of the presentation by bringing a third party into it.* If you're having a phone conversation, you can invite the third party in by using the three-way calling feature of your phone. If you're presenting to someone in person, call the third party into the room if they're nearby or use the speaker phone. (I've had speaker phones installed at home, in the office, and in all my cars since the technology became available, just so I could use this practice.) The third person into the conversation may be someone with a stake in what you're discussing, an outside expert with no interest beyond helping some colleagues, or a mutual friend who might be good for a few laughs. A large benefit comes from redirecting the rhythm of the presentation, which may give you a Breathing Space for more time to think, to look at your notes, or simply to come back, after the interruption, with a new tone of voice.

Call a break. During meetings or formal presentations that run for an hour or longer, sometimes you can create a Breathing Space in the most literal sense—simply call a break. For sessions that are ninety minutes or longer, I recommend that you *schedule* a break to show respect for your participants.

Create audience interaction. *Having your audience talk among themselves is an excellent way to break down peer-to-peer barriers that can be a source of tension in the room.* There are any number of ways to accomplish this, depending upon the context. Most involve asking the audience to break up into smaller groups and interact with one another either intellectually or physically. Each group may consist of two people or up to ten, depending upon the overall size of the audience. Then, rather than conducting a quiz to be answered individually, for example, you can have each group decide collectively on a response. More seriously, you may decide to have the groups discuss some business that is central to the success of the meeting, such as a particular change in the bylaws of an organization. Whatever the case, the groups then report back to you and the overall audience. In this way, first, connections are built among audience members—who are temporarily focused on one another rather than the presenter. Second, the audience then returns its focus to you with a sense of accomplishment and connection to the material that you're presenting.

Ask the audience to read something. *One easy way to get the audience eyeballs off you is to direct them to a handout.* Many presenters are in the habit of passing out reams of information at the beginning of a meeting or presentation. I strongly discourage this approach, which can lead to your audience going off into **Freelance Breathing Spaces** at the very time you want them focused on you. Much better is to hold on to your handouts and have a plan for when you will pass them out, distributing only those materials that are needed to advance your presentation at any given moment. Of course, this has the added benefit of creating multiple Breathing Spaces throughout your presentation.

Ask them to write. In addition to asking your audience to read something, you can pass around pencil and paper and get them writing. Ask questions relative to a subject you're addressing and go around the table (in a small group) or just request that people call out (in larger groups) to share their answers with the rest of the audience. The act of audience writing affords you a Breathing Space, creates further engagement with the material by giving your audience a stake (now that they've expended effort), and adds a change of pace to your presentation. For all these reasons, in very small groups or even one-on-one, if there's a whiteboard present I often ask another person to perform "scribe" duties rather than writing on my own. That way, I'm not lecturing at them, I'm not at risk of "cooking the books" by recording just what I want, and I can focus on what the audience has to say. They are participating directly in my communication to them.

Use mini-skits. Sometimes one of the best ways to break down barriers is to get a few people from the audience to come up to the "stage" and help you create a moment of dramatization. This could be done in an amusing fashion or it could be very serious, depending upon the context. In the first instance, for example, you may be asking people to do something a little silly or read from a brief script. On the other hand, positioning people at the center of attention may be a way of illustrating to a jury how certain individuals were standing when a crime was committed. In any case, while mini-skits (not to be confused with mini-skirts!) can have an impromptu element, it is very important that you launch into them only with proper preparation and consideration of the potential consequences for your presentation. During mini-skits, the attention may briefly leave you, but you must always keep the acting under control by playing director. *If mini-skits are well planned and managed, they can be a powerful way to make an emotional connection to your audience.*

When planning to employ the above practices, consider that introducing a Breathing Space too abruptly can have a jarring effect on your audience, which could cause you to lose them for a brief period. For this reason, I suggest that you start by involving the audience in simple ways, such as asking for a show of hands, and then move them into more intense activities. By the Law of Inertia, once you get them moving even a little bit in your direction it will become easier to move them toward increasingly greater involvement.

That's Entertainment

Johnny Carson observed that "People will pay more to be entertained than educated." As Dale Carnegie often pointed out, the successful communicator understands that people follow their emotions as much as they do their rational mind. So it's just human nature for any audience not to want to face a wall of talk. Keeping this in mind will enable you to move to a deep sense of rapport with your audience, so that you can command not only their attention but their engagement.

If you need a role model, there's no one more adept at engaging her audience than Oprah Winfrey, who uses most of the techniques we've discussed in this chapter. Turn on the television and just watch how she handles her presentations to her guests and her audience. Unfortunately, she does have at least one technique that's unavailable to most of us: When she needs a Breathing Space, she can call for a commercial break!

Oprah knows that when it comes to audience engagement the trick is to remember that any good presentation is a participatory experience. *One of the key questions to ask yourself when drafting your 3-D Outline and making other preparations is "How much of the time should I be talking versus encouraging other people to talk?"* The answer depends upon the context, but keep in mind that sometimes the most productive presentations result when the presenter isn't even speaking for a majority of the time.

Think about some of the oldest kinds of presentations we know of, teaching and preaching. The format of religious ceremonies has inevitably undergone a sort of natural selection process over the millennia, so this is an instructive example to look at. If you can't get the flock to attend the service every week, it doesn't matter how right you are in your beliefs—that audience will find a preacher who can deliver the goods in a more palatable way. While styles have changed over the centuries, it is certainly true today that people do not go to most churches and listen to a pastor droning on without interruption for two hours. Everyone else in that church—even those with prescribed responsibilities—is a member of a kind of audience. And during most church services the pastor has many Breathing Spaces and opportunities for audience involvement. In the course of a given service, different laypeople may read from scripture, the choir may sing, the offering may be collected, the audience may participate in communion, there may be a report from the alderman or announcements to the congregation, etc. All these pieces relieve the pastor of some of his burden while reminding the audience that they constitute a community of like-minded individuals. They are not there to be lectured to, but to participate—even though, in some sense, the pastor is in fact making a presentation to them.

Similarly, think about the experience of teaching, in school or in the context of training a new employee or coworker. While it is true that many of us have suffered through classes where we struggled to stay awake, the most successful teachers throughout history have been the ones who found ways to engage their audience. The great Greek philosophers didn't simply lecture their students. Rather, they often listened to their students' questions and assertions and responded in kind to these forms of audience involvement. That's one reason why much of Plato's surviving work is in the form of dialogues. Similarly, one of my partners, George Lowe, recalls how much he enjoyed the experience of engineering school, where class formats often interspersed straight lectures with the showing of slides and practical, hands-on exercises for the students. The result of this approach, we all know, is a more enriching learning experience. Why not add this kind of variety when making other kinds of presentations?

If you're not fully convinced of the importance of audience involvement for Presentation Mastery, consider this set of statistics. The average adult retains

- 10 percent of what he or she reads
- 20 percent of what he or she hears
- 30 percent of what he or she sees
- 50 percent of what he or she hears and sees
- 70 percent of what he or she says
- 90 percent of what he or she says and does

Create Breathing Spaces in your presentations to give yourself a rest and to fully engage your audience. By doing so, you are guaranteed to achieve greater audience retention of your message.

✓
Very Important Points

- The Breathing Space is often an opportunity to get your audience personally involved in the presentation by giving them something to do that supports your communications objectives while drawing attention away from you.

- Having someone else speak not only helps direct attention away from you, it also changes the dynamic in the room by introducing the power of Authority or Social Proof.

- Sometimes getting the audience to hone in on an inanimate object is as good as having them focus on another person.

- Conducting a written quiz creates lots of Breathing Space and audience involvement.

- When possible, set your audience up to win.

- Often when we're in the midst of a one-on-one presentation, opportunities arise to change the tenor of the presentation by bringing a third party into it.

- Having your audience talk among themselves is an excellent way to break down peer-to-peer barriers that can be a source of tension in the room.

- One easy way to get the audience eyeballs off you is to direct them to a handout.

- If mini-skits are well planned and managed, they can be a powerful way to make an emotional connection to your audience.

- One of the key questions to ask yourself when drafting your 3-D Outline and making other preparations is "How much of the time should I be talking versus encouraging other people to talk?"

CHAPTER 12

Essential #8: Flex for Success

Tailor the Presentation to Keep Your Audience Focused

Many moons ago, the chamber of commerce of a small rural town in Maine engaged a man from the agricultural college to give a talk to local farmers. The man was coming from a long way off, so he set out early on a sunny but crisp winter morning. Those were the days before satellites and weather-predicting supercomputers, and as the ag man traveled he began to encounter some unexpected elements, first in the form of fast-moving clouds, then a light freezing rain turning to snow. But the man had made a promise, so he pressed on.

Pretty soon, the snow began to fall steadily, and that gave way to even more of the white stuff, which was now being propelled by driving winds. A full-blown nor'easter had erupted, but the ag man had made a promise, so he plodded on.

Finally, just before the appointed time, the man pushed himself with great effort through the door of the grange hall, stomped the snow off his shoes, and hurried to the head of the room. The weather seemed to have delayed most of his audience, so he decided to wait. After fifteen minutes, however, only one lone soul had shuffled in. The ag man looked at his watch and then turned to the old man in overalls who appeared to be his only audience.

"Well," said the ag man, "it's long past the time I'm scheduled to begin, and the wind is howling outside. What do you think I should do?"

The other fellow tugged on his overalls and scratched his fore-head with his thumbnail, then looked the ag man straight in the eye and said, "Sir, I may just be a poor farmer from Down East, but there's one thing I do know. If only one horse comes to the barn, a man's still got to feed him."

"Okay," replied the ag man. "I didn't mean any disrespect." And he stepped to the podium and commenced his talk.

As you might imagine, the ag man, who was looking out into rows and rows of empty chairs, began rather haltingly, but it was his nature to press on, and he did. He had made a lot of speeches before, and after a few minutes he came to ignore the peculiar circumstances and settled into his usual rhythm. Pretty soon he felt completely comfortable and had just really begun to hit his stride when he noticed that the farmer was refer-ring repeatedly to his watch. Suddenly feeling self-conscious again, the ag man groped for a way to wind down his talk and awkwardly brought it to a conclusion. Then he walked over to the farmer and asked earnestly, "So, how do you think it went?"

The farmer looked at his boots, put on his hat as if getting ready to go, and then met the ag man's eye.

"Well, sir," he said, "I may be just a poor farmer from Down East, but there's another thing I do know. If only one horse comes to the barn, a man doesn't give him the whole load."

This joke, which I learned from my colleague Greg Kaiser, hits upon a mistake that inexperienced presenters make all too often. Like an actor who hasn't heard the director shout "Cut!" they plow ahead even when it has become clear that their audience is beginning to focus its attention elsewhere and a change of approach is in order. *Masterful presenters, on the other hand, have the wherewithal to respond to their audience or to their own internal gyroscope by adjusting their presentation style to keep the audience focused on their presentation.*

Since the human mind can process information approximately four times faster than we talk, even an inherently interesting presentation is rife with opportunities for your audience to tune out. And once you've begun to lose their attention, it is very difficult to get it back. *You must have an awareness at all times, using your Sensory Acuity, of how your audi-ence is responding to what you have to say.* Then you must make adjustments, some subtle and some profound. But this does not mean ad-libbing. The underlying principle that I teach my clients is the concept of **Planned Spontaneity.** *The more prepared you are going in to your presentation, the better positioned you will be to react spontaneously to your audience in a way that keeps getting your message across.*

The same principle applies whether we're conducting a business meeting or sitting at the dining room table at home with our family trying to "present" a message or make a point. At dinner there are many distractions—food being passed, side conversations, dishes banging, people kicking one another under the table—but often a family meal is our only opportunity to raise certain issues. Whether you're discussing where to take a vacation, your children's homework habits, or even an illness in the family, you must read the mood of your family audience and adjust your presentation to keep them focused on your message. Flexibility becomes the key.

Your Turn

Mark Twain once said, "It takes about six weeks to prepare a good ad lib comment." While Twain exaggerated, he was referring to a very real central irony concerning spontaneity: In order to be effectively spontaneous, you must be prepared. But, of course, you have to do so without seeming like you're reading from a script.

I once saw an interview with Tom Hanks's brother, who is himself an actor. For his first film role, the younger Hanks asked his brother whether he could offer any advice. Yeah, Tom replied, no matter how many takes you have to do, always deliver your lines as if you're speaking them for the first time. When Kim coaches her author clients before they go on book tour, she teaches this exact advice. Her clients travel from one city to the next, day after day. One moment they're in Atlanta and the next second they're in Portland, facing interviewers over and over about the same book, responding to the same questions, to the point where they often can't even remember what city they're in. The most important rule for a touring author to learn and the best skill to have is always to answer the questions as if they're being asked for the very first time. Keep it fresh, keep it exciting, and keep it interesting. When it's just no longer possible to pretend a certain question is new, Kim advises her client to say, "That's a great question and one I often get asked." Then continue with the answer, but always give it a new slant.

You will have noticed by now, I hope, that I don't advocate the cookie-cutter form of presentation preparedness. Every person is different, which means that every audience is unique. And, as a result, no two presentations are really the same. All of the practices in this book are best employed when you can do so from a position of naturalness, using your own wits along with the general principles that you've learned. Yet it is also true that the freedom to be yourself while making successful presentations comes from being so comfortable with your preparation that you can achieve mastery. That's why I don't talk about spontaneity, which might be fun but carries with it no sense of purpose. Instead, *I teach Planned Spontaneity, which is the ability to adapt to a situation while continuing to reach for your presentation goals.*

It so happens that I've coached for about a third of all the major automotive brands available in the world, so I've learned a bit about cars along the way. One of the things I picked up is that the turning radius of autos has much improved over the past ten years, which means today's cars can change direction with fewer steps and less effort than past models. Think of Essential #8 as the turning radius of your presentation skills. The less effort it takes to change direction, the easier it will be for you to take yourself where you want to go.

The presenter's turning radius is not so much slave to the laws of physics, as with a car, but dependent upon the laws of human nature. When the time comes to veer off course, it will hurt your presentation if the tires are screeching and you're seen to be wrestling with the steering wheel. You want to be smooth. Yet you also want to be sincere. Most people have an internal bunk detector. That's why responding to surprises doesn't mean launching into a snow job; it means being prepared to adjust within the context of your presentation objectives. The Presentation Arsenal that you learned about in Chapter 8 is essential to your ability to tailor your presentations on the fly. It constitutes a reserve of sincere, honest material that can get you out of a tight spot, if necessary, or simply help you better illustrate a point.

Over the next few pages, we'll take a look at some of the kinds of changes you may be required to make from time to time in order to demonstrate Presentation Mastery.

Why Change?

Many of us have heard that the definition of insanity is performing the same task repeatedly while expecting different results each time. In this context, one of the things we learned in our chapter about Neurolinguistic Programming bears repeating: The person with the most flexibility has the best chance of achieving the outcome he or she desires. This is true in every aspect of our quest for success, from the goals we set for ourselves to our attempts to achieve happiness. And, of course, it is especially relevant to our presentations. Why is this so? Because people—meaning members of our audience—relish naturalness and abhor the stilted. A person who delivers his presentation without demonstrating flexibility is not responding to his audience. *So if all our preparation leads to a rigid and seemingly scripted presentation, we will not have maximized our opportunity for success.*

Let's briefly examine why flexibility is such an important—and powerful—force in our lives. In *Who Moved My Cheese?* Dr. Spencer Johnson created an allegory about four mice who live in a maze. Everything is going along swimmingly at first because they all know where to find the cheese, which is their main goal in life. Then, one day, the cheese moves. Those mice who are willing to accept this change and adjust to it soon learn how to thrive again, while those who resist the notion that their cheese has moved do not do well.

Dr. Johnson's book became a huge best-seller a few years ago because it dealt very elegantly with a fundamental fact: Life itself is about change, and those who adapt will achieve a greater level of success and happiness than those who refuse to do so. Here are the seven insights that Dr. Johnson presents in his nifty little book, along with my commentary on how this applies to one's Presentation Universe:

- *Change happens.* Just because you prepared for your presentation doesn't mean everything will go as anticipated. Despite your best efforts, the environment might work against you, the equipment

might stall or even break down, the audience might not be as expected, you might have made a mistake in your preparation, or
any number of things might occur that you cannot control
through preparation alone. By accepting that change happens,
you can expect the unexpected. Nothing, then, should be a complete surprise to you when you make your presentation.

- *Anticipate change.* Since change is inevitable, why not get out
  ahead of it by planning your presentation for any contingency?

- *Monitor change.* Keep your eye out for changes that may be
  coming over the horizon. Remember the old story about the
  frog and the boiling water? If you drop a frog into boiling water,
  he jumps out. But if you put the frog in cool water and gradu-
  ally increase the temperature, he'll boil to death. By looking out
  for those things that can adversely impact your presentation,
  you will be in a position to respond more effectively when
  things aren't going your way.

- *Adapt quickly to change.* Don't wait until your presentation is
  over to respond. The Master Presenter tailors his presentation to
  his audience and continues to adapt at the first sign of trouble.

- *Change.* Nor should you always wait for your audience to force
  you to adjust your presentation. If you see a better way to get to
  your point, take it.

- *Enjoy change.* As you learn to incorporate the essentials in this
  book into your own effortless presentation style—in other
  words, as these things become part of your unconscious competence—you will find that change is not something to fear. It is
  something to celebrate. By sticking to the substance of your
  message while tailoring it to fit your audience's needs, you will
  best achieve your presentation goals, and triumph.

- *Be ready to change quickly again and again.* As you expand your
  Presentation Universe to include all the presentation opportuni-

ties in your day, remember to remain flexible at every opportunity, not just once or twice.

So what kinds of changes should we expect to have to make while facing presentation opportunities? The specific adjustments may be as varied as life itself. Yet we can review the types of situations one is most likely to face, so, as Dr. Johnson suggests, we are prepared to anticipate the change, monitor for the change, and quickly adapt to the change.

Perhaps the greatest potential disappointment for a presenter arises when he fails to establish rapport with his audience. As we have discussed throughout this book, without that essential connection the chances of succeeding in your other presentation goals are greatly reduced. So if you feel the attention of your audience slipping away, remember all the practices that you have learned and be ready to employ them in ways other than planned. For example, create a Breathing Space where you otherwise might not have had one or poll audience members to figure out why you feel your presentation is going off the tracks. Then, of course, be prepared to take different approaches than you had planned and to make adjustments based upon audience feedback.

Sometimes—especially in more intimate and less formal scenarios—our presentation may be interrupted by people coming and going. Know beforehand what you will do if someone walks in on your presentation. If you are conducting a meeting and the boss enters late, be prepared to bring him up to speed with a quick recap. If you are down on one knee proposing to your girlfriend in a public place, know that you are susceptible to interruption and have a plan for that contingency—either to bull your way forward or roll with the punches. A friend of Joel's proposed to his wife-to-be in Times Square on New Year's Eve. When the people around him realized what was happening, they began to cheer—and he was ready with a bottle of champagne and a dozen plastic cups for sharing the moment. To this day his wife talks about how the inclusion of a dozen total strangers oddly enhanced the romanticism of the marriage proposal. Without those extra cups, it may not have been as sweet.

The timing of this man's proposal was essential because he wanted to be drinking champagne as part of an engaged couple while the new year rolled in. Time is one major factor that often changes our presentation approach. Perhaps we've been told that we have an hour to make a major presentation, but the previous presenter runs long and our time is cut in half. Maybe we go to ask our boss for a raise, thinking we'll get five minutes, and before we open our mouth he invites us to lunch, so now we have an hour. We should always know how we'll handle having to squeeze our time or stretch it as circumstances warrant.

As we've discussed in other chapters, the environment is a significant, often overlooked factor in our presentation success. That's why it is very important not only to choose your setting wisely, if possible, and familiarize yourself with it, but also to monitor your surroundings constantly with an awareness that they may impact your effectiveness. To take an obvious example, if the skies clear and the sun begins pouring through the window, don't wait for the room to heat up before adjusting the HVAC. Not so obvious, perhaps, is to remember that we can often initiate a change of venue if the environment is working against our presentation. If you're trying to win a point with a retailer and you feel the counter has become a barrier to communication, for instance, you may ask him to step over to look at something in the store that you can use as an impromptu prop to make a point. So, while the environment can change your presentation, remember that you can also change your environment.

One thing you can't alter is the fact that people sometimes make mistakes. Of course, proper preparation will prevent chronic mistakes, but on occasion you may still forget your handouts or misunderstand what the host has asked you to do. In these circumstances, you must be ready to adjust to the new reality. Don't dwell on the mistake. Focus on the solution and you may very well find that the omission—whatever it is—can be more easily rectified than first thought. When all else fails, don't be afraid to admit when you don't know.

If your presentation involves equipment, rehearse a few times for the possibility that the equipment will fail. If you've thoroughly followed the practices in this book, the possibility of surprise equipment failure should be minimal. But, let's face it: stuff happens. A circuit breaker could blow or your laptop might die in the middle of your slide deck. The key, again, is not to allow this kind of thing to take all the wind out of your sails. Whatever you do, don't spend fifteen minutes waiting on a repair or, even worse, trying to do it yourself. Equipment that dies in the midst of your presentation is spilt milk. Be prepared with handouts that replicate what you're trying to show, or just force yourself to move on. If you've rehearsed without the equipment, you should be able to flow seamlessly away from the problem.

Finally, what if something even more fundamental interferes with your presentation plans? What if you misunderstood who would be in the audience or the audience has arrived at the presentation with the wrong information about what to expect from you? Generally speaking, the solution is not to plow ahead as if this misunderstanding never occurred. Instead, you must try to find common ground between you and your audience by asking questions of their expectations. Then do your best to accommodate what they were looking for, presuming you can do so within the realm of your expertise. (Never fake it; that does more harm than good.) Even if you're not perfect, they will appreciate the effort.

Park It!

Of course, life is complicated. It is not *always* desirable to change your presentation just because your audience may have had a different expectation. For example, if your son thought you came into his room to discuss baseball, but you feel you really need to present to him about how to resist the temptations of drugs, adjusting from your topic to his would be counterproductive. Fortunately, there is an easy tool that is available for keeping your presentation on-message. Trainers call it the **Parking Lot.**

In business settings—particularly in the context of a meeting with a defined agenda—*the Parking Lot is a way to respect material that may arise during the course of the meeting but the immediate discussion of which is inconsistent with the goals of the meeting.* I suggest that the presenter or facilitator briefly note at the beginning of a meeting that she is setting up a Parking Lot for items that fall into this category. Then the list of these items can be kept on a section of the whiteboard or on a separate piece of paper. By enforcing this kind of discipline on the audience, the presenter acknowledges the validity of tangential subjects without allowing them to interfere with the meeting's purpose. You may then choose to set aside time at the end of the session for discussion of Parking Lot items, to make arrangements to see people with narrow or specialized interests at another time, or to commit to specific follow-up actions to deal with those items.

While the Parking Lot may seem like a very corporate concept involving whiteboards and meeting agendas, like most of the practices in this book it can be much more broadly applied with a little creativity. Families might keep their own list of issues to be addressed, so if a family member attempts to disrupt your presentation by introducing a different subject, you can add it to the list for a future discussion and continue on. In even less structured environments, you may simply acknowledge your audience's other issues and agree to address them after your presentation or at a later date. Don't just ignore them, however. By showing respect for your audience's ideas—even when they're unexpected—you will strengthen the rapport you have, making your presentation that much more effective.

Sorry to Interrupt—Not!

At one time or another in their lives, most people find themselves falling into an undesirable pattern of behavior. For example, using profanity regularly is a pattern. So are most compulsions. Many people get into a pattern of responding to criticism in a certain way. They may even respond to constructive criticism with arguments and denials. If you have futilely reacted to their reactions with continued insistence that you are "only trying to help," consider the possibility that you and the other person have established a pattern for this situation. Without a way to break that pattern, you will replay the same old record over and over. In fact, the more you try to change, the more deeply ingrained the behaviors will become.

The way to break out of damaging patterns is to interrupt them. In the above situation, you need to take another approach, perhaps by just grinning and declaring, "Boy am I glad to be alive!" This completely unexpected behavior will break the pattern for both you and the other person, and the behaviors may change going forward.

In similar fashion, the Master Presenter must always be on the lookout for inadvertent patterns that could harm her ability to build rapport and communicate effectively. As the saying goes, if you find yourself standing in a hole, the first thing to do is stop digging. If a certain approach is not working with a certain audience, that means you need to change it. Try to do so with a **Pattern Interrupt.**

Sometimes we must adjust our presentations based upon outside factors such as the ones mentioned earlier. In other cases, we must know when to initiate the change ourselves by perceiving when we have fallen into an unproductive pattern in our communication. In the context of Presentation Mastery, *the Pattern Interrupt is an attempt to change emotional direction—sometimes our own, but usually that of our audience.* Therefore all those things we know to have powerful effects on our emotional state are also potential pattern interrupters: tone of voice, body language, the environment, and visual and aural stimulators, to name a few.

Say you're presenting to your child's school board in order to request more money for the music program. Budgets are tight and the school board members are on the defensive, sitting with their arms crossed. Rather than press on in frustration, you decide to lower your voice, which may cause the board members to lean forward in order to hear you better. This interrupts the pattern through a major change of tone and by completely altering their body language, which is suddenly in a more receptive posture. In another approach to this situation, you may have prepared an audio- or videotape of your child's school band, which you trot out when you begin to sense resistance to your message. The audio and video, too, can serve as Pattern Interrupters. What about the environment? While in this instance you can't control the standard environmental factors like the lighting or HVAC, you *can* stand up and walk over to the side of the room while you're addressing the board. This will break the pattern because everyone will have to turn to follow your voice. If you have a knack for the dramatic, you might even throw open a window, seemingly in order to point out across the quad. What you're really doing, however, is again finding a way to break the pattern. Any of these steps would be more effective than simply continuing to drone on in the face of an unreceptive board.

Preparation at every level is essential in order to deliver effective presentations the majority of the time, but we must never allow our preparation to become a detriment to our success. What we have to say during the presentation is important, of course, but without proper rapport that content is sure to be lost. Therefore, *our focus must always be on the audi-*

ence, not ever only on our agenda. Yes, maintaining our composure requires knowing our stuff to the point where we can deliver the message with unconscious competence. But we must also be on the lookout for things that may distract from our presentation. The Master Presenter tailors the presentation to his audience and constantly stands ready to adjust to keep them focused.

✓
Very Important Points

- Masterful presenters have the wherewithal to respond to their audience or to their own internal gyroscope by adjusting their presentation style to keep the audience focused on their presentation.

- You must have an awareness at all times, using your Sensory Acuity, of how your audience is responding to what you have to say.

- The more prepared you are going into your presentation, the better positioned you will be to react spontaneously to your audience in a way that keeps getting your message across.

- Planned Spontaneity is the ability to adapt to a situation while continuing to reach for your presentation goals.

- If all our preparation leads to a rigid and seemingly scripted presentation, we will not have maximized our opportunity for success.

- The Parking Lot is a way to respect material that may arise during the course of a meeting but the immediate discussion of which is inconsistent with the goals of the meeting.

- The Pattern Interrupt is an attempt to change emotional direction—sometimes our own, but usually that of our audience.

- Our focus must always be on the audience, not ever only on our agenda.

PART III

MAKING IT WORK

Presentations in Your Life

CHAPTER 13

On Your Mark and Get Set

*Assessing Presentation Effectiveness
and Changing Your Habits*

One of the thoughts in my own Presentation Arsenal is something the well-known college basketball coach Bobby Knight once expressed. He said that what distinguishes winners from everyone else is not the *will* to win—nearly everybody has that. *What distinguishes winners is the will to prepare to win.* Knight is a complex character, infamous for certain inexcusably bad behaviors that I don't ever condone. But in sports, more than any other aspect of life, we can easily measure success in the win/loss column. I detest Knight's temper tantrums, but anyone looking at the stats has to admit that the man knows how to reach his goals.

The simple desire to succeed has never led to great achievement in any endeavor, and in and of itself it will not make anyone a successful presenter. When I was standing in the ballroom of that hotel in Seattle some twenty years ago, I had more desire to succeed than you could fit in the Grand Canyon. But I didn't have the means to succeed because I did not yet grasp the presentation practices that I was seeking. I now know that great presenters—like all people of achievement—don't take anything for granted. They do not ignore the fact that they are coming to the presentation with personal baggage; they neutralize their weaknesses before they set out. They do not assume that the purpose of their presentation is self-explanatory; they seek the foundation of that purpose. They do not presume that their audience will respond favorably to their presentation; they condition that audience to respond favorably. They do not proceed unvaryingly through their presentation; they arm themselves with the tools to respond to and involve their audience.

Some people spend a good deal of their professional lives making formal presentations. For most, however, the majority of our presentations are impromptu affairs: the unexpected phone call, the office drop-in, the chance meeting. People who excel in these situations have *presence*. They often command our attention not by accident but because they have prepared themselves ahead of time by turning this book's practices into habits. As a consequence, they have the confidence to seize their opportunities. When the moment comes, they are ready to act in that moment. That's what makes Presentation Mastery the key to professional success and personal power.

Now You Know

In 1980, on the television show *60 Minutes*, Roger Mudd asked Senator Ted Kennedy why he wanted to be president. When Kennedy responded with a long, confused answer, millions of viewers thought the bungled reply revealed a personal ambivalence toward the senator's own political ambition. They quickly drew the conclusion that Kennedy was only running for president in order to please others, not because he really wanted the office. This single, failed presentation led to a crisis of confidence among his supporters that inevitably ended in the failure of his entire campaign.

I wrote this book because I want *your* campaign through life to get the kind of traction that Ted Kennedy's bid for president never got. *You can have all the right ideas, all the best intentions, and all the talent in the world, but if you don't know how to present yourself and your ideas you will be selling your ambitions short.* As we have seen, this is true whether your goal is to become president of the United States or whether you're just determined to get an acquaintance to accept your advice. *Our lives are interwoven with presentation opportunities, from the moments we spend with our families and friends to the time we devote to our careers or pastimes.* On a professional level, the quality of our presentations will directly influence our career and business goals, which can significantly affect our wealth and happiness. And the same is true for the communication in all our relationships. The list of presentation types is substantial. In business it includes sales presentations, training sessions, speeches, meetings, media appearances, e-presentations in all their forms, branding messages, phone pitches, facilitated events, seminars, and one-on-one opportunities. In your personal life it involves presentations to influence or persuade, teaching sessions, speeches, meetings, e-mail, personal branding messages, facilitated events, group instruction, phone calls, and one-on-one conversations. The very comprehensiveness of these lists ought to remind us that these opportunities play a hugely important part in every aspect of our lives.

I have worked with all kinds of individuals over the years, in many cases as part of my profession and in others simply because people asked. I have watched as the steps toward Presentation Mastery improved the professional lives of corporate executives, as well as their personal lives. I have seen improved presentation skills build stronger relationships at all ages and in all contexts. I have witnessed small children grow confident as they began to learn this previously undiscovered secret of success. People in all stations of life have the ability to inspire more, inform better, and influence with increased effectiveness when they begin to comprehend the practices that you've learned in this book. They have a greater measure of control over their interactions with people, and this inspires confidence, which accelerates their effectiveness that much more.

When we began this book, we set out to increase your awareness of the role presentations play in many people's success and happiness, and I hope we have done so greatly. Equally important was our aim to inspire you to action on behalf of your own improvement. You read a good many stories of Presentation Masters in this book, from Bill Porter the door-to-door salesman to businessmen Mike Perkins and Scott Klein, to our fictional barista, who was a composite of several people I know. I hope these stories have motivated you to act by demonstrating that the practices in this book really do work to improve people's personal achievement and happiness. These people are reaching their life goals not only because of their awareness, but because they have incorporated these practices into every aspect of their lives. As Stephen Covey noted, success requires more than awareness. *It comes when people turn what they've learned into the daily habits that breed success.* This is as true for your presentation effectiveness, of course, as it is for any other form of self-improvement.

Now that you are nearing completion of this book, the results you reap in meeting your presentation opportunities will depend on two final steps. First, honestly evaluate where you stand in relation to achieving your desired outcomes. Then, resolve to turn the Eight Essential Practices of Successful Presenters into habits that you carry wherever you go.

Who's to Judge?

Throughout this book we have driven home the point that the success of your presentations depends not only on what you say and do, but also upon what your audience perceives your message to be. I can stand before an audience, move my lips, and tell them that I'm happy to be there, but if my shoulders are slumped and my energy is low and there are tears of sadness running down my cheeks, they will leave that presentation knowing that I was *not* happy to be there.

Naturally, your presentation success will first and foremost be measured by your audience. In a one-on-one presentation, it may be easy to learn whether your audience has received your message convincingly, because he or she will tell you directly or behave in some way that indicates whether you have succeeded. For example, if you've just made a sales presentation, the result will speak for itself when you get the sales order (or—heaven forbid!—don't). If you're attempting to convince your daughter to treat her baby brother more nicely, you'll soon know the results of that presentation, too. But when you're presenting to a medium-sized or large group, it may become difficult to discern how your message has been received by everyone. What do you do in that circumstance? It's simple. As always, *if you want to know what the audience is thinking, ask them.* You may do so by soliciting either formal or informal evaluations of your performance.

Besides satisfying your curiosity, evaluations provide an opportunity for participants to give feedback to meeting organizers (praise or criticism), bring closure to the event, and help solidify audience buy-in to the message of the session. They also capture and convey valuable information to presenters and meeting organizers relative to the quality of the results and the satisfaction level of the participants. Finally—and in some ways most significant for you—they provide important clues on how to improve your personal performance and how future sessions can be enhanced.

In many situations, you'll want to get some kind of formal feedback from your audience so you can find out what they perceived as most and least effective in your presentation. This is especially true in problem-solving and instructional contexts, where you may have no way to solicit their opinions other than a formal evaluation sheet that you provide for your audience. When presenting to a particularly large audience, since you can't speak to all of them individually and people may be likely to reserve comment, it is essential to formalize feedback if you want to learn anything about how your presentation went over. Of course, if you receive a standing ovation and they start cheering for an encore, you may feel that you know what they thought. Even in a rare case like that, though, it is helpful to obtain more specifics so you can employ the true strengths of that presentation at future opportunities.

Basic evaluations can be done easily by passing around a paper survey that lists the elements of your presentation, asks the audience for feedback through some kind of scoring system, and provides a space for comments. Using this approach, the audience can evaluate your session in just a few minutes. More detailed evaluations are appropriate for training courses and longer seminars if the course will be repeated in the future, because it's important to identify specific elements of the program that worked well, along with those that need improvement. These kinds of evaluations should also be keyed to the agenda and provide numerical ratings and space for comments.

When employing paper evaluation forms, keep a few things in mind. First, pass the forms out before the presentation begins or—if it's a long presentation such as a full-day seminar—at least before the time of the final break. If your audience understands early that they'll be asked to evaluate you, they are more likely to make time to do so at the end in their own minds. And if the evaluation form touches upon the takeaway you're hoping for—for instance, by asking for their opinion about particular content in the presentation—then the form itself is an opportunity to reinforce your message. Second, remember not to make the evaluation form so detailed that it shows disrespect for an audience member's time. Evaluation forms generally should not take more than three to five minutes for someone to fill out.

Interactive methods that gain more information may require more time than evaluation forms, depending on group size, but they have the potential to greatly reinforce the audience takeaway. You can encourage live evaluations by asking sub-groups or individuals to "call out" their feedback on a rotating basis: verbally, by writing on flip charts, or by having one designated person at each table report on their group's work. It helps to request that the callouts specify both positive and negative items, so ask for pairs of comments—one item each of "what worked" and "what needs improvement." If time is limited, ask for one-word evaluations, or one word each for positives and improvement opportunities. On a personal level, you can and should do a similar thing. When presenting to a family member, for example, it's always useful to ask things like "Am I making sense?" "Do you understand where I'm coming from?" or "Is there a way I could be more clear?" These constitute another means of getting an informal, on-the-spot evaluation of your presentation. Posing these questions may also help you create a personal style that will become a part of who you are—less the "lecturing" mother, father, or spouse who dictates family rules or plans, and more of a sensitive and open-minded person.

For other large audience situations where paper won't work, you can take a few moments to do your own real-time surveying. Throw out a specific question and ask for a show of hands **(Verbal Surveying)** or select a few individuals randomly and ask them to share their feedback with the rest of the audience **(Targeted Polling).** You also can do a follow-up survey via e-mail with or without a link to your web site.

Using a web-based feedback form can be useful for drawing people out, but it lacks the immediacy of in-room methods. As a result, many people will not respond, but an incomplete evaluation from your audience is better than none at all. I always solicit audience reviews in one fashion or another. Then I study the results, which will guide both the content and the practices of my future presentations.

How'm I Doing?

It will not come as a surprise to you that I put a lot of stock in the similar root of the words "presentation" and "presence." *People who have presence are not simply prepared for a single moment—they are prepared to meet all presentation opportunities that arise in their lives.* Aspiring to be like these Master Presenters means always finding ways to improve your readiness, and this becomes a positive, almost automatic habit rather than a chore.

When Ed Koch was mayor of New York City, at every opportunity he famously asked of its citizens, "How'm I doing?" This seemed almost radical at that time, but it brilliantly had the effect of communicating to his constituents that he cared about what they thought.

Unfortunately, we can't always ask our audience how we're doing with our presentation style. You're not going to pass out evaluation forms at your next cocktail party, and you'd feel pretty foolish pulling aside the clerk at Sears to inquire about how your presentation is coming off. On the other hand, you *can* ask whether your audience needs clarification or additional information. Sometimes, though, you just have to evaluate yourself, which you can now do with greater clarity within the context of the Eight Essentials we introduced in Chapters 5 through 12.

Think again about all the types of presentation opportunities that arise in your life. In Chapter 4, we defined our Presentation Universe by type of presentation. This time, let's evaluate ourselves by the environments in which our opportunities arise.* I've identified ten contexts in which I make most of my presentations: family, career, spiritual, friendships, neighborhood, community, general business, personal business, charitable, and sports. These places, in effect, are the planets in my Presentation Universe. In order to evaluate how you've been performing in your Presentation Universe, take a few moments to rate yourself based upon how frequently you achieve your presentation objectives:

Context	Opportunities	Rating (1–10)
FAMILY	Examples: dinner table, homework, outings, weekend time, bedtime, spouse various, kids various	
CAREER	Examples: interviews, investor relations, partner communications	
SPIRITUAL	Examples: worship, Sunday school, meetings, outreach, small group meetings	

(continued on next page)

---

*Visit http://www.tonyjeary.com/presentationuniverse for a free electronic copy of this table.

Context	Opportunities	Rating (1–10)
FRIENDSHIPS	Examples: telephone, e-mail, dates, networking, moral support	
NEIGHBORHOOD	Examples: cleaners, book store, video store, grocery store, policemen, trash people, gardener, service station	
COMMUNITY	Examples: neighbors, associations, government, clubs	
GENERAL BUSINESS	Examples: customers, references, decision-makers, networking, speeches, staff meetings, e-mails, telephone	
PERSONAL BUSINESS	Examples: attorney, stock broker, real estate broker, accountant, agent, financial advisor, personal coach	
CHARITABLE	Examples: events, fund-raising prospects, school	
SPORTS	Examples: games, coaches, team members, teaching	
TOTAL (Best Score = 100)		

The above list of Contexts is keyed to my general list, but yours may very well be different, as we discussed when we introduced the Presentation Universe concept earlier in the book. Whatever your priorities are, remember that *a Presentation Master achieves the majority of his or her desired outcomes almost ALL the time.* If you scored between 0 and 71, you have basic presentation skills or lower. A score between 70 and 89 indicates advanced skills, and any higher score means you are approaching Presentation Mastery.

Naturally, there are different ways to assess yourself. For example, you can examine the totality of your presentations or home in on an individual one. In cases (or contexts) where you are not achieving your goals, revisit the presentation in your own mind and break your effort down into the Eight Essentials with which you are now familiar. Then, of course, focus your self-improvement efforts on the weakest points. In this way, you can strive for continual self-improvement, as I do. And it doesn't matter whether your starting point is one of conscious incompetence or unconscious competence because you are judging yourself not against others but only in the framework of your performance within your own Presentation Universe.

Make photocopies of the above rating sheet and evaluate yourself regularly. The first couple of times it will be difficult to score, but don't agonize over things like whether to enter a 6 or a 7 in the box. The important thing is to zero in on where you stand this week versus where you stood last week. That's what continual self-improvement is all about.

You Must Remember This . . .

As I was writing this book, a close friend's mother had to visit the hospital. I am at that age when many of my friends' parents have gotten on in years. Many are suffering from various old-age ailments, some of them very grave, and this particular woman has a number of maladies that mostly affect the elderly.

One day, she suffered a bad fall and was taken to a local hospital by ambulance. For anyone, the hospital is a place of high stress and bone-numbing uncertainty that can bring out the worst in all of us. Older people, especially, become frustrated by the creeping helplessness they often feel as a consequence of their receding roles in life, and this sensation frequently manifests itself as anger and resentment. So it was with my friend's mother. By the time my friend arrived, her mother had managed to insult and alienate just about every doctor and nurse who had tried to come to her aid. She had criticized their attentiveness to her and had questioned their competence. Needless to say, the woman was not winning friends in that hospital. And—much to her frustration—she also was not influencing the people to whom she had to entrust her care. As a result, she could not receive the attention that she required, and the medical staff was having trouble finding ways to alleviate her discomfort. My friend—who happens to be well versed in the practices you've read about in this book—realized that her mother's life wasn't just a series of presentations, it *depended* upon a series of presentations.

My friend quickly observed, first, that her mother did not understand her audience. She had been addressing them like the hired help rather than as the skilled professionals they were. Then, in rapid succession, it dawned on my friend that her mother was not preparing her audience for the important message she wanted to communicate ("I'm in severe pain and I need help now"), did not understand the "whys" behind her message, and had made no effort to put herself or her audience in the proper mental state to receive her presentation quickly and get on with her care. Of course, all of this was understandable given the woman's vulnerable position. But if she could have focused even for a few moments through the pain and frustration, she might have moved much closer to the outcome she desired.

The old woman had been in the hospital for three hours when her daughter arrived, but had not yet received the level of care required to make her more comfortable. After assessing the situation, my friend called the doctor and nurses aside and took corrective action. She began by saying that she realized they all wanted to help her mother and she was sure that they could, because she understood this to be the best hospital in the entire city. Then she continued by suggesting that her mother was really a nice old lady who was in tremendous pain. Once they had relieved that pain, she observed, they could look forward to having a far more cooperative and pleasant patient. Then she reminded them *why* her mother had some resistance to her own care: She had fallen at home and couldn't get up, but was a fiercely independent woman who had irrationally hindered efforts to bring her to the hospital. In the course of the conversation, my friend also learned something that she knew would favorably influence her mother.

She then brought the staff into her mother's room and reintroduced them to her mother by name. She gently held her mother's wrist as she observed that this was the same doctor who had recently helped her mother's friend in need (the important thing she had just learned). And she reviewed the fact that the staff and her mother had the same outcome in mind: getting her out of pain and out of the hospital as quickly as possible. Pretty soon the communication between patient and caregiver finally began flowing in earnest. In fact, within an hour, as a result of these presentations, my friend's mother was relatively pain free. And over the following days, her relationship with the staff improved so much that she became one of their favorite patients. When she was released a few weeks later, they all gave her a warm good-bye.

Now that we're moments from the conclusion to this book, I hope you have already identified some of the practices my friend used to get her mother's situation under control. She invoked the Liking principle, Future Paced the staff, addressed the "whys," prepared her audience, and Anchored the message of Social Proof for her mother with a touch on the wrist, among other things.

When she performed these practices, she did so mostly unconsciously, in keeping with her status as a Master Presenter. Only later did she reflect on the practices she used and how she might improve them in the future. Now that you are on the road to Presentation Mastery, you can begin to recognize these practices in yourself and others.

I have built and developed many millions of dollars worth of adult learning programs over the years, so I understand how important some kind of memory peg can be in helping you retain an entire program of knowledge. To reinforce your takeaway from this book, I've worked the Eight Essentials into a mnemonic: I P-R-E-S-E-N-T. The order of these letters matters no more than the order of the Essential Practices. As you may have observed, four of the practices pertain primarily to readiness and four are focused primarily on delivery. Any one of these Essentials will improve your presentation skills, and taken together they will help you exponentially.

I P-R-E-S-E-N-T:

I is for Involve your audience.
P is for Prepare your audience.
R is for Research your Presentation Arsenal.
E is for Explain "Why" before planning "How."
S is for State management: achieve proper mental states.
E is for Eliminate "unknowns" by turning them into "knowns."
N is for kNow your audience.
T is for Tailor the presentation throughout to keep your audience focused.

Whenever you're preparing for a particular presentation or for the readiness that makes all impromptu presentations more effective, remember your I P-R-E-S-E-N-T essentials (in the Resources section, you'll find a table that you can reproduce and put in your pocket). Review them in the car on the way to the grocery store. Think about them before social events. List them on a pad in preparation for business meetings. Jot a mental note before you coach the soccer game. They will make your life and work better and more productive. .

My colleagues and I have helped tens of thousands of people around the globe become better presenters. Along with my coauthors and business partners, I most sincerely hope that this book has already begun to assist you in achieving your life goals. If it has, we would love to learn your story, which you may pass along by contacting me through any of the means listed in the Resources section. In fact, my organization is willing to go a step further than just soliciting your opinion. As part of my philosophy of always exceeding expectations, we will give all readers of this book a free Presentation Mastery Profiler. You can get yours by logging on to *www.tonyjeary.com/profiler.*

The more people who learn these presentation practices the better. I envision a world where we all can perform at our best most of the time and where today's misunderstandings become tomorrow's opportunities for growth and achievement. My organization has devoted countless hours to arriving at the Essentials that you've now read about. If you agree that they can change the lives of your family, friends, and colleagues, please tell them so. When I was sixteen somebody gave me a copy of Dale Carnegie's *How to Win Friends and Influence People.* It was a gift in every sense of the word, one that had a huge impact on my life and my career, and that influenced me in ways I hope my book will influence you and yours.

It is my sincerest wish that you now fully appreciate the impact that presentations have on your personal and professional effectiveness. What others may consider a casual chat you now see as an opportunity to employ your newly learned presentation skills and assert your influence. What some view as a speech, you understand to be a series of interactions with your audience. What I have come to believe is the largely undiscovered secret of success, you have now discovered. The techniques and practices for achieving your most desired outcomes rest at your fingertips. Make them your own and apply them to your Presentation Universe. Armed with this knowledge, you will greatly advance yourself and your causes, so long as you continue to keep in mind that *life is a series of presentations.*

✓
Very Important Points

- What distinguishes winners is the will to *prepare* to win.

- You can have all the right ideas, all the best intentions, and all the talent in the world, but if you don't know how to present yourself and your ideas you will be selling your ambitions short.

- Our lives are interwoven with presentation opportunities, from the moments we spend with our families and friends to the time we devote to our careers or pastimes.

- Success comes when people turn what they've learned into the daily habits that breed success.

- If you want to know what the audience is thinking, ask them.

- People who have presence are not simply prepared for a single moment—they are prepared to meet all presentation opportunities that arise in their lives.

- A Presentation Master achieves the majority of his or her desired outcomes almost ALL the time.

- Remember I P-R-E-S-E-N-T:

  I is for *Involve your audience.*
  P is for *Prepare your audience.*
  R is for *Research your Presentation Arsenal.*
  E is for *Explain "Why" before planning "How."*
  S is for *State management: achieve proper mental states.*
  E is for *Eliminate "unknowns" by turning them into "knowns."*
  N is for *kNow your audience.*
  T is for *Tailor the presentation throughout to keep your audience focused.*

Resources

Support for Your Life's Presentations

- Tony Jeary High Performance Resources at your service
- Assessments and prescriptions
- Training and self-development materials
- Coaching and consulting
- Coming Attractions

What are your next steps?

By now, you are convinced that Life really Is a Series of Presentations. You've decided that it's important to pay more attention to your daily presentation opportunities. You need to take a closer look at your own capabilities in each type of presentation and set a course for improvement. You need a plan and may need help. What you do know for sure is that you want to achieve your presentation objectives more of the time and that sitting still is not an option. The next few pages will give you some ideas about how to get underway and where to get help.

"It is not necessary to change. Survival is not mandatory."
W. Edwards Deming

First, let's start with how to access the team at Tony Jeary High Performance Resources. TJHPR is located in Flower Mound, Texas, near the Dallas–Fort Worth Airport. Here's the contact information:

Telephone Numbers: ·
- Toll-free: 1-877-2-INSPIRE
- Direct: 817-430-9422
- Facsimile: 817-430-9424

Web site: http://www.tonyjeary.com

Mailing and Shipping Address:
8105 Firestone Drive
Flower Mound, Texas 75022

TJHPR's vision is that Presentation Mastery is on its way to becoming a movement. This book, and others to come, will help millions of people realize the dramatic improvements in impact that can flow from better presentations. We are leading this movement and have designed and developed many resources that can help you even more. More are on the way. Later in this section we'll highlight a few of our offerings that were available at press time.

Next, before you write down your action plan, we recommend that you visit the TJHPR web site and take advantage of the Presentation Mastery Profiler. You can access this personal profiler at **http://www.tony jeary.com/profiler.** When you've completed this instrument—by answering a few simple questions in less than ten minutes—you'll have a description of who you are as a presenter and a prescription for how to begin your personal journey toward greater presentation success.

Once you have an idea of what you need to work on, we suggest that you develop a simple action plan. You may want to focus initially on a certain type of presentation (e.g., one-on-one, meetings, sales, etc.), a specific purpose (persuasion, informational, etc.), or a specific context (e.g., work, family, community, etc.). You can pick up a template at **http:// www.tonyjeary.com/actionplan** or build your own, but the main thing is to commit to starting your own development program.

Most action plans will include some intensive reading and study of materials that will support your own presentation improvement objectives. We believe that learning the "language" of the presentation world is an important building block. By subscribing to our free electronic newsletter, you can get regular tips on presentation improvement and begin picking up on the terminology we use to talk about the mechanics of presentations and the presentation planning process. At **http://www.tony jeary.com/ezine** you can view archived editions and subscribe.

If your primary presentation improvement focus is work related, there are unique ways that TJHPR can help your company or organization. We offer training and consulting programs that can be tailored to your specific needs and budgets. We can do the work for you or train your trainers for internal cascades. Take a look at **http://www.tonyjeary.com/ organizationsupport** for some ideas, and give us a call.

Tony can help you personally "jump start" a movement in your company or organization through keynote speeches. His personal touch, delivered in a dynamic way, can accelerate awareness of the need for improved presentation effectiveness and provide high-value "business entertainment" for major meetings and events. He can bring years of expertise to your events in pre-planning sessions and on-site dress rehearsal coaching. He also is available for special business strategy sessions at your location or in his Success Studio. **Contact Tony's booking manager Dan Miller at 817-430-9422 or Dan@tonyjeary.com** to discuss your need or possible opportunity.

Life Is a Series of Presentations is also available from Vision Point as a video-based training course for *your* facilitators. This comprehensive package includes VHS video or DVD, a facilitator guide, participant materials, and more—everything required to present this valuable training in your organization. *Call 1-800-300-8880 today for a FREE preview.*

Need media presentation coaching? Don't miss opportunities that can vastly improve your life, career, or business. Contact Kim at kimfromla @earthlink.net to find out what her company, Kim-from-L.A. Literary & Media Services (kimfromla.com), can do for you. She will teach you how to communicate more effectively during interviews by helping you to develop your message as well as coaching you on how to deliver it concisely and passionately. As Kim says, "It takes more than a great idea, it takes the perfect pitch!"

If you're into electronics and high-tech, we have several presentation software products that can help both you and your organization manage your presentation knowledge database, build consistent cascading messages, and advance your CBL (computer based learning) efforts. At **http://www.tonyjeary.com/software** you can check out our *Mr. Presentation Wizard, Total Recall,* and other software to enhance your presentation effectiveness.

Toastmasters International

This is the world's largest organization devoted to communication excellence. Through local clubs, Toastmasters offers you the opportunity to learn effective communication through practical experience. It is a nonprofit, self-supporting group of individuals who meet on a regular basis to develop basic speaking skills. Various certifications are available, guided by manuals provided to the national organization. The structure is very valuable, and support is excellent, making this one of the best things you can do to increase your confidence in front of audiences. It's very affordable and there is most likely a meeting group in your area. I attended weekly years ago when I entered the training industry, and I recommend it highly. Contact Toastmasters at: P.O. Box 9052, Mission Viejo, CA 92690. Call 949-858-8255.

Please write us with ideas, suggestions, and questions. **Send to info@ tonyjeary.com.**

Presentations Magazine

Presentations is the only magazine written exclusively for people who create and deliver presentations. Each month, *Presentations* reviews the latest presentation technology and trends, offers professional techniques and how-to tips to enhance both your design and delivery skills, and covers "best presentation practices" of leading presenters and organizations worldwide. Whether you've achieved presentation Mastery or not, if you create and deliver presentations then *Presentations* is the magazine for you. Go to *www.presentations.com* for a free subscription.

However you choose to proceed, whether through one of our products, training, and consulting services, or through Tony's individual attention, we are committed to helping both individuals and organizations move ahead on the road to Presentation Mastery.

I	Involve Your Audience	*BENEFIT*	Engages, manages attention, and enhances audience buy-in
		AVOIDS	Inattention, lack of retention
P	Prepare Your Audience	*BENEFIT*	Maximizes initial audience influence
		AVOIDS	Confusion, lack of relevance
R	Research Your Presentation Arsenal	*BENEFIT*	Saves time during preparation and insures consistency
		AVOIDS	Inconsistency, wasted time, duplicated effort
E	Explain "Why" Before Planning "How"	*BENEFIT*	Heightens influence and persuasion (people are more likely to respond positively when given a reason to do so)
		AVOIDS	Lack of relevance, confusion, little buy-in
S	State Management: Achieve Proper Mental States	*BENEFIT*	Insures that you communicate with your audience in the most suitable way possible
		AVOIDS	Misunderstandings, communication gaps, boredom, lessened influence
E	Eliminate "Unknowns" and Turn Them into "Knowns"	*BENEFIT*	Confidence
		AVOIDS	Surprises, looking foolish/unprepared, stress
N	kNow Your Audience	*BENEFIT*	Determines communication preferences, thereby increasing the success of your presentation
		AVOIDS	Mismatched expectations, frustration
T	Tailor Your Presentation Throughout	*BENEFIT*	Creates and maintains interest and supports acceptance of your message
		AVOIDS	Boredom, inattention

Visit http://www.tonyjeary.com/ipresent for a free color download of this document.

Glossary

3-D Outline: A trademarked outline format that includes the What, Why, and How aspects of a presentation and is used for planning purposes. Most presentation outlines only cover the "whats"—dimension one. Dimension two is the "why" and dimension three is "how." Agendas and other presentation materials may be derived from the 3-D.

aligning: Achieving an understanding among meeting or presentation participants as to the purpose of the meeting or presentation and the roles of attendees.

Anchoring: The process by which any stimulus or representation (external or internal) gets connected to and triggers a response. Note that Anchors can be set up intentionally or occur naturally.

audience: Any person or group of people to whom you are presenting.

Audience Champion: A person in the audience who will openly support the presenter and reinforce his or her message.

Authority principle: The sense that we are inclined to show automatic respect to symbols of expertise such as titles, uniforms, or academic degrees, regardless of the substance behind these symbols.

automatic compliance: The "pre-programmed" response to a verbal trigger.

Basic Desires (sixteen): According to the research of Dr. Steven Reiss, the building blocks that constitute all our personalities and form the foundation for all our behavior: Power, Independence, Curiosity, Acceptance, Order, Saving, Honor, Idealism, Social Contact, Family, Status, Vengeance, Romance, Eating, Physical Activity, Tranquility.

Breathing Space: An opportunity to direct the attention of the audience away from the presenter in order to involve the audience more through a change of pace, and to give the presenter a moment to collect his or her thoughts. Examples include showing a video, directing someone else to comment, or having audience members write something down—so their eyes come off the presenter for a few seconds or a few minutes.

cascading messages: The consistent filtering down or across of messages throughout an organization or group, for instance from a top executive down to her direct reports down to their direct reports and so on. Messages can also cascade across to other departments, and sometimes even upward in an organization.

Chunking: The act of mentally moving ourselves or our audience from details to abstractions, or vice versa.

Chunking Down: The act of mentally moving from an abstract concept to some specific ways that concept can be put into action, thus changing your perspective.

Chunking Up: The act of mentally moving from the specific parts of a plan to the abstract concept of why that plan is important.

CLASS R: A mnemonic for remembering Dr. Robert Cialdini's Influencers: Commitment and Consistency, Liking, Authority, Social Proof, Scarcity, and Reciprocation.

Commitment and Consistency principle: The tendency of people not to want to change their way of doing things, though their inclination is to keep going forward once they have taken even tentative steps in a particular direction.

Creative Confusion: The technique that takes advantage of the mind's discomfort with confusion by intentionally introducing that confusion in order to gain attention for a command or directive upon which the presenter wants the audience's minds to settle.

Critical Success Factor Sheet: A summary of the key questions and answers required to achieve the highest performance in an important situation. Can be an effective tool in one's Presentation Arsenal.

DISC Profiler: A model refined by Dr. Michael O'Connor that enables us to categorize the personality types in our audience based upon where their behavior falls on two continua, between Outgoing (Fast-Paced) and Reserved (Methodical) and between Task-Oriented and People-Oriented. Sample characteristics are as follows: **D:** Dominant, Direct, Determined, Demanding, Decisive; **I:** Influencing, Inspirational, Interactive, Interested in people; **S:** Steady, Stable, Supportive, Status quo, Shy; and **C:** Cautious, Calculating, Compliant, Conscientious, Contemplative.

Eight Essential Practices of Successful Presenters: Involve your audience; Prepare your audience; Research your Presentation Arsenal; Explain "why" before planning "how"; State management: achieve proper mental states; Eliminate "unknowns" by turning them into "knowns"; kNow your audience; and Tailor the presentation throughout to keep your audience focused.

Electronic Arsenal: The part of your Presentation Arsenal that consists of virtual weapons such as e-mails, web bookmarks, 3-D Outlines, presentation scripts, and notes, slide decks, and other digitized documents.

Freelance Breathing Space: When, contrary to the intentions of the presenter, a member of the audience has stopped paying attention to the presenter.

Future Pacing: Focusing the mind of your audience on the pleasant outcome of a requested action in order to gain possible compliance.

Hard Copy Arsenal: The part of your Presentation Arsenal that consists of books, printed pictures, magazine articles, newspaper stories, etc., often stored in a desk, file cabinet, or briefcase.

Hierarchy of Needs: According to Abraham Maslow, the five sequential stages or phases of life that roughly correspond to and dictate our deepest desires: food, sex, and shelter; safety; belonging or social contact; esteem and status; and self-fulfillment.

Host Introduction: The opportunity for a third party to acquaint the audience with the presenter's background, highlights of the content of the presentation, and notes on the context and importance of the material to the audience. A strong Host will enhance the presenter's credibility and open the audience's mind to the ideas to be conveyed.

Inhibitors: Insecurities that become magnified when we present and can consequently sabotage the effectiveness of our message. Inhibitor types are Pleasing, Impostor Syndrome, Perfectionism, Egomania, Peter Pan Syndrome, Defensiveness, Aloofness, Good Student Syndrome, and Tenseness.

JukeBox Journey: Developed by Al Lucia and Donna Long, the employment of music to create memory anchors and to inspire action.

Law of Requisite Variety: In any system of machines or human beings, the element (or person) with the widest range of variability will be the controlling factor in that system.

Leading: Exhibiting behavior that differs from the other person's as a way of generating some new response on his or her part.

Liking principle: Our tendency to be receptive to messages from people who like us and who are like us.

lobbying: Before a presentation, reaching out to prospective attendees ahead of time to influence them if you expect your presentation to address a controversial subject or a matter of high importance to you or the group.

Looping: A technique that, by exploiting the audience's natural desire for completion, maintains their attention by interrupting a thought and then moving on to other things.

Matchers and Mismatchers: One way people filter information. Matchers prefer to seek out similarities. Mismatchers look for differences.

Material Arsenal: The part of your Presentation Arsenal that consists of clothing, props, and the tools (e.g., the right kind of markers for whiteboards) you need to maximize use of presentation equipment.

Mental Arsenal: The part of your Presentation Arsenal that consists of interesting stories, facts, and figures that you can readily recall for use in impromptu or other presentations.

Mental State: The frame of mind of a person at any given moment that may affect his or her receptivity to a message or the ability to deliver a presentation effectively.

metaprograms: Mental patterns that we use as subconscious filters to form internal images and ideas when we are confronted with a choice that must be made.

mirroring: Subtle imitation of another person's gestures, facial expressions, body language, and tone of voice in order to facilitate rapport.

muscle memory: Behavior so ingrained through repetition that it has become nearly automatic.

Neurolinguistic Programming (NLP): The study and use of language as it impacts the brain and, therefore, our behavior. A study of excellence that models how individuals structure their experience.

Pacing: What practitioners of NLP call the entire process of matching the behaviors, beliefs, or ideas of your audience.

Parking Lot: A list of non-core items and issues that arise during a meeting or presentation that are noted for disposition at the end of the session if time permits, or set aside for future discussion.

Pattern Interrupt: Breaking undesirable patterns of behavior by introducing an abrupt change.

Peer-Trust Transference: The employment of Social Proof to earn the confidence of one's audience through the use of words or other reinforcement from an audience peer or peers.

Planned Spontaneity: Prior preparation that enables you to respond to an audience in impromptu fashion with material designed for specific contingencies and held in reserve. The better prepared you are the more spontaneity you can bring to your presentations with confidence.

Political Mapping: Assessing the importance of various stakeholders in a meeting or other presentation in order to determine the impact they may have on your desired outcomes.

Pre-Contact: Reaching out to an audience before a more formal presentation in order to prepare them to be more receptive during the event.

presentation: The act of working to impact, change, or reinforce the content and state of another person's mind and/or actions.

Presentation Arsenal: A battery of weapons that consists of quotes, stories, statistics, printed and other visual material, wardrobe, electronic files we keep, and anything of substance that can help us make future presentations more colorful and effective.

Presentation Mastery: The ability to achieve all your presentation objectives nearly all the time.

Presentation Universe: All the presentation opportunities in a person's daily life, both personal and professional.

Pre-Work: Tasks that a presenter asks his or her audience to perform before attending the presentation, such as a background reading assignment.

production before perfection: The principle that we must not allow the fear of potential missteps to prevent us from taking effective action now.

rapport: The sense of connection that puts a presenter and his or her audience on the same "wavelength."

Reciprocation principle: The sense that we have an obligation to repay a debt, favor, or concession. Also the process of establishing and maintaining a relationship of mutual trust and understanding between a presenter and his or her audience, enhancing the ability to generate desired responses.

Reporter's Questions: A series of questions the presenter asks himself or herself to become certain that he or she has minimized the risk of failure and maximized the opportunity for success—who, what, when, where, why.

Scarcity principle: The inclination to desire most those things we believe are in shortest supply, including information.

Sensory Acuity: The full employment of one's senses in order to understand the audience and the environment in which a presentation is being made. Also, the process of learning to make finer and more useful distinctions about the sensory information we receive from the world.

sensory modalities: The ways we receive information, usually with a preference either for visual, aural, or kinesthetic modes.

Social Proof principle: The sense that we have more confidence in a given course of action or belief if we see other people acting or believing the same way. Examples include testimonials, endorsements, and reference letters.

stages of learning (four): The steps in our mastery of a skill or set of skills, from Unconscious Incompetence to Conscious Incompetence to Conscious Competence to Unconscious Competence (automatic performance).

State: See Mental State.

Subconscious Desires (seven): The predisposition of every audience member to want to belong, to be respected, to be liked, to be safe, to succeed, to find romance, and to be inspired or enthused.

Subconscious Tensions (four): Friction in a presentation scenario that may interfere with the presenter's ability to maximally deliver the message. They are tension between each member of the audience and other audience members; tension between audience members and the presenter; tension created by the materials the presenter has given the audience; and tension between audience members and their environment.

surveying for content: As part of Pre-Contact, the use of formal or informal surveys to find out where members of the audience stand on issues that may arise during the presentation and how specific elements of the presentation may be received.

surveying for technique: As part of Pre-Contact, the use of formal or informal surveys to find out likes and dislikes of the audience with regard to props, presentation tools, handouts, presentation techniques, and venue.

Targeted Polling: Calling on specific members of the audience and asking them to share their feedback with the rest of the group, giving the presenter the ability to tailor the remaining portion of the presentation to more successfully impact the audience.

Three-Dimensional Outline: See 3-D Outline.

Verbal Surveying: Asking questions of the audience (in general, not a specific person) to obtain usable feedback, and to maintain connectivity and engagement.

Recommended Reading

In addition to the books listed in the bibliography, all of which I highly recommend, I also suggest the following titles. They are among my favorites and I know you will find them valuable.

Alessandra, Tony, Ph.D. and Michael J. O'Connor, Ph.D. *The Platinum Rule: Discover the Four Basic Business Personalities—and How They Can Lead You to Success.* Warner Books, February 1998.

Blanchard, Ken and Sheldon Bowles. *Raving Fans: A Revolutionary Approach to Customer Service.* William Morrow & Company, May 1993.

Canfield, Jack, Mark Victor Hansen, and Les Hewitt. *The Power of Focus: How to Hit Your Business, Personal and Financial Targets with Absolute Certainty.* Health Communications, October 2001.

Cathcart, Jim. *Relationship Selling: The Key to Getting and Keeping Customers.* Perigee, October 1990.

Carlson, Richard. *Don't Sweat the Small Stuff.* Hyperion, January 1997.

Gitomer, Jeffrey. *The Sales Bible.* William Morrow & Company, November 1994.

Gross, T. Scott. *Microbranding: Build a Powerful Personal Brand & Beat Your Competition.* Leading Authorities, January 2002.

Hubbard, Elbert. *A Message to Garcia.* Peter Pauper Press, August 1983.

Jeary, Tony. *How to Gain 100 Extra Minutes a Day.* Tony Jeary High Performance Resources, 2000.

Jeary, Tony, and George Lowe. *The Secrets of Meeting Magic Revealed.* Walk the Talk, 2001.

Jeary, Tony. *Success Acceleration: Proven Strategies to Put You on the Fast Track to New Levels of Achievement.* River Oak, July 2002.

Jeary, Tony, George Lowe, Sara Bowling and Marc Harty. *TOO Many E-mails.* Tony Jeary High Performance Resources, 2003.

Jones, Charlie "Tremendous." *Life is Tremendous.* Executive Books, September 1968.

Lang, Doe. *The Charisma Book, What It Is and How to Get It.* Putnam, August 1980.

Levinson, Jay Conrad. *Guerrilla Marketing.* Houghton Mifflin, March 1984.

Morley, Patrick. *The Man in the Mirror: Solving the 24 Problems Men Face.* Zondervan, August 1997.

Nelson, Bob. *1001 Ways to Reward Your Employees.* Workman, September 1993.

Parinello, Anthony. *Selling to VITO: The Very Important Top Officer.* Adams Media, May 1994.

Sjodin, Terri L., CSP. *New Sales Speak: The 9 Biggest Sales Presentation Mistakes & How to Avoid Them.* John Wiley & Sons, November 2000.

Tracy, Brian. *Goals!: How to Get Everything You Want—Faster Than You Ever Thought Possible.* Berrett-Koehler, March 2003.

Qubein, Nido R. *How to Be a Great Communicator: In Person, on Paper, and on the Podium.* John Wiley & Sons, September 1996.

Rohn, Jim. *7 Strategies for Wealth & Happiness: Power Ideas from America's Foremost Business Philosopher.* Prima, October 1996.

Waitley, Denis E. *The Psychology of Winning.* Berkley Pub Group, 1984.

Ziglar, Zig. *See You at the Top.* Pelican, June 1982.

Bibliography

Arnot, Robert. *The Biology of Success*. Little, Brown & Company, 2000.

Brady, Shelly. *Ten Things I Learned from Bill Porter*. New World Library, April 2002.

Brockovich, Erin with Marc Eliot. *Take it from Me: Life's a Struggle but You Can Win*. McGraw-Hill/Contemporary Books, October 2001.

Carnegie, Dale. *How to Win Friends and Influence People*. Holiday House, December 1937.

Cialdini, Robert B. *Influence: The Psychology of Persuasion*. William Morrow & Company, 1984.

Covey, Stephen R. *The 7 Habits of Highly Effective People*. Free Press, August 1989.

Csikszentmihalyi, Mihaly. *Flow*. HarperCollins Publishers, March 1991.

Davidson, Jeff. *Breathing Space: Living and Working at a Comfortable Pace in a Sped-Up Society*. Breathing Space Institute, February 2000.

Davis, Bette and Michael Herskowitz. *This 'N That*. Putnam Pub Group, February 1990.

Jeary, Tony. *Inspire Any Audience: Proven Secrets of the Pros for Powerful Presentations*. Honor Books, January 1998.

Jeary, Tony. *Speaking From the Top*. Biztank, January 2001.

Jeary, Tony and George Lowe. *Presenting Your Business Visually*. Tony Jeary High Performance Resources, 2001.

Jeary, Tony and George Lowe. *We've Got to Stop Meeting Like This!* Provant, 2000.

Jeary, Tony, George Lowe and Greg Kaiser. *Presentation Mastery*. Tony Jeary High Performance Resources, 2003.

Jeary, Tony with Mark Pantak and Kevin Grant. *Communication Mastery Training Manual*. Tony Jeary High Performance Resources, 1997.

Johnson, Spencer. *Who Moved My Cheese?* Putnam Pub Group Paper, September 1998.

Lucia, Al and Donna Long. *Rock Your Way to Happiness: Harmogenize! A Fun Way to a More Fulfilling Life*. Jukebox Pub Group, December 1999.

Pritchett, Price. *Mindshift: The Employee Handbook for Understanding the Changing World of Work*. Pritchett Pub Co., October 1996.

Reiss, Steven. *Who Am I?: The 16 Basic Desires That Motivate Our Actions and Define Our Personalities*. J. P. Tarcher, August 2000.

Robbins, Anthony. *Unlimited Power*. Nightingale-Conant Corporation, September 1989.

Walters, Barbara. *How to Talk With Practically Anybody About Practically Anything*. Doubleday, June 1970.

Index

Kim Dower is known throughout the publishing and publicity world as Kim-from-L.A., the name of the company she founded in 1985. Kim-from-L.A. Literary & Media Services specializes in book publicity and in training and coaching authors, speakers, business people, and experts of all kinds in how to best present themselves to the media.

Kim has advised hundreds of high-profile authors—including celebrities and business leaders—teaching the presentation skills necessary to come across in both a professional and provocative way. An expert at showing her clients how to formulate the content of their message as well as teaching them how to deliver it clearly, concisely, and passionately, Kim has also created national marketing and publicity campaigns for a wide range of literary and commercial fiction and nonfiction.

Kim lives in Los Angeles with her husband and son.

J. E. Fishman, who has fifteen years of book publishing experience, is also co-owner of Salem Saddlery in North Salem, New York, and Millerton, New York (www.salemsaddlery.com). A former senior editor for Doubleday and a former literary agent, he lives with his wife and daughter in North Salem.

About the Authors

Tony Jeary is known across the globe as Mr. Presentation—the leading authority on Presentation Mastery. He is the personal coach of CEOs and presidents at Ford Motor Company, EDS, Texaco, Shell, Wal-Mart, SAM's Club, Qualcomm, and New York Life. He has mentored business leaders in thirty-six countries on five continents.

His organization, Tony Jeary High Performance Resources, designs and develops unique products and services to enable their clients to accelerate their success . . . personally *and* professionally. Tony's focus includes fostering Presentation Mastery, a business movement that pivots on the concept of strategically elevating the art of presentations. He advises his clients to establish the role of Chief Presentation Officer (CPO) in order to harness the power of presentations at all levels.

In order to be near his family, he often works from his Studio, a half-million-dollar presentation laboratory. The Studio provides his high-achieving clients with a unique, private setting in which to create some of the world's most influential presentations. Here he deploys more than two decades of dedicated research and best practices to forward the strategic agendas of both individuals and organizations.

Tony is dedicated to his motto, "Give value, do more than expected." He believes that life really *is* a series of presentations, and his new vision is to inspire *all* people to use Presentation Mastery to enhance their effectiveness and quality of life.

Tony is a devoted husband and the father of two daughters. He lives just outside of Dallas, Texas. He is committed to furthering the success of his church and community.